The Surveillance Century

The Surveillance Century

How Data Replaced the Spy

By

Ronan Khoury

Vij Books
New Delhi (India)

Published by

Vij Books
(Publishers, Distributors & Importers)
4836/24, 3rd Floor, Ansari Road
Delhi – 110 002
Phone: 91-11-43596460
Mobile: 98110 94883
e-mail: contact@vijpublishing.com
www.vijbooks.in

ISBN: 978-93-47436-60-4 (PB)

This book was developed using advanced writing tools to support the drafting and ideation process. All content has been thoughtfully curated, refined, and reviewed to ensure quality and relevance.

Contents

Introduction

A city camera blinks, innocuous and unremarkable, perched on a lamppost above a busy intersection. It captures a face—a face that belongs to someone who walked the same route yesterday, the day before, the week before. The software does its work, matching contours and angles against an invisible ledger of identifiers. Somewhere, an algorithm marks a minor deviation: this person lingered near a public square longer than usual. A flag appears, quiet and unassuming, on a digital dashboard. No officer knocks on a door. No dossier is stamped *SECRET*. And yet the effect is coercive. Not immediate in the dramatic sense of espionage novels, but profound in its reach: the algorithm's gaze shapes opportunity, risk, and autonomy without fanfare.

Elsewhere, an insurance app quietly recalculates a premium. Not because of a new accident report or a fraudulent claim, but because subtle behavioural signals—acceleration patterns in a vehicle, frequency of urban foot traffic, even app usage—have shifted. The client remains oblivious. The result, however, is real: higher costs, restricted coverage, subtle pressure to conform. Across the city, these instances multiply. Individually, they appear trivial. Collectively, they constitute a lattice of influence, quietly rerouting lives, choices, and freedoms.

This book is about that lattice. It follows the relocation of power from the visible world of human spies, dossiers, and clandestine operations to a digital ecosystem of pipes, platforms, and predictive systems. These are not science-fiction inventions; they are infrastructures that already operate in plain sight. Yet their logic—data becoming knowledge, knowledge becoming control, and control normalised—is rarely interrogated. *The Surveillance Century* seeks to do exactly that: to map this transition, illuminate its mechanisms, and equip readers with the tools to recognise where influence is exerted, often invisibly, on their daily lives.

The transformation at the heart of this century is subtle yet structural. Intelligence, once episodic and selective, has become continuous and ambient. The spy, whose work relied on patience, deception, and social skill, has been supplanted by systems that collect indiscriminately and analyse algorithmically. Metadata—call logs, location traces, browsing histories—has proven more informative than the content it frames. Small, seemingly innocuous datasets, once scattered and fragmented, now fuse into high-resolution portraits of human behaviour. In this context, surveillance is no longer an episodic drama; it is infrastructure, quietly embedded in the routines of life.

To understand the significance of this shift, it helps to consider its historical antecedents. Espionage has always been a domain of human ingenuity and subtlety: the couriers who moved microfilm across Europe, the agents who infiltrated foreign ministries, the analysts who pieced together fragments of intercepted communication. These practices were resource-intensive, episodic, and inevitably limited in scope. Digital systems, by contrast, operate on a scale that the Cold War intelligence apparatus could scarcely imagine. A single smartphone generates data traces far more detailed than a dozen human tails could compile in a week. And unlike spies, these systems do not tire, negotiate, or err in human ways; they apply statistical inferences relentlessly and globally.

Yet this is not merely a story of technological capability. It is a story of incentives, economics, and power. Platforms externalise labour to users, transforming everyday interactions into behavioural data streams. Engagement becomes intelligence. Likes, shares, comments, and even scrolling patterns feed sophisticated models of preference, association, and influence. Corporations, insurers, and government agencies alike consume these models, often under different banners but with similar objectives: to predict, to influence, to manage risk. The architecture of surveillance is therefore not a novelty of authoritarianism alone—it is embedded in democratic societies, in commercial imperatives, in routines we have come to accept as convenience.

The consequences are both immediate and insidious. Predictive policing maps crime not only to streets but to individuals, allocating attention and resources with statistical precision, yet without recourse for those wrongly flagged. Corporate espionage moves quietly through supply chains, cloud systems, and software libraries, reshaping market competition while eluding traditional legal oversight. Risk scores—whether for credit, insurance, or employment—travel invisibly between sectors, adjusting life chances in ways we seldom observe, let alone contest. Every digital interaction, every passive collection point, becomes a node in an ever-expanding network of observation and inference.

And yet, amid this ubiquity, visibility is rare. The public experiences the effects of surveillance but rarely its mechanisms. The seams of influence—algorithms, data pipelines, predictive models—remain opaque. What appears to be chance, friction, or misfortune is often the outcome of systems designed to shape behaviour, optimise efficiency, or mitigate risk. The challenge, then, is not merely technical; it is civic and ethical. How does society regulate power that is diffuse, embedded, and algorithmically enacted? How do individuals maintain autonomy when so much of their social and economic reality is mediated through predictive systems?

Recurring throughout this book is the motif of flow. In the era of the spy, intelligence was bounded, episodic, and stored in static dossiers. In the era of the data century, influence is continuous, mobile, and networked. Information moves in pipelines, sometimes across borders and sectors, often invisibly. Control is exerted less through possession than through shaping the conditions under which choices are made. Understanding this shift—from static secrets to flowing signals—is essential. It allows us to see that contemporary surveillance is less about intrusion in the dramatic sense and more about structuring the very options available to individuals and communities.

The chapters that follow explore this transformation from multiple angles. We begin by tracing the pivot from human intelligence to server-based observation, examining how cost, scale, and digital infrastructure have redefined what intelligence gathering looks like. We then move into mass collection and the quiet commercialisation of personal data, showing how consent is often manufactured and how metadata operates as a powerful predictor of behaviour. Social media intelligence demonstrates how everyday communication becomes a tool for influence and control, while predictive policing and corporate cyber espionage reveal the tangible consequences of algorithmic inference.

Later sections consider the mathematics of sorting and the moral economy of scoring: how predictive models reproduce bias, amplify small errors, and institutionalise inequality. Legal and corporate governance frameworks are examined critically, revealing the loopholes, misalignments, and blind spots that permit pervasive surveillance to persist. Finally, the book engages with resistance, civic responsibility, and accountability, offering both pragmatic tools for citizens and a vision for institutions that restore proportionality, discretion, and dignity to the exercise of knowledge.

By framing surveillance as a relational, infrastructural phenomenon rather than a series of episodic intrusions, this book challenges conventional assumptions about privacy, autonomy, and power. It argues that the most insidious forms of control are often invisible precisely because they feel mundane—insurance premiums, social media feeds, minor policing decisions. These effects, however, accumulate, shaping opportunities, reinforcing inequalities, and structuring behaviour at scale. Recognising these mechanisms is the first step toward asserting meaningful limits and designing systems that respect both security and human dignity.

This is, ultimately, a book about seeing the unseen. It asks the reader to examine how ordinary practices—signing in to a platform, driving through a city, browsing online—become threads in a vast network of observation. It explores the tension between efficiency and autonomy, prediction and consent, governance and control. And it offers a guiding principle: the legitimacy of surveillance is inseparable from its transparency, proportionality, and accountability.

As the century progresses, the questions will only grow sharper. Which data should governments collect, and under what authority? How should commercial actors balance innovation against the public good? What rights, recourse, or oversight are adequate when algorithms shape life chances invisibly? These are not abstract or distant queries; they are decisions being made now, every day, through the quiet actions of code and pipeline, sensor and server.

The chapters ahead are an invitation to trace these flows, to interrogate systems, and to equip oneself with the analytical tools necessary for both comprehension and critique. They aim to make visible the invisible, to reveal the architecture of influence, and to suggest pathways for reclaiming agency in a world where data has become both the medium and the instrument of power. In doing so, *The Surveillance Century* is a guide for understanding, challenging, and, where necessary, reshaping the forces that quietly govern modern life.

Chapter 1

From Shadows to Servers

On a chilly evening in a European city, a lone intelligence officer once followed a target through winding streets, noting habits, acquaintances, and routines. Each observation required stamina, patience, and careful documentation. A single misstep—an alert neighbour, a mistimed turn—could unravel weeks of work. Today, a different kind of surveillance operates silently in the background. Metadata from a mobile phone, collected automatically, can trace the same route, mark deviations, and reveal networks of association—all without a human shadowing a single step. The shift is subtle yet seismic: intelligence has moved from the episodic drama of human spies to the continuous infrastructure of digital observation.

This pivot is neither abstract nor accidental. It reflects a structural transformation in the logic of intelligence itself. Human intelligence (HUMINT) relied on proximity, interpersonal skill, and episodic interventions. Signals intelligence (SIGINT) and open-source intelligence (OSINT) exploit communication channels, public and private, at scale. Today, data brokers aggregate fragmented digital traces, creating persistent, high-fidelity portraits of behaviour that HUMINT could only approximate. Collection is no longer costly; storage is no longer prohibitive. The act of observing, once labour-intensive and limited in reach, is now practically infinite. A single call record can substitute for a tail that would have demanded multiple operatives over days. A chain of geolocation pings replaces dozens of carefully orchestrated stakeouts. The implication is profound: intelligence has become infrastructure—persistent, flowing, and woven into the fabric of daily life rather than punctuated by dramatic operations.

As intelligence migrated from agents to servers, so too did the operational theatre. Pipelines and APIs replaced clandestine meetings and locked briefcases. The strategic value of knowing *what moves through a system* increasingly outweighs the value of possessing any individual secret.

Platform access logs, for example, reveal patterns of social interaction, routine, and preference that agents once cultivated painstakingly by hand. In a single dataset, one can observe the habits, affinities, and influence of thousands of individuals simultaneously. The emphasis has shifted from possession to control of flow, from episodic interception to continuous monitoring. The city itself—its sensors, cameras, and networked devices—functions as a distributed observatory. The architecture is designed not around dramatic discoveries, but around constant, low-friction visibility.

The transformation is amplified by the rise of social platforms, which have externalised much of the labour of observation to their users. Likes, shares, and friend graphs generate high-resolution behavioural maps without any explicit reporting. Each interaction, incentivised by engagement algorithms, becomes a data point; every digital choice contributes to an intelligence mosaic more complete than any spy's notebook. Users unwittingly participate in a global observation project, producing insights that corporations and governments alike can leverage. Social networks have not merely hosted communication—they have created an infrastructure for perpetual intelligence gathering, one that scales far beyond the capabilities of traditional human operatives.

This chapter also traces the commodification of risk. Risk scores are no longer confined to insurance actuaries or financial analysts; they traverse sectors, shaping credit limits, employment prospects, and even policing priorities. A person flagged as a potential fraud risk can find that flag echoed across multiple services, producing cascading consequences. Intelligence is no longer only about knowledge for decision-making—it is knowledge packaged, marketed, and deployed as a product. Every sector that touches daily life—from banks to local authorities—now participates in an ecosystem where predictive evaluation drives tangible outcomes. The metrics are algorithmic, the effects pervasive, and the feedback loops largely invisible to those subjected to them.

Finally, the chapter considers the quiet normalisation of these processes. Convenience habituates the public to constant observation: single sign-on services, frictionless app access, personalised recommendations. Choice architectures make opting out difficult, socially awkward, or technically inconvenient. Habits once mundane—logging in to a service, sharing a location, authorising a payment—become vectors for continuous monitoring. These systems are not imposed by force; they are welcomed, engaged with, and gradually internalised. Surveillance, in this sense, is not merely tolerated—it is normalised, almost invisible in its ubiquity.

From Shadows to Servers is a chapter about scale, structure, and subtlety. It situates the reader in a world where intelligence no longer requires drama, discretion, or human presence in the traditional sense. It introduces the motifs and mechanisms that will recur throughout the book: infrastructure over episodic action, flow over possession, participation over imposition, and risk as both tool and product. Readers will encounter stories and analyses that show how what was once the province of spies has become the background hum of modern life, shaping behaviour, influencing opportunity, and quietly conditioning choices. By the end, the familiar streets, apps, and platforms of contemporary existence will be seen not as neutral tools, but as integral components of a vast, infrastructural intelligence apparatus.

The chapter opens a lens onto this transformation, inviting reflection on both technical sophistication and societal consequence. It challenges the reader to reconsider assumptions about surveillance: to see beyond headlines of scandal or cyberattack, and to understand intelligence as a flowing, structural force. The world of observation is no longer confined to shadows—it exists in servers, pipelines, and platforms, quietly shaping the possibilities of everyday life. As you turn the page, the question becomes immediate: how do we live under conditions where the gaze is omnipresent, subtle, and yet profoundly consequential?

The Long Pivot

For much of the twentieth century, the practice of intelligence was a matter of shadows, patience, and physical proximity. A case officer trailing a diplomat, a field agent cultivating sources in a foreign ministry, or a courier ferrying sensitive documents across a continent—these were the rhythms of HUMINT, human intelligence, painstakingly accrued and episodically deployed. Every observation demanded attention, discretion, and an infrastructure of trust: a single error could compromise months of effort. Scale was inherently limited. No matter the ingenuity of a spy, intelligence collection was bounded by the constraints of time, personnel, and geography.

Now consider a single mobile phone. Metadata alone—a log of calls, texts, locations, and duration—can reveal the patterns of a life with a precision that would have required weeks of surveillance by a team of human operatives. Each ping, each tower connection, each transaction contributes to a map not just of movement but of social networks, routines, and influence. HUMINT's episodic interventions have been supplanted by continuous, ambient observation. The shift is structural, not merely technological: intelligence has migrated from the discrete realm of human agents to the pervasive infrastructure of networks and servers.

This pivot did not occur overnight. Signals intelligence (SIGINT) had long expanded the reach of states, intercepting radio, telegraph, and later digital communications. Open-source intelligence (OSINT) similarly evolved from library research and press monitoring to systematic, automated harvesting of publicly available digital traces. Each stage lowered the cost of collection and storage, gradually rendering what was once scarce and labour-intensive abundant and instantaneous. What took weeks, months, or even years in the HUMINT era—mapping associations, monitoring communications, inferring loyalties—can now be executed algorithmically, at near-zero marginal cost, over millions of individuals simultaneously. The economic implications alone are profound: surveillance is no longer a scarce resource to be rationed; it has become a continuous, scalable process.

The transformation is perhaps most evident when comparing operational techniques. Where a human tail once followed a suspect through streets and cafés, today metadata reveals the same patterns invisibly. Each connection logged—who called whom, when, and for how long—reconstructs social networks in exquisite detail. Patterns emerge without any physical proximity: the moments of hesitation at intersections, the meetings inferred through co-location data, the frequency of interactions—all form a mosaic richer than any single operative could compile. Intelligence has become infrastructural rather than episodic. Observation is no longer a rare intervention; it is a persistent backdrop, woven into the fabric of daily life.

Yet the shift is not merely about quantity. The nature of insight itself has changed. HUMINT relied on interpretation, intuition, and human judgement; SIGINT and OSINT exploit scale, correlation, and pattern recognition. Where a field agent might deduce relationships through conversation and context, metadata allows algorithms to quantify, cross-reference, and predict interactions at a scale that defies human comprehension. The epistemology of intelligence—what counts as evidence, what justifies suspicion, what reveals influence—has migrated from the qualitative to the quantitative, from subjective appraisal to systemic measurement. The result is a form of knowledge that is continuous, machine-mediated, and, crucially, infrastructural.

This infrastructural turn extends beyond state intelligence. Commercial data brokers have constructed a parallel architecture, harvesting fragments of digital life—loyalty card transactions, web browsing histories, app usage—to create detailed profiles. These profiles are traded, merged, and resold, forming an ecosystem in which private sector systems mirror, and often exceed, the capabilities once confined to government espionage. The structural shift is therefore societal as well as technical: the capacity for continuous observation and inference is embedded in everyday commerce and communication, not just national security operations.

It is tempting to underestimate this transformation because it is so gradual, so embedded in convenience. The human observer has vanished from view, replaced by automated systems that never tire and never forget. Yet their effect is tangible. A person's social ties, spending patterns, commuting routes, and online interactions—all formerly private, ephemeral, and scattered—are now available as enduring, analysable data. Metadata, once dismissed as trivial by those accustomed to content-heavy intelligence, has revealed itself to be extraordinarily potent: it can predict relationships, habits, and behaviours with remarkable accuracy, often more effectively than direct observation. The scale and granularity are unprecedented, and the infrastructure that supports this observation is invisible to those it monitors.

Perhaps the most significant consequence is epistemological: intelligence is no longer occasional insight; it is persistent, flowing, and infrastructural. Where a spy might have known a target's routines over a month, a modern dataset can reconstruct years of patterns, and do so across millions of individuals simultaneously. The paradigm has shifted from episodic discovery to continuous mapping. Knowledge itself has become a substrate of control, embedded in the pipelines and repositories that capture the minutiae of everyday life. Surveillance has ceased to be an exceptional activity and has become a persistent condition of existence.

The Long Pivot is therefore both structural and conceptual. It is a shift in how intelligence is produced, what counts as actionable knowledge, and how control is exercised. In the HUMINT era, observation was scarce and judgements were local; in the SIGINT/OSINT era, observation is abundant and judgements are systemic. The scale, speed, and persistence of data collection have redefined the very terrain of intelligence: no longer a theatre of episodic operations, but an infrastructure that permeates public and private spaces alike. A phone call, a credit card swipe, a social media interaction—each contributes to a persistent, machine-readable record, forming the raw material for inference, prediction, and intervention.

This infrastructural perspective illuminates the stakes of the contemporary surveillance environment. It is not merely that intelligence is easier to gather; it is that the logic of intelligence has changed. Collection is continuous, knowledge is algorithmically codified, and influence can be exerted subtly, invisibly, and at scale. The very frameworks of privacy, autonomy, and accountability are challenged by systems that operate independently of episodic human discretion. And because the infrastructure is embedded in ordinary life, it is largely imperceptible to those affected.

As digital traces accumulate, they constitute a lattice of observation in which patterns emerge without human orchestration. The challenge for citizens, policymakers, and scholars is to recognise this lattice, to understand its operational principles, and to consider what limits, safeguards, and ethical frameworks are appropriate. What was once exceptional—surveillance requiring deliberate effort—is now ambient. What was once episodic—intelligence gleaned through human skill—is now continuous, systemic, and infrastructural.

In tracing this transformation, one sees that the story of intelligence is no longer about individual spies or dramatic coups. It is about the quiet, unrelenting construction of knowledge infrastructures that organise and regulate social life. Metadata, pipelines, and brokerage networks are the contemporary instruments of observation. The pivot from HUMINT to SIGINT, OSINT, and data brokerage is not a footnote in history; it is the defining characteristic of a surveillance century, reshaping how power operates, how privacy is experienced, and how societies are governed.

The Long Pivot thus leaves a pressing, unresolved tension: intelligence is no longer a scarce resource but an ambient condition. The tools that allow insight also allow manipulation. The flows of data that illuminate behaviour also constrain it. Understanding this shift is not merely an academic exercise—it is a prerequisite for navigating a world in which the invisible architecture of observation has become both omnipresent and indispensable. The question lingers, uncomfortably: how does one live knowingly under the gaze of an infrastructure designed to see all, yet to reveal nothing?

Pipes, Not Plots

In the mid-2000s, a team of analysts in a European intelligence agency discovered a pattern that would have taken field operatives months to map manually. Platform access logs—records of who accessed what, when, and from where—revealed networks of association among targets of interest. Individuals who had never met physically, never exchanged a word, were linked through digital traces: a shared set of files, overlapping logins, common endpoints. Patterns that spies once cultivated through months of painstaking observation now emerged in minutes, extracted from the invisible flow of information. The operative's notebook, once sacrosanct, had been replaced by servers and pipelines.

The operational theatre of intelligence has shifted from plots to pipes. Traditional espionage valued possession: a stolen document, a secret conversation overheard, a dossier acquired. Today, the strategic advantage lies less in holding a particular secret and more in controlling the flow of information. The concept is subtle but transformative: knowing *how data moves*, where it originates, and how it circulates is more valuable than the individual pieces themselves. A single classified email, once a triumph to acquire, is now often trivial compared with a stream of metadata that traces networks, behaviours, and influence patterns over time. Intelligence has become less about isolated events and more about the persistent currents through which information circulates.

Networks, APIs, and data pipelines constitute this new operational theatre. Each pipeline—whether an application programming interface connecting a platform to its users, a server log capturing transactions, or a series of automated queries aggregating disparate data—functions as a conduit for intelligence. Unlike traditional espionage, these conduits operate continuously, silently, and at global scale. Control of these flows permits the construction of real-time models of behaviour, social interaction, and influence. An analyst does not need to infiltrate an organisation physically when access to its digital infrastructure produces equivalent or superior insight. In this environment, the question is not what you know, but what you can monitor as it moves and morphs across the system.

Consider the example of social media platforms. Friend graphs, access logs, and engagement histories form a lattice of associations, revealing not just connections, but patterns of influence, frequency of interaction, and latent networks that would have required human operatives months to chart. A single algorithm can flag emerging clusters, detect central actors, and trace the diffusion of ideas with a precision and speed unimaginable in the HUMINT era. The operational advantage is inherent in the capacity to observe the *flows*, not merely the nodes. Each interaction contributes to a living map of social behaviour, and control over the pipeline allows for interventions and predictions that are both subtle and extensive.

This paradigm extends beyond the digital realm into every connected infrastructure. Financial transactions, e-commerce interactions, travel itineraries, and sensor readings from urban environments all feed pipelines of intelligence. What once required painstaking investigation—a physical tail on a suspect, a series of interviews, a careful triangulation of movement—can now be inferred from patterns in aggregate digital flows. The logic is consistent: it is more efficient and more powerful to monitor streams than to seize individual items. Flow becomes a form of knowledge, and knowledge becomes leverage.

The architecture of these pipelines is designed for resilience, continuity, and scalability. Data is rarely isolated; it is ingested, transformed, combined, and routed across systems. APIs serve as both gateways and control points: who can read, write, or transmit data becomes a vector of influence. Logs record interaction, not as static proof of fact, but as material for pattern recognition and predictive modelling. Even deleted content leaves traces, because flows leave residue in caches, backups, and derivative analyses. Intelligence agencies, corporations, and other actors no longer pursue discrete plots—they manage, curate, and interpret the circulation of information itself.

Yet with this transformation comes new tensions. Control of flow is potent precisely because it is often invisible. Individuals may not realise that their behaviour, interactions, and digital footprints are continuously being harvested, aggregated, and analysed. Systems designed to optimise experience—recommendation engines, notification algorithms, seamless authentication—simultaneously serve as intelligence infrastructure. The ordinary act of logging into a platform is also the initiation of observation, producing streams of data that feed analytical models. The theatre of surveillance is everywhere, yet it is designed to appear nowhere.

In this environment, the stakes of intelligence are both practical and ethical. Controlling pipelines can pre-empt threats, shape markets, or influence social dynamics. But the same control, exercised without accountability, produces asymmetries of power that are structural rather than episodic. Whereas a spy's intrusion could be detected, contested, or mitigated, a continuous flow embedded in infrastructure is far harder to escape or resist. The consequences are subtle yet profound: behaviours are shaped, opportunities constrained, and autonomy circumscribed long before any conscious decision is made.

The pivot from plots to pipes also reframes what it means to be an operative, an analyst, or a policymaker. Technical expertise—understanding APIs, server logs, data flows—becomes as crucial as interpersonal skill. The ability to map interactions, detect anomalies, and anticipate emergent patterns is the contemporary analogue of fieldcraft. Influence and control now reside in architects of infrastructure as much as in traditional agents. The operational theatre is everywhere data flows, and mastery over those flows constitutes strategic advantage.

Even ordinary interactions contribute to these pipelines. Every login, click, and message is a trace in a living network. The invisibility of these operations does not diminish their power; if anything, it enhances it. Intelligence is exercised not through overt acts but through shaping the conditions under which individuals operate. Platforms, servers, and pipelines are instruments of observation and intervention, embedding influence into the architecture of everyday life. The result is a subtle but pervasive form of control: systemic, continuous, and inescapable.

Pipes, Not Plots thus illuminates a fundamental reorientation in the practice of intelligence. Knowledge is no longer a matter of singular secrets or episodic interventions. Its value lies in the persistence, movement, and circulation of information. Control over the pathways of data—the flows—enables insight, prediction, and influence at a scale far beyond traditional methods. The quiet power of observation now resides in systems and architectures rather than individuals; in flow rather than possession.

The implications are both profound and unresolved. As intelligence becomes infrastructural, citizens, institutions, and societies confront a new challenge: how to navigate a world in which surveillance is continuous, distributed, and largely invisible. The operational theatre has shifted from the dramatic to the infrastructural, from the episodic to the perpetual. And in this world, the question is no longer simply what is known, but how the flow of knowledge shapes lives before they are even consciously lived.

The Platform Turn

In 2010, a university researcher in the United States noticed an unusual pattern while studying social networks. By mapping the "friend graphs" of a few hundred volunteers, she could predict not only who was likely to be acquainted with whom, but also identify clusters of influence, latent communities, and even potential behavioural tendencies. What was striking was that the data emerged almost entirely from voluntary actions: profiles, friend requests, likes, and shared posts. Users had become unwitting cartographers of their own social landscapes, generating intelligence with each interaction.

The phenomenon at play is what one might call the platform turn. Social platforms, by design, have externalised surveillance labour to their users. Whereas traditional intelligence relied on analysts, agents, and informants to gather information, contemporary networks leverage the activity of millions, translating ordinary behaviour into high-resolution behavioural maps. Every click, comment, and friendship contributes to a continuously updated model of human association. The labour of observation, once scarce and human, is now distributed and algorithmically aggregated. Users generate the raw material, while platforms orchestrate its collection, classification, and deployment.

This model rests on the subtle architecture of incentives. Engagement is the currency: likes, notifications, and feedback loops encourage repeated interaction, and each interaction produces a trace. These traces are aggregated into patterns that are extraordinarily revealing. Friend graphs, for instance, act as ready-made intelligence: they expose networks of influence, centrality, and connectivity without the need for covert operations. Patterns that once required months of painstaking fieldwork—observing gatherings, tracking communication, noting relationships—can now be inferred instantaneously. The architecture of the platform turns everyday activity into persistent, machine-readable intelligence.

The implications extend far beyond social curiosity. Intelligence agencies, marketers, and commercial actors exploit these flows. Access to friend graphs and engagement metrics enables predictions of social dynamics, identification of key actors, and, in some cases, manipulation of behaviour. The labour of surveillance is outsourced: users generate insight about themselves and their networks, often without awareness of its analytical value. The sophistication lies in scale and subtlety. No single action is inherently revealing, yet the accumulation of millions of such actions produces a portrait of remarkable accuracy. Behaviour becomes data; data becomes prediction; prediction becomes influence.

Yet the platform turn is not merely a technical achievement—it is a social reconfiguration. By externalising surveillance, platforms shift the burden of observation from formal agencies to everyday life. Privacy is eroded not through coercion but through participation. Users willingly disclose information, normalising a system of continuous observation. The very mechanisms that encourage sociality—friend recommendations, activity feeds, interactive content—simultaneously constitute intelligence-gathering instruments. In this sense, sociality and surveillance are co-constitutive: each reinforces the other.

The creation of behavioural maps is both opportunistic and structural. Algorithms do not merely record interactions; they interpret, classify, and anticipate. Central nodes within networks are identified, communities mapped, and influence scored. Friend graphs can indicate not only direct connections but also secondary or latent affiliations, revealing pathways of communication and potential leverage points. Intelligence emerges less from the secrets people keep than from the patterns in which they participate. Knowledge, in this architecture, resides in flow, in relational data, rather than in discrete events.

There is a philosophical dimension to this transformation. The platform turn alters the agency of users: their interactions are simultaneously expressions of self and contributions to collective intelligence systems. Autonomy becomes interlaced with infrastructure. Every choice to "like" or "share" is a data point; every networked interaction is a contribution to a mapping of society itself. Yet most users remain unaware of the scale and sophistication of the intelligence they generate. The labour is hidden, its consequences dispersed across commercial and state interests. Surveillance becomes ambient, participatory, and structurally embedded.

The scale of this labour externalisation also shifts the balance of power. Traditional espionage depended on elite operatives and targeted interventions. Platforms invert this paradigm: intelligence now arises from mass participation, continuously collected and algorithmically analysed. Human effort is multiplied by the ubiquity of interaction. A single operator no longer needs to cultivate sources; algorithms parse millions of voluntary contributions to identify networks, detect trends, and predict behaviour. The operational advantage lies not in the secrecy of the observer but in the orchestration of the observed.

Moreover, this orchestration enables predictive capacities that HUMINT could only dream of. Social graphs allow inference of not just existing relationships but emergent patterns: who is likely to influence whom, which clusters may react to stimuli, and how information propagates across communities. The very structure of networks is an intelligence asset. Platforms transform every interaction into a vector for analysis and intervention, effectively turning sociality itself into a data-generating infrastructure.

Yet the turn is double-edged. While platforms amplify insight, they also blur lines of consent, accountability, and ethics. Users become both subjects and instruments of surveillance. Platforms, incentivised by engagement and monetisation, optimise for data generation as much as user experience. The consequences ripple through commercial, social, and political spheres. Friend graphs can be leveraged to influence elections, target advertising, or identify potential vulnerabilities. The invisible architecture of observation grows dense and persistent, producing influence long before conscious action is taken.

The Platform Turn thus reveals a structural pivot in intelligence itself. Knowledge is no longer solely produced by specialists; it emerges from the ordinary, everyday activity of millions, captured, classified, and interpreted by algorithms. Control resides not in access to secrets but in the orchestration of participation. Behavioural maps are generated automatically, continuously, and at scale, creating a form of insight that is systemic, infrastructural, and enduring.

The unresolved tension lies in awareness and agency. Users contribute willingly to these systems, yet rarely comprehend the scope of their participation or the power it yields. Platforms have become arenas where self-expression, social interaction, and intelligence production coalesce. Influence is embedded in infrastructure; observation is inseparable from engagement. In this environment, the familiar acts of liking, sharing, and connecting are not just social—they are components of a distributed intelligence apparatus that shapes behaviour, networks, and decisions in ways both subtle and profound.

The chapter leaves a question lingering in the mind of the reader: when surveillance labour is outsourced to the very subjects of observation, what is left of autonomy, discretion, and resistance? Friend graphs, once an academic curiosity, have become instruments of systemic influence. The platform turn has reshaped the social landscape into a living intelligence network, invisible yet consequential, continuous yet granular.

Understanding this pivot is essential to navigating a world in which participation itself produces insight, and insight becomes power.

Risk as a Product

In 2017, a consumer in a major European city discovered that a credit card application had been automatically declined. There was no fraud, no default, no late payment. The rejection came from an opaque risk score assigned not by a bank officer but by a machine, synthesising historical transactions, spending patterns, geolocation traces, and social network data. Months later, that same score affected eligibility for rental insurance and even online lending platforms. The consequences were invisible yet tangible: opportunities curtailed, premiums adjusted, reputations indirectly shaped. The financial system, long perceived as neutral and procedural, had become a pipeline of predictive judgements. Risk had been commoditised, packaged, and sold as a service.

Risk scoring has evolved from an internal tool to a cross-sector commodity. Where banks once assessed creditworthiness solely through financial history and personal interviews, algorithms now integrate vast quantities of behavioural, social, and transactional data. Insurers, e-commerce platforms, and even policing agencies purchase, exchange, and apply these scores, often without transparency. A single risk indicator can travel between domains: a fraud score derived from online purchases may influence credit approval, insurance premiums, and even policing priorities. The abstraction of risk into a portable metric has transformed it into both product and infrastructure, shaping lives in ways previously reserved for formal intelligence assessments.

This transformation rests on the logic of scale and prediction. Traditional risk assessment was episodic and local: an underwriter reviewed an application, weighed the applicant's history, and rendered a decision. The modern model relies on data pipelines, aggregating myriad signals from multiple sources to produce a probabilistic forecast. Metadata, transaction logs, browsing patterns, and social connections converge to estimate the likelihood of adverse events. The predictive value of these assessments increases with volume and diversity, creating an ecosystem in which knowledge about potential behaviour can be applied preemptively. Risk becomes actionable before the event, guiding decisions across sectors and contexts.

Consider the integration of fraud scores across finance and insurance. An algorithm detecting irregular credit card usage can flag a consumer not only for immediate intervention but also for downstream assessment: insurers may adjust coverage, lending platforms may alter thresholds, and background risk databases may update, influencing unrelated applications. The same principle applies to policing: data-driven risk assessments are used to allocate patrols, monitor individuals, and predict hotspots, often based on aggregated commercial indicators rather than direct observation. The portability of these scores transforms them into instruments of control, quietly shaping access and opportunity.

The production and circulation of risk as a commodity also reflects broader economic and structural incentives. Firms specialising in scoring and predictive analytics operate as intermediaries, translating behavioural and transactional data into standardised metrics. Their clients—banks, insurers, government agencies—require a uniform signal to guide decision-making at scale. The labour of intelligence, once performed in-house by underwriters or analysts, is now outsourced to data brokers and algorithmic platforms. Individuals participate passively, generating the very patterns that feed these assessments, while institutions apply the outputs as if they were objective measures. The perceived neutrality of the score masks its contingent, constructed nature.

Yet the very abstraction that makes risk a product also introduces systemic vulnerability. Scores are built on historical behaviour, but behaviour is not uniform or neutral. Socioeconomic status, geographic location, and demographic factors implicitly shape the data used to train models. A single high-risk flag may propagate across sectors, amplifying disadvantage in unforeseen ways. The probabilistic nature of risk assessment obscures causality: individuals may be penalised for correlations rather than actions, and interventions may reflect structural bias as much as individual behaviour. The portability of risk, while operationally efficient, compounds the consequences of error.

Moreover, the commodification of risk reconfigures the relationship between citizen and institution. Access, opportunity, and oversight are increasingly mediated by invisible metrics. The individual experiences the effect—credit denied, premium increased, patrol allocation—but rarely understands the mechanisms or provenance of the score. Accountability is diffuse: the originator of the score may be a commercial entity, the implementer a bank or insurer, and the affected individual largely excluded from the process. Power resides in control of the predictive model and the data flows feeding it, not in formal authority or legal sanction.

Risk scoring also illustrates the expansion of intelligence beyond state actors. Governments, long the primary purveyors of predictive knowledge, now operate in an ecosystem alongside commercial platforms. Data flows between sectors blur traditional boundaries: what begins as financial monitoring can influence law enforcement, social welfare eligibility, or employment screening. The movement of risk as a product creates a lattice in which prediction, opportunity, and control are distributed across multiple actors, each with distinct incentives but convergent interests in reducing uncertainty. Intelligence is no longer episodic or centralised; it is continuous, transactional, and embedded in infrastructure.

The philosophical stakes are equally profound. The abstraction of behaviour into quantifiable risk metrics transforms human life into a series of probabilities, pre-emptively judged and operationalised. Autonomy becomes mediated by the opacity of algorithms: one's choices and past interactions are refracted through predictive models that determine eligibility, pricing, and surveillance. The individual is both subject and object: generating data through participation, yet constrained by the outputs of the systems their participation fuels. Freedom is negotiated not with institutions in the open but with infrastructures whose logic is continuous, automated, and largely hidden.

Risk as a product also challenges assumptions about causality and responsibility. When scores influence policing, credit, and insurance simultaneously, the impact of a single data point can be amplified, diffused, and repurposed in ways impossible for any human to trace. Feedback loops emerge: high-risk designations can produce behaviours that reinforce the initial assessment, creating self-fulfilling prophecies at scale. The invisibility of these mechanisms complicates accountability, both ethically and legally. Errors are no longer local; they are systemic, propagating quietly through interconnected networks of prediction and intervention.

Yet despite these tensions, the logic of risk as a product is compelling to institutions. It offers efficiency, scalability, and predictive power. It aligns with the structural imperatives of modern governance and commerce: decisions must be rapid, continuous, and informed by heterogeneous data. The alternative—episodic, context-limited assessment—appears inefficient and incomplete. The modern infrastructure of risk scoring satisfies the imperatives of both scale and anticipatory control, transforming prediction into an instrument of governance and commerce.

The circulation of risk across sectors, its packaging as a commodity, and its invisibility to those affected marks a profound shift in the nature of power. Knowledge has become portable, predictive, and pre-emptive. Control now flows through data pipelines, algorithms, and commercial intermediaries. Individuals are governed less through explicit rules and more through the consequences of system-generated assessments. The stakes are no longer merely procedural; they are existentially practical, influencing access, opportunity, and freedom in the everyday.

Risk as a Product reveals the structural logic underlying these transformations. Scores are not neutral measures; they are operationalised, marketable, and applied across domains. They convert uncertainty into actionable intelligence, yet in doing so, they create dependencies, amplify inequalities, and shift discretion from human judgment to automated infrastructure. The challenge for modern societies is to recognise how risk circulates, to interrogate the assumptions built into its production, and to consider mechanisms of oversight that are commensurate with its reach and power.

The tension at the heart of this system is unmistakable: the very tools designed to quantify and mitigate uncertainty also redistribute power, shape opportunity, and pre-empt behaviour, often invisibly. Fraud scores, credit indices, predictive policing metrics—all demonstrate that risk is now a commodity, flowing between sectors, shaping lives, and embedding influence in ways that are continuous, automated, and largely imperceptible. The question that lingers, unanswered, is whether society can reconcile the efficiency of predictive systems with the imperatives of accountability, equity, and human dignity.

The Quiet Normalisation

A commuter in a major city opens a transport app on their phone. Within seconds, the application confirms the fastest route, suggests a coffee shop en route, and automatically updates payment details. The user has traded a fragment of personal data—a location ping, a preference, a travel history—for convenience. Few pause to consider the consequence: each interaction is captured, logged, and integrated into a network of behavioural data. Individually, these moments feel trivial. Collectively, they constitute a lattice of observation, one that increasingly shapes choices and constrains options without explicit consent. Convenience has become a mechanism for habituation, gradually embedding surveillance into the routines of daily life.

The process is subtle because it is seductive. Frictionless experiences—single sign-on, autofill passwords, recommendation engines—offer immediate rewards in return for data. Users rarely perceive the trade-off: privacy is exchanged for speed, efficiency, and usability. These architectural choices are not incidental; they are designed to maximise participation while minimising friction. A single login using a central account can unlock dozens of services, each collecting data that contributes to persistent behavioural profiles. What appears as seamless access is in fact an intricate form of observation, habituated through repetition and necessity. Opting out is not simply inconvenient; it becomes socially and functionally awkward, penalising those who attempt to reclaim discretion.

The mechanisms underlying this habituation extend beyond interface design. Choice architectures—how options are presented, default settings configured, and permissions framed—structure behaviour at scale. Defaults are rarely neutral. They guide users toward data disclosure, embedding patterns of participation in ways that feel natural and unremarkable. Notifications, prompts, and nudges encourage engagement, while privacy controls are often buried, complex, or confusing. Participation is incentivised; non-participation is penalised by friction, reduced functionality, or social isolation. In effect, convenience becomes the conduit through which surveillance is normalised.

This process is amplified by the layering of systems. Single sign-on, for instance, allows a user to access multiple platforms with a single set of credentials. The immediate benefit is clear: no repeated logins, no forgotten passwords, no friction. The invisible consequence is less obvious: each interaction, across multiple services, can be correlated, traced, and aggregated, producing a continuous, high-resolution profile of the user. Metadata flows seamlessly, often across commercial and governmental boundaries, forming persistent records of behaviour that were once ephemeral. Infrastructure designed for usability doubles as intelligence architecture.

The behavioural implications are profound. Humans are conditioned to seek convenience, to rely on seamless functionality, and to defer attention to privacy decisions. This conditioning accelerates the internalisation of surveillance. What was once exceptional—explicit tracking, warrantless observation—is now routine. Habits become pipelines of data generation, normalised through iterative interaction. The very act of participation is both contribution and compliance: users unknowingly generate the intelligence that platforms, corporations, and states consume. In this sense, normalisation is not enforced; it is voluntarily internalised.

Yet the ethical dimensions are complex. Systems are rarely malevolent by design; their primary goal is engagement, retention, or efficiency. Nevertheless, their effects are structurally coercive. By shaping the architecture of choice, they create circumstances in which opting out is impractical, socially awkward, or technically difficult. Behaviour is subtly guided, autonomy constrained, and consent diluted. The ubiquity of convenience masks the presence of observation: the more integrated these systems become into everyday life, the less visible the trade-offs, and the more difficult it is to assert agency.

The phenomenon extends beyond individual interfaces to entire ecosystems. Social media, e-commerce, urban mobility platforms, and smart home devices all operate on similar principles. Each system encourages participation, captures behavioural signals, and integrates them into larger data infrastructures. Cross-referencing enables inference: location data from a transit app can inform advertising; online purchases can calibrate credit risk; streaming habits can indicate lifestyle preferences. Surveillance is embedded in the experience itself, inseparable from the convenience that sustains it.

This embedding has political and social implications. As convenience becomes a structural norm, citizens experience surveillance not as a distant or exceptional imposition, but as a routine aspect of everyday life. Expectations shift: privacy is gradually redefined downward, consent becomes perfunctory, and transparency is obscured by the sheer complexity of interlinked systems. Behaviour is shaped by the affordances of technology rather than conscious decision-making, and the distribution of power moves quietly from the individual to the infrastructural operators who design, manage, and monetise these flows.

The process also alters the perception of risk. Users habituated to frictionless systems rarely perceive the consequences of cumulative data collection. The costs of participation are deferred, dispersed, and intangible. Yet the intelligence generated can influence opportunities, access, and social standing, often in ways the individual cannot anticipate or contest. Risk, in this context, is asymmetrical: the institution benefits from insight, while the user experiences indirect consequences, usually after the fact. Convenience, therefore, becomes a mechanism of structural power, embedding influence without overt coercion.

Ultimately, the quiet normalisation of surveillance is not a story of coercion or overt control; it is a story of subtle habituation, infrastructural embedding, and iterative participation. Every frictionless login, every autofill payment, every recommended choice contributes to a system in which observation is continuous, pervasive, and largely imperceptible. The architecture of convenience serves simultaneously as a vector of empowerment and a conduit of intelligence. Users participate willingly, yet the very act of participation constructs the lattice of surveillance that shapes daily life.

The tension is inherent: societies prize efficiency, connectivity, and seamless access, yet these same qualities embed forms of observation that are persistent, pervasive, and difficult to resist. As convenience becomes normalised, the boundaries of autonomy, privacy, and control are redrawn imperceptibly, shaping behaviour before conscious reflection occurs. The challenge is recognising this quiet shift, understanding the infrastructure of habituation, and considering what forms of oversight, design, and civic awareness might reclaim agency in a world where convenience is inseparable from surveillance.

Chapter 2

Mass Collection Without Asking

In a quiet suburb, a resident checks their smartphone as they leave the house. A notification pops up: "Allow [App] to access your location?" The options are framed as convenience versus obstruction. One tap grants persistent access, the promise of personalised service outweighing an abstract notion of privacy. Unbeknownst to the user, that single decision initiates a cascade of collection: geolocation traces aggregated, behavioural patterns recorded, metadata harvested, and sold or shared across networks of commercial and governmental actors. No consent in the ordinary sense was exchanged; what appears as choice is engineered to produce compliance.

This is the new architecture of mass observation: data gathered quietly, continuously, and often without meaningful permission. Traditional notions of surveillance—covert operations, warrant-protected searches, targeted observation—have been eclipsed by ambient collection. Sensors embedded in phones, vehicles, and home devices, combined with software that nudges users to disclose information, have created a system in which participation is both voluntary and unavoidable. Consent, once the moral and legal linchpin of intelligence gathering, has been reframed as a transactional formality. In practice, it functions more as a mechanism of habituation than genuine authorisation.

The process is commercial as much as it is technical. Behind the interfaces of apps and devices lies a sprawling marketplace of data brokers. Each micro-interaction—clicking an ad, visiting a page, scanning a loyalty card—produces a fragment of identity. Individually, these fragments appear insignificant; aggregated, they form a detailed portrait that can travel across sectors, informing credit assessments, employment screening, and even policing. Ad-tech segments originally designed for targeted marketing are repurposed to construct social and behavioural profiles, often with scant regard for the consent of the people whose data underpins them. The ease of collection masks the complexity and reach of these transactions, allowing information to circulate widely while remaining invisible to its subjects.

Metadata, in particular, illustrates the surprising potency of these collections. Simple logs of communication—call times, durations, participants—can reveal hierarchies, relationships, and influence networks more effectively than the content itself. Analysts can map leadership roles in organisations, anticipate coordination between actors, or infer behavioural patterns without ever intercepting a message. The sharp edges of metadata lie in its abstraction: it transforms incidental traces into predictive intelligence, quietly redefining the boundaries between public and private life.

The proliferation of sensors amplifies this effect. Internet of Things devices, urban cameras, retail beacons, and connected vehicles act as ambient collectors, tracing movements and behaviours across contexts. When data from home assistants is combined with location services and transaction logs, the result is a comprehensive portrait of daily life. Cross-context leakage—where insights from one domain inform analyses in another—creates a level of surveillance continuity previously unimaginable. Observation is no longer episodic or targeted; it is continuous, woven into the very infrastructure of contemporary living.

Public authorities have increasingly leveraged this ecosystem through partnerships with commercial providers. Agencies can purchase datasets that, while generated for advertising or commercial purposes, provide indirect access to behavioural patterns without the procedural safeguards associated with formal warrants. This practice raises profound questions about accountability, oversight, and the ethical limits of surveillance. By capitalising on the data produced by private platforms, state actors can bypass traditional constraints, creating a legal and moral grey zone where influence is exerted without transparency.

Taken together, these dynamics illustrate a fundamental transformation in the nature of observation. Mass collection is no longer exceptional, episodic, or contingent on human discretion; it is ambient, continuous, and infrastructurally embedded. Participation—whether through interaction with apps, engagement with platforms, or use of connected devices—becomes both the medium and the method of intelligence generation. Individuals contribute to their own observation, often without awareness or recourse. The cumulative effect is a system in which behaviour, preference, and movement are continuously mapped, analysed, and monetised.

This chapter examines the mechanics, marketplaces, and consequences of this shift. It interrogates the myths of consent that underpin app ecosystems, the commercial logic of data brokerage, the predictive power of metadata, the pervasiveness of sensors, and the interpenetration of state and private infrastructures. In doing so, it frames mass collection not as a series of isolated incidents, but as an integrated system whose operation reshapes autonomy, accountability, and social life.

By highlighting both the scale and subtlety of contemporary collection practices, the chapter prepares the reader to see how modern surveillance is operationalised without overt coercion. Convenience, contractual nuance, and infrastructural ubiquity serve as instruments of observation, habituating the public to practices once exceptional. The stakes are profound: understanding these dynamics is essential for recognising when and how data transforms into influence, and for evaluating what protections, remedies, and oversight are feasible in a world where participation itself generates intelligence.

Mass collection without asking is thus both a technical and civic phenomenon. It challenges assumptions about consent, transparency, and agency. It demonstrates how ambient infrastructures can shape behaviour, encode patterns, and produce predictive insights that traverse commercial and public domains. And it leaves a central question unresolved: how can individuals, institutions, and societies navigate a reality in which observation is ubiquitous, choice is engineered, and influence is exercised continuously before it is consciously perceived?

Consent That Wasn't

On a crisp morning, a commuter unlocks their smartphone and is greeted with a familiar prompt: "Allow [App] to access your location while using the app?" Two options are presented: "Allow" and "Ask Me Later." The default is obvious, the path of least resistance inviting. One tap, almost reflexive, grants persistent access. The commuter's movements, routines, and preferences are now being captured, aggregated, and potentially sold or shared. The decision feels voluntary, even trivial. Yet beneath the surface, consent has been engineered, nudged, and subtly coerced. What appears as an act of personal agency is, in reality, a carefully orchestrated surrender of privacy.

This phenomenon—widespread and largely unexamined—is central to the contemporary architecture of data collection. App ecosystems rely on the illusion of consent: legalese and interface design combine to manufacture permission that is technically explicit but substantively hollow. Users are prompted to accept terms they rarely read, while defaults and incentives subtly guide behaviour. "Consent" has become a performative gesture rather than a meaningful check on power, a veneer that legitimises extraction while concealing the mechanisms of surveillance.

The design of consent in digital environments is deliberate. Interfaces employ dark patterns—subtle cues, obfuscations, and manipulations—to steer users toward data disclosure. Choices that appear neutral are structured to maximise participation, minimise friction, and normalise sharing. Consider location prompts: they may frame persistent tracking as a convenience, offer time-limited alternatives that subtly encourage permanence, or obscure the extent of monitoring. In these moments, the architecture of decision-making shapes behaviour more powerfully than any overt mandate. Users comply not out of coercion, but because the design of the interface makes refusal cumbersome, inconvenient, or socially awkward.

Legal mechanisms compound the effect. Terms of service and privacy policies are long, densely written, and peppered with technical and legal jargon. Few users read them; even fewer comprehend them. Yet these documents provide formal justification for data collection and sharing, creating the appearance of informed consent. The combination of behavioural nudges and legal formality produces a consent architecture that is simultaneously persuasive, performative, and permissive. Participation is encouraged, refusal penalised subtly, and oversight rendered difficult.

The consequences of this engineered consent extend far beyond individual apps. Once granted, data flows into networks, brokers, and analytics systems that recombine, repurpose, and distribute information. A location permission given to a navigation app may inform advertising segments, underpin credit assessments, or even influence law enforcement resource allocation. Consent, as it is operationalised, is disconnected from control: users authorise collection in one context, but the downstream uses of that data remain opaque and largely irreversible. The promise of autonomy is undermined by the scale and fluidity of modern data pipelines.

These patterns illustrate a broader philosophical tension. Consent, historically understood as an ethical and legal safeguard, is being reframed as a procedural ritual. Individuals appear to choose, yet the structural conditions of choice—default settings, interface design, opaque legalese—predetermine outcomes. The gap between formal permission and substantive control grows with each iteration of app design, data aggregation, and platform integration. Autonomy becomes performative: exercised in appearance but constrained in effect.

The operational implications are equally significant. Data collected under the guise of consent feeds predictive models, risk scores, and behavioural maps. Metadata harvested from routine interactions—frequency of app usage, geolocation patterns, or device identifiers—can produce insights that would have required active human observation in the pre-digital era. The surrender of information, subtle and habitual, is the engine of mass intelligence infrastructure. Users participate willingly in the production of data that is subsequently leveraged for purposes they may neither foresee nor endorse.

Notably, the design of these consent mechanisms is not universally malicious. Developers prioritise usability, engagement, and commercial viability. Yet even well-intentioned design can serve as a conduit for surveillance: convenience is inseparable from observation, and participation is inseparable from extraction. The ease of access, the clarity of interface, the promise of immediate utility—all serve to normalise a culture in which privacy is voluntarily surrendered and observation is taken for granted.

The patterns of engineered consent also shape social norms. When millions of individuals habitually accept tracking prompts, default permissions, and opaque policies, the behaviour becomes standard. Expectations of privacy are recalibrated downward, not through legislation or coercion, but through habituation. Consent is internalised as a routine: a prerequisite for participation, a frictionless step in a digital habit loop. The infrastructure of observation becomes invisible, because it is simultaneously necessary, convenient, and normative.

The tension is inherent: users engage in acts that appear autonomous, yet the architecture surrounding those acts systematically channels behaviour toward compliance. Legal formalities, interface defaults, and social pressures converge to produce consent that is largely illusory. The ethical question is not simply whether individuals agree, but whether they have meaningful capacity to do otherwise. In a system designed to maximise participation and data extraction, genuine refusal becomes difficult, socially awkward, and functionally limited.

The consequences ripple beyond the individual. Once data has been collected under manufactured consent, it enters commercial, analytical, and governmental networks. Location data may inform urban planning models or targeted advertising; usage patterns may shape risk assessments or predictive policing algorithms. Each act of "permission" contributes to an infrastructure that anticipates, influences, and constrains behaviour at scale. Consent, stripped of substantive power, becomes both procedural and performative: a justification for observation, rather than a guarantee of autonomy.

Consent That Wasn't reveals the gap between formal approval and practical control. The mechanisms that produce this gap—dark patterns, legalese, defaults, and nudges—are integral to contemporary data ecosystems. They normalise participation in mass observation, habituate behaviour to continuous tracking, and obscure the true scope of collection. Users believe they are choosing; the system ensures that the choice is structured, channelled, and predictable.

The unresolved tension remains: as convenience, habit, and interface design entangle with legal forms, how can individuals exercise meaningful control over their personal information? When consent is engineered rather than freely given, when participation itself produces intelligence, and when opting out carries friction or exclusion, the ethical, civic, and practical questions multiply. The chapter invites readers to interrogate these mechanisms, to recognise where consent is performative, and to consider the implications of living in a world where the appearance of choice conceals pervasive observation.

The Data Broker Bazaar

In a fluorescent-lit office in suburban Virginia, analysts sifted through thousands of data points purchased from commercial brokers. Each record appeared innocuous: a catalogue of online purchases, a set of app interactions, a list of subscriptions. Individually, the entries were fragments of ordinary life, easily dismissed. Yet when fused, they created an extraordinarily detailed portrait of a person—preferences, routines, social connections, and even potential vulnerabilities. Ad-tech segments, initially designed to target consumers with personalised advertisements, were repurposed for employment background checks and credit assessments. In this marketplace, the small becomes comprehensive, and the trivial becomes consequential.

The commercial trade in personal data—what has come to be known as the data broker industry—is vast, opaque, and structurally transformative. Firms acquire fragments of behaviour from myriad sources: loyalty programmes, e-commerce histories, mobile apps, social media engagement, and public records. Each dataset, on its own, is limited; it reveals a sliver of habit, preference, or identity. But brokers specialise in fusion. By linking disparate datasets through identifiers, algorithms can reconstruct robust identities that span sectors, geographies, and digital contexts. The resulting profiles are high-resolution: predictive, portable, and operationally valuable across finance, insurance, marketing, and even security domains.

Consider, for instance, the lifecycle of an online advertising segment. A consumer interacts with a travel app, browses boutique hotels, and follows a set of lifestyle influencers. The ad-tech segment capturing these behaviours may later be combined with subscription data from a fitness service and payment records from a retail chain. Individually, none of these datasets reveals more than a partial truth. Together, they allow a broker—or a client purchasing the composite profile—to infer income brackets, travel habits, social networks, and even personality traits. This fusion transforms ephemeral interactions into durable intelligence.

The operational logic of this system rests on scale and inference. Small datasets are building blocks; the intelligence emerges from integration and analysis. The process is underpinned by identifiers—email addresses, device IDs, mobile numbers—that allow records to be linked across platforms. Advanced algorithms detect correlations, patterns, and predictive signals that would be invisible to a human observer. Brokers do not merely sell raw data; they sell insight, often in the form of pre-packaged scores, segments, or behavioural predictions. The labour of intelligence, once human and episodic, is now automated, distributed, and commoditised.

This marketplace is not limited to commercial convenience. Increasingly, entities beyond marketing exploit brokered data for operational purposes. Employers, insurers, law enforcement agencies, and even political operatives can purchase profiles that were originally generated for advertising. An individual's online browsing, combined with purchase histories and social graph data, can influence hiring decisions, creditworthiness assessments, and risk evaluations. The portability of intelligence across sectors blurs traditional boundaries, turning disparate data streams into systemic instruments of influence and control.

The consequences for individuals are profound precisely because they are largely invisible. Few are aware that their online behaviours are constantly harvested, aggregated, and sold. Even fewer understand how these composite profiles migrate between sectors, shaping opportunities and constraining options. The opacity of the data broker ecosystem compounds the effect:

the provenance of the information is often indiscernible, and recourse is limited. Consent, even when nominally granted for a specific platform or purpose, rarely extends to the full lifecycle of data once it enters the bazaar. Participation—whether through app usage, loyalty programmes, or online activity—becomes involuntary contribution to a pervasive intelligence infrastructure.

The trade in fused identities also reshapes the epistemology of observation. The insights derived from aggregated datasets often surpass the utility of direct human observation. Behavioural patterns, social connections, and predictive signals can be inferred without any direct interaction or surveillance in the conventional sense. For example, call graphs and co-location patterns can indicate network centrality or leadership within groups, while purchase histories can reveal lifestyle and risk profiles. The intelligence generated in this way is structural: it exists independently of episodic human scrutiny and persists continuously, feeding decision-making systems that operate at scale.

Yet the system is neither omnipotent nor entirely deterministic. Fusion algorithms are sensitive to input quality, gaps, and biases. Errors in linkage, misclassification, or sampling can propagate through analyses, producing distorted or unfair conclusions. Nevertheless, the very design of the market ensures that partial, probabilistic intelligence is actionable. In practice, even imperfect profiles can influence decisions, constrain opportunities, and shape behaviour. The commercial logic prioritises usability and predictive value over completeness or accuracy, embedding the consequences of error into the architecture itself.

Ethically and philosophically, the data broker bazaar raises profound questions. Autonomy is compromised not by overt coercion, but by the invisible circulation of personal traces. Individuals may consent to one service, yet find their behavioural footprint repurposed for contexts they never authorised. The fusion of small datasets into comprehensive identities transforms incidental acts—clicking a link, scanning a loyalty card—into instruments of influence. Participation in daily life becomes inextricably entwined with observation, prediction, and commercial exploitation. The marketplace produces a kind of ambient intelligence: pervasive, continuous, and largely imperceptible.

The scale and opacity of this infrastructure also shift the locus of power. Where once human analysts controlled access to knowledge, the brokers' algorithms and the architecture of fusion now dictate who is observed, how insight is produced, and where influence is exercised. The operational advantage lies not in the volume of data alone, but in the capacity to integrate, analyse, and distribute intelligence. Power resides in the orchestration of flows rather than the collection of discrete items. Control of the marketplace—the ability to fuse, segment, and deploy profiles—becomes strategic leverage.

For individuals and societies, the implications are urgent. The very structure of data brokerage challenges conventional notions of privacy, consent, and accountability. Behavioural fragments, scattered across platforms and domains, coalesce into enduring profiles whose influence is far-reaching yet largely opaque. The consequences traverse commercial, civic, and legal spheres, influencing credit, employment, insurance, and law enforcement. What begins as seemingly innocuous interaction becomes part of a dense lattice of observation, prediction, and control.

The Data Broker Bazaar thus illuminates the mechanics, scale, and stakes of contemporary commercial surveillance. It shows how small datasets, seemingly innocuous on their own, are fused into comprehensive identities that traverse sectors, influence decisions, and shape lives. The infrastructure of brokerage converts everyday behaviour into intelligence, often without consent, awareness, or recourse. Participation in the digital economy becomes, therefore, both voluntary and inescapable: the act of living and interacting online feeds a system that maps, predicts, and ultimately governs opportunity and influence.

The tension is intrinsic: the bazaar is both efficient and opaque, pervasive yet largely invisible, commercial in design yet civic in consequence. The systems that enable it are engineered for usability, engagement, and monetisation, yet they embed structural observation that shapes lives. The unresolved question lingers: in a world where identity is increasingly constructed from aggregated traces, how can autonomy, accountability, and recourse be meaningfully preserved?

Metadata's Sharp Edges

In 2013, a team of analysts studying social movements in a major city faced a peculiar challenge. They had limited access to the contents of communications: the messages themselves were encrypted, deleted, or simply unavailable. Yet patterns began to emerge—not from the words, but from the traces surrounding them. By mapping call records, timestamps, and routing information, they identified central figures, inferred networks of coordination, and even anticipated meetings. The content of the messages, they realised, was often less informative than the metadata accompanying them. In that moment, the invisible scaffolding of communication revealed its extraordinary power.

Metadata—literally "data about data"—is often dismissed as incidental or trivial. Yet its analytical potency is immense. Every phone call generates a record: who called whom, when, for how long, and where. Every email produces headers indicating sender, recipient, timing, and routing. Every social media post carries digital footprints of engagement, location, device, and connection. Aggregated across networks, these ostensibly minor signals allow analysts to construct predictive models, trace relationships, and anticipate behaviour with a precision that raw content alone rarely achieves. In effect, metadata sharpens the view of reality, often outperforming the information it surrounds.

The strength of metadata lies in its abstraction. While content may require interpretation, context, and subject-matter expertise, metadata provides a structural map of activity. Call graphs, for instance, reveal the topology of social networks: nodes representing individuals, edges representing interactions. Analysis of such graphs can indicate central actors, bridge figures, and clusters of influence. Leadership roles, authority structures, and lines of coordination emerge not from what was said, but from who communicates, how often, and in what patterns. The insights are systemic: they illuminate relationships and dynamics that human observation might miss, even with full access to content.

The modern landscape amplifies this effect. Smartphones, IoT devices, wearable sensors, and digital platforms generate a constant stream of metadata. Location pings, app usage logs, transaction records, and device identifiers create a continuous map of behaviour. Unlike content, which may be ephemeral, encrypted, or selectively shared, metadata is pervasive, persistent, and readily structured for analysis. Its ubiquity allows for large-scale inference: patterns across time, space, and networked interaction become intelligible. Intelligence infrastructures now treat metadata as both a lens and a foundation, enabling insights that human-centric observation alone cannot provide.

Consider, for example, the predictive capacities of communication metadata. During the Arab Spring, analysts noted that the temporal and structural characteristics of calls—frequency, clustering, and centrality—could reveal leadership within activist networks before any content was decrypted. Similarly, law enforcement agencies have used mobile and social media metadata to anticipate gatherings, identify influencers, and map relationships among criminal organisations. Metadata transforms the ephemeral into the persistent, the private into the inferable, and the distributed into the centralised for analytical purposes.

The commercial sphere mirrors these capabilities. Marketing and advertising sectors have long exploited metadata for behavioural inference. Patterns of purchase, browsing, and interaction allow the creation of predictive profiles: who is likely to respond to an offer, what products are correlated with certain behaviours, and how social networks propagate influence. The analytical approach is identical in form to state intelligence: abstracting signals from actions, connecting nodes across networks, and predicting behaviour based on structural patterns. The difference lies not in method but in context, consent, and consequence.

Yet metadata carries unique ethical and philosophical tensions. Unlike content, which carries overtly expressive meaning, metadata is often invisible to the individual. A person may be unaware that the timing of calls, the co-presence of devices, or the sequence of interactions produces actionable insight. The power asymmetry is profound: observation occurs continuously, automatically, and without deliberate disclosure. The individual generates intelligence simply by participating in the infrastructure of daily life. Autonomy becomes mediated not by what is said, but by how, when, and with whom it occurs.

The analytical advantages of metadata also illuminate its limitations. Interpretation is probabilistic: patterns may suggest influence, centrality, or intention without certainty. Noise, errors, and incomplete datasets can produce misleading inferences. Yet even imperfect, partial metadata can generate operationally useful intelligence. In practice, small signals, aggregated and correlated, often suffice to reveal networks, predict behaviour, and inform intervention. The sharp edges of metadata lie precisely in this asymmetry: its subtlety belies its power, and its abstraction both conceals and amplifies influence.

Metadata's structural advantages extend to scale and persistence. Unlike content, which may be ephemeral, deleted, or contextually ambiguous, metadata can be captured continuously, structured automatically, and analysed at large scale. Network visualisation, temporal sequencing, and predictive modelling transform raw traces into intelligible patterns. Intelligence production shifts from episodic, human-centric observation to continuous, systematised inference. Metadata is no longer an adjunct to content; it is often the primary medium through which actionable insight is derived.

This raises profound implications for privacy, agency, and societal norms. Individuals routinely generate metadata—through calls, messages, online activity, and sensor interaction—without awareness of its inferential potential. Unlike content, metadata is rarely subject to legal protections, consent mechanisms, or social scrutiny. Its collection, aggregation, and analysis operate largely invisibly, yet with real-world consequences: risk scores, policing priorities, and behavioural predictions may all be informed by traces that the individual perceives as mundane. The ordinary, everyday act of participation becomes a vector for systemic intelligence.

The utility of metadata also reframes the ethics of surveillance. Because it reveals networks, influence, and coordination, it confers predictive power disproportionate to the visibility of its subjects. Traditional paradigms of oversight and accountability, designed around the interception of content, struggle to accommodate the persistent, infrastructural nature of metadata collection. Citizens are observed not through direct scrutiny, but through the indirect traces of their activity, yielding insight that is both pervasive and elusive.

Metadata's Sharp Edges thus exemplifies a fundamental shift in how knowledge is produced, structured, and operationalised. It demonstrates that intelligence does not require access to explicit content; understanding emerges from the architecture of interactions, the patterns of communication, and the temporal and spatial sequencing of behaviour. Call graphs, device logs, and interaction networks form a lattice of insight that maps relationships, predicts influence, and guides decision-making. In this landscape, metadata is not secondary—it is primary, infrastructural, and often more potent than the content it surrounds.

The unresolved tension is both practical and moral. As infrastructures capture and interpret metadata continuously, individuals generate intelligence without awareness or explicit consent. The subtlety of metadata's inferential power renders oversight difficult, ethical frameworks tentative, and autonomy partially illusory. The challenge, ongoing and urgent, is recognising the centrality of metadata in contemporary surveillance: understanding how it shapes networks, predicts behaviour, and influences outcomes, while grappling with its hidden consequences for agency, accountability, and societal norms.

Sensors Everywhere

On a busy city street, a pedestrian passes a café, a bank, and a boutique store. Above, traffic cameras record motion and density; the café's Wi-Fi beacon registers device identifiers; the bank notes a familiar card transaction; the boutique tracks browsing behaviour through an indoor sensor network. The pedestrian's smartphone communicates intermittently with nearby base stations, while a connected car logs speed, location, and route. Individually, each sensor captures a fragment of activity. Together, they produce a continuous, multidimensional portrait of movement, preference, and routine—a portrait the individual has neither consciously authorised nor fully perceived.

This proliferation of ambient collection points—the Internet of Things, urban cameras, and retail beacons—is emblematic of contemporary surveillance. Observation is no longer episodic or targeted; it is woven into the infrastructure of daily life. Sensors embedded in homes, streets, and vehicles continuously capture behaviour, often in ways designed for convenience, security, or commercial insight. The extraordinary subtlety of this system is that the collection is largely invisible: the pedestrian receives no alerts, signs, or consent prompts, yet their interactions are persistently recorded, correlated, and analysed.

The operational power of such sensors lies in their ubiquity and integration. A smart thermostat notes presence and activity patterns, an assistant device registers queries and commands, and a wearable tracks biometrics and mobility. Individually, each device produces modest utility. When combined, however, they form a continuous behavioural trace that extends across contexts: home, car, street, and commerce. Cross-context leakage emerges, allowing inference that bridges what were previously separate spheres. A shopper's movements in a store can be linked to commuting habits, online purchasing patterns, and social interactions, producing insights that no single device or context could reveal.

Retail beacons provide a tangible example of this integration. Designed to enhance marketing, they track in-store movement, dwell times, and product engagement. That data, when combined with online purchasing, loyalty programmes, and geolocation information, can create predictive models of behaviour, preferences, and social influence. The ostensibly simple act of walking through a store becomes a point of observation that contributes to a wider intelligence infrastructure. Patterns once inferred through human observation—frequency of visits, preferred pathways, and associative behaviours—are now automatically logged, correlated, and monetised.

Urban cameras amplify this effect. Municipal and commercial networks monitor streets, public squares, and transportation hubs. Facial recognition, licence plate readers, and motion analytics provide temporal, spatial, and social data. Integrated with other sensor outputs, these data streams allow analysts to reconstruct movement patterns, identify regular contacts, and anticipate future behaviour. Observation is no longer limited to what is visible in one context; the fusion of multiple sensor types generates a synthetic continuity that is both persistent and predictive.

The integration of sensors extends to vehicles and transportation systems. Modern cars transmit telematics data to insurers, manufacturers, and third-party platforms, including speed, route, location, and usage patterns. When combined with smartphone location data, retail interactions, and urban surveillance, these datasets can map an individual's routines with remarkable precision. A route taken once or twice can be linked to habitual commuting, revealing work schedules, social contacts, and lifestyle patterns. Cross-context leakage amplifies the predictive value of otherwise innocuous signals.

These capabilities highlight a central paradox: systems designed for convenience, security, and efficiency simultaneously enable pervasive observation. Smart home devices optimise energy use, wearables monitor health, and connected vehicles provide navigation assistance. Yet each interaction feeds an infrastructure of intelligence. The utility offered to individuals obscures the scale and persistence of data collection, habituating users to surveillance while embedding the traces of their lives across commercial, municipal, and state networks.

The commercial dimension of sensor networks is particularly notable. Retailers, insurers, advertisers, and data brokers integrate outputs from IoT devices, location tracking, and social engagement to construct rich behavioural profiles. Sensor data is no longer ephemeral; it is aggregated, correlated, and retained. Inference derived from one context informs predictions and decisions in another. A pattern observed at home may influence marketing online; an urban route may adjust insurance premiums; repeated footfall in a commercial district may calibrate risk assessments. The subtle, systemic nature of these flows challenges traditional notions of consent, privacy, and control.

The philosophical implications are profound. Individuals generate intelligence simply by moving through the world, interacting with devices, and participating in infrastructural systems. Autonomy is mediated not only by the choices made but by the traces left behind. These traces are persistent, combinable, and highly predictive. Behavioural insight arises not from coercion or interrogation, but from the ambient ecology of sensors. The ordinary routines of life—commuting, shopping, exercising—become data points in continuous observation networks.

Yet the analytical utility of sensors comes with limits and risks. Data quality, accuracy, and completeness can vary. Devices may misreport, aggregate improperly, or fail to capture context. Cross-context fusion can produce misleading inferences or false correlations. Nevertheless, even partial datasets, when integrated at scale, provide operationally significant insight. The predictive power of ambient collection frequently surpasses human intuition, particularly in detecting patterns across time, location, and networked activity.

The systemic consequence is a reconfiguration of power. Control resides less in isolated surveillance events and more in the orchestration of continuous data flows. Observers—commercial or governmental—can analyse, predict, and intervene in behaviour without individual awareness. The distribution of sensors converts ordinary space into a persistent intelligence infrastructure, where every movement, transaction, and interaction contributes to a broader understanding of activity. Surveillance is no longer episodic; it is embedded, ambient, and inseparable from everyday experience.

Sensors Everywhere illuminates this transformation. IoT devices, urban cameras, retail beacons, and connected vehicles form a continuous mesh of observation, producing high-resolution intelligence from ordinary life. Cross-context data integration amplifies predictive power, revealing patterns that would have remained opaque in isolated contexts. The infrastructure of sensors, once auxiliary and specialised, has become central to contemporary surveillance, embedding influence and observation into the rhythm of daily life.

The unresolved tension remains stark: convenience, efficiency, and insight are inseparable from continuous observation. Individuals interact, move, and participate in their environment, unaware of the intelligence generated in parallel. The very systems designed to enhance experience, manage energy, and facilitate commerce simultaneously produce data that can be aggregated, analysed, and repurposed in ways that shape behaviour and opportunity. The challenge lies in recognising the ubiquity of ambient collection, understanding the flows it produces, and considering the ethical, civic, and personal implications of living in a world where every sensor contributes to the invisible architecture of observation.

State on Tap

In 2015, a federal agency in the United States quietly purchased a commercial dataset encompassing millions of mobile device locations, financial transactions, and consumer preferences. No subpoena had been issued; no warrant had been sought. The transaction was framed as a routine procurement of "market intelligence," yet the intelligence produced was indistinguishable from traditional investigative data. Analysts could reconstruct movement patterns, identify associations, and infer routines—capabilities that would previously have required formal judicial oversight. By tapping into the commercial ecosystem, state actors bypassed procedural barriers, gaining access to behavioural insights at scale while remaining ostensibly within the bounds of legality.

This example illustrates the emergence of public-private partnerships as a central feature of modern intelligence. Governments, constrained by legal frameworks and resource limitations, increasingly rely on commercial intermediaries to obtain data that would otherwise require direct surveillance or judicial authorisation. Telecommunications metadata, credit histories, location signals, and consumer behaviour logs flow seamlessly from private repositories into state analytic systems. The result is a form of indirect observation: data is acquired legally from third parties, yet used operationally in ways that replicate the capabilities of traditional intelligence collection, often without the procedural safeguards historically associated with state surveillance.

The strategic logic is clear. Public agencies face a tension between legal constraints, resource scarcity, and operational imperatives. Procurement from commercial data sources offers scale, speed, and breadth that would be infeasible through conventional collection methods. In many cases, these datasets are already structured for analysis, enriched with predictive models, and updated continuously. What once required surveillance teams, field agents, and court orders can now be accessed through contractual agreements and licensing arrangements. Intelligence, in this context, becomes infrastructural: pipelines of information flow directly from the marketplace into operational systems.

The implications of this model extend beyond efficiency. When agencies acquire datasets designed for marketing, credit scoring, or behavioural analysis, the original consent frameworks for data collection often remain limited or ambiguous. Individuals may have agreed, nominally, to data collection for commercial purposes, yet their information is now leveraged for state intelligence operations. The procedural justification is indirect: no warrant is required when the state is a client of a commercial service. The result is an accountability gap, where observation occurs continuously and at scale, yet oversight is fragmented and attenuated.

Consider location data. Mobile applications routinely track user movement for convenience, advertising, or analytics. When aggregated by brokers, anonymised or pseudonymised datasets are sold to governments, which can reconstruct patterns of travel, identify habitual routes, and correlate behaviour across contexts. Even without directly identifying an individual, analysis can reveal networks, predict activities, and inform operational decisions. The capacity to combine multiple commercially sourced streams amplifies intelligence potential, raising questions about the boundary between private commerce and state surveillance.

The ethical tension is amplified by opacity. Citizens rarely know that their participation in commercial ecosystems may indirectly feed government analysis. Even when privacy policies exist, they rarely articulate the full chain of potential downstream uses. The law, in many jurisdictions, treats data obtained from third parties as separate from data collected directly by the state, creating a loophole that permits effective surveillance without transparency. The infrastructure of observation is embedded not in the state's direct actions, but in the commercial ecology of data aggregation, sharing, and resale.

These dynamics illustrate a broader shift in the locus of intelligence power. Control is exercised not only through collection, but through access and orchestration of flows. Agencies that can tap into commercial networks gain insight proportional to the scale and richness of those datasets. Influence and oversight become a matter of contractual and infrastructural leverage rather than episodic investigation. Intelligence becomes ambient, persistent, and, in effect, outsourced.

At the operational level, indirect access enables predictive capacity previously unattainable. Behavioural modelling, anomaly detection, and network inference can all be conducted on datasets obtained from third-party sources. Agencies can identify patterns of movement, social connections, and risk factors without initiating conventional surveillance.

The result is a continuity of intelligence production that mirrors traditional HUMINT or SIGINT capabilities, yet exists outside the standard regulatory frameworks. The distinction between commercial insight and state intelligence is increasingly blurred.

The political and civic consequences are substantial. By relying on commercially sourced data, states can circumvent safeguards designed to protect civil liberties: warrants, judicial review, and transparency requirements. Accountability is diffuse; responsibility for collection and analysis is distributed across private firms and public agencies. Individuals affected by analysis often remain unaware of the sources or methods that influence decisions about them. The architecture of indirect access raises questions about consent, proportionality, and the limits of lawful observation.

This model also highlights the evolving relationship between privacy, commercialisation, and governance. Data generated for one purpose—consumer convenience, marketing, or operational efficiency—is repurposed for state intelligence. The consent and expectations surrounding that data are often limited or ambiguous. Individuals are enrolled in a system of observation by virtue of participation in the commercial ecosystem. Autonomy is mediated through indirect channels: the state observes, not by intrusion, but by tapping pre-existing flows.

State on Tap reveals the structural logic of these partnerships. Governments acquire insight, scale, and continuity without direct surveillance; companies monetise their data infrastructure; and individuals, largely unaware, contribute continuously to an intelligence lattice. This arrangement raises enduring questions about transparency, oversight, and the ethical boundaries of observation. The operational benefits are clear, yet the implications for privacy, agency, and democratic accountability are profound and largely untested.

The tension is intrinsic: efficiency and predictive power are gained at the cost of procedural safeguards, consent clarity, and civic visibility. Public-private partnerships create a subtle form of surveillance, embedded in commerce and contractual arrangements, that is both pervasive and difficult to contest. As state actors increasingly rely on these infrastructures, the challenge becomes recognising the boundaries of lawful observation, assessing the adequacy of accountability mechanisms, and grappling with a world in which indirect access produces intelligence that is both ubiquitous and largely invisible.

Chapter 3

Social Media Intelligence

In the aftermath of a protest in a major European city, analysts pieced together a startling mosaic from the digital detritus left behind. Geotagged photos, shared hashtags, and ephemeral live streams—each fragment seemed innocuous alone. Yet by cross-referencing timestamps, shadows in images, and landmarks captured in videos, it was possible to map the locations of key organisers, reconstruct their movements, and anticipate subsequent gatherings. No informants had been placed; no covert surveillance teams shadowed individuals. The intelligence emerged from the everyday traces left on social media, a testimony to the unprecedented resolution of contemporary observation.

This is the new frontier of intelligence: platforms once conceived for social connection, self-expression, and entertainment have become high-fidelity sensors of human behaviour. Open-source intelligence, once the purview of niche analysts with binoculars and microfiche, has become a default practice across agencies, corporations, and independent investigators. The proliferation of digital interaction produces continuous, granular signals—images, text, likes, retweets, geolocations—that, when aggregated and analysed, yield insights rivaling or surpassing traditional human intelligence. In this context, the act of posting, sharing, or even observing can inadvertently generate information that is operationally consequential.

The power of social media intelligence lies not only in what is explicit, but in the patterns, correlations, and emergent behaviours that can be derived from large-scale analysis. Virality, for example, functions as a form of signal detection. Rapid dissemination of content—trends, memes, or emergent hashtags—can indicate emerging social currents, potential flashpoints, or collective sentiment shifts. Analysts can detect these patterns early, informing interventions or policy responses. Yet virality is also noisy: automated bots, coordinated manipulation, and platform-specific amplification can distort signals, introducing uncertainty into otherwise precise predictive models. Understanding the dynamics of virality is as much art as it is science, requiring discernment and contextual literacy.

Beyond trends, the battlefield of narratives has become central to social media intelligence. Coordinated campaigns, whether orchestrated by states, commercial entities, or activist networks, operate across platforms with remarkable sophistication. Influencers seed ideas, memes, and messages into micro-communities; automated moderation and platform takedowns attempt to curtail dissemination. The interplay between propagation and suppression forms a narrative battlespace in which control over perception, association, and sentiment is contested in real time. Unlike traditional intelligence, where information flows through controlled channels, social media intelligence operates in a dense, distributed, and participatory ecosystem.

Micro-communities function as high-resolution sensors within this ecosystem. Small, tightly connected groups often reveal behaviours, trends, and associations invisible at the macro level. Analysts can observe engagement patterns, social cohesion, and emergent dynamics in these communities, producing insight into broader networks. Yet the ethical stakes are acute: many micro-communities include vulnerable individuals or populations. Studying them for intelligence purposes raises questions of consent, harm, and moral responsibility. The richness of insight is inseparable from ethical complexity, requiring careful deliberation and proportionality.

The temporality of social media further complicates intelligence practice. Posts can be deleted, accounts deactivated, or content obscured behind privacy settings. Yet third-party caches, archiving tools, and scraping technologies often preserve traces long after apparent deletion. The persistence of these digital shadows allows for reconstruction, historical analysis, and longitudinal insight, but also introduces questions about context, interpretation, and the evolving nature of digital evidence. Intelligence derived from social media is both immediate and archival, ephemeral and enduring, creating a paradox in which the present is archived even as it unfolds.

The implications of social media intelligence are profound and multifaceted. Knowledge can be generated without traditional surveillance apparatus, yet the same mechanisms that enable insight also amplify risk: errors propagate quickly, automated systems can misinterpret signals, and the opacity of platforms can obscure accountability. Intelligence now operates at the intersection of technology, society, and ethics, requiring practitioners to navigate platforms as complex systems, and citizens to contend with the fact that ordinary online activity produces enduring informational traces.

This chapter traces the emergence of social media as both sensor and archive, signal and battleground, microcosm and systemic instrument. It examines the rise of open-source intelligence from a niche craft to a ubiquitous practice, the predictive potential of viral signals, the contested landscape of narratives, the observational acuity of micro-communities, and the archival persistence of digital traces. Together, these dynamics illustrate a fundamental transformation in how knowledge is produced, structured, and operationalised in the twenty-first century.

The tension is both operational and ethical. Social media intelligence offers unprecedented visibility into human networks, yet it operates in spaces where consent is diffuse, boundaries are porous, and signals are entangled with manipulation. Analysts gain insight from behaviours that are simultaneously public and private, visible and ephemeral. The chapter invites readers to understand these complexities: to see how social media functions as an intelligence infrastructure, to appreciate the subtle interplay of participation and observation, and to consider the implications for privacy, autonomy, and power in a world where posting a photograph or sharing a message may generate insight far beyond its apparent intention.

Open Source, Closed Effects

In 2014, a single photograph circulated online depicting a remote military installation. To most viewers, it was just an image—shadows stretching across a courtyard, the glint of a rooftop, a tree in the foreground. Yet analysts equipped with geospatial software and open-source techniques were able to determine the location, orientation, and even the time of day the photograph was taken. Within hours, the image had become intelligence: a precise map of facilities and patterns of activity, derived entirely from information publicly available. No espionage was required; no clandestine assets were deployed. The intelligence was drawn from what was openly shared, yet its effects were as consequential as any traditional covert operation.

This episode exemplifies the rise of open-source intelligence, or OSINT, from a marginal craft into a standardised tool for analysts, corporations, journalists, and independent investigators alike. What was once a niche skill—combining satellite imagery, news reports, and publicly available records—has now become a default practice in a world saturated with digital traces. Social media posts, photographs, videos, blogs, and forum discussions constitute a vast reservoir of observable behaviour. Each data point is banal in isolation, but aggregated and analysed, these fragments reveal patterns, affiliations, and vulnerabilities that rival or surpass traditional intelligence collection.

The power of OSINT lies in its dual nature: it is both openly accessible and operationally potent. Analysts can geolocate images by examining shadows, landmarks, or topography; infer routines by aggregating timestamps across posts; and identify associations through social network mapping. These capabilities reveal the latent structure of social, political, and economic life, translating ostensibly public signals into actionable knowledge. The paradox is striking: information freely shared, intended for casual consumption, can yield closed effects far beyond the intentions of those who produced it.

Social media and open platforms have amplified these dynamics. A single tweet or photo can ripple across networks, providing insight into personal habits, organisational behaviour, or regional conditions. Analysts exploit patterns in timing, language, and content to infer context and forecast outcomes. Geolocation through visual cues, frequency of posts, and cross-platform correlations allows OSINT practitioners to construct predictive models with remarkable fidelity. The richness of open-source data renders traditional barriers to intelligence—such as physical proximity or direct observation—less relevant. Knowledge can be derived without ever touching the target, and with a transparency that belies its operational impact.

Yet OSINT is not without complication. The abundance of signals introduces both opportunity and noise. Viral content, memes, and coordinated misinformation campaigns can obscure true patterns and amplify false conclusions. Automated systems, while capable of processing vast datasets, may be confounded by manipulation, disinformation, or cultural nuance. Analysts must exercise judgment: the capacity to observe is not synonymous with the capacity to interpret. The closed effects of OSINT are contingent on understanding context, assessing reliability, and integrating diverse sources, all while contending with the performative nature of online behaviour.

The evolution of OSINT also reshapes the operational landscape. Traditional intelligence depended on controlled sources, clandestine access, and episodic operations. Open-source methods invert this paradigm:

intelligence emerges from participation, visibility, and accessibility. Platforms once designed for connection, expression, or commerce now function as instruments of observation. Every post, share, or image contributes to a collective substrate that can be algorithmically or manually analysed. The very openness of these systems enables predictive power, yet also embeds ethical and practical dilemmas.

Consider the implications for social networks. Connections, likes, check-ins, and shared content are not merely social gestures; they form a lattice of potential insight. Friend graphs, group affiliations, and engagement patterns reveal influence, centrality, and activity hubs. By aggregating public data, analysts can infer organisational hierarchies, map social movements, and identify emergent actors. The closed effects of these analyses—coordination disruption, risk assessment, policy intervention—demonstrate that visibility carries operational consequences, even when the information itself is unclassified, public, and ostensibly benign.

The ethical dimension is similarly complex. OSINT operates in the interstice between legality, consent, and expectation. Individuals freely share content for social purposes, yet the aggregation and analytical interpretation can produce insight that they never intended to disclose. The architecture of the digital environment amplifies traceability, persistence, and inference, creating a scenario in which voluntary transparency generates unintended operational outcomes. Participation in public discourse becomes intertwined with the generation of intelligence. Autonomy is subtly mediated by the infrastructural visibility of online activity.

The shift from niche craft to default practice reflects both technological capacity and organisational adaptation. Analysts, journalists, NGOs, and state agencies increasingly rely on OSINT for verification, monitoring, and predictive insight. Software tools automate extraction, geolocation, and correlation, while human expertise contextualises findings. The skill lies not in acquiring information, but in discerning signal from noise, tracing connections across platforms, and anticipating implications. Open-source data is abundant, yet intelligence emerges only through synthesis, interpretation, and operationalisation.

This transformation is structural. OSINT demonstrates that intelligence production no longer depends solely on clandestine methods or human assets. Instead, visibility itself is leveraged as infrastructure. Geolocated images, social feeds, and public records collectively generate insight at scale. What appears accessible, routine, or trivial can, when systematically analysed, produce effects equivalent to traditional surveillance. The paradox of "open source, closed effects" captures the tension at the heart of contemporary intelligence: openness enables observation, yet operational consequences are both real and enduring.

The unresolved tension remains profound. As participation in public digital spaces generates intelligence without coercion, individuals, organisations, and societies confront questions of consent, accountability, and privacy. OSINT blurs the line between public and operationally consequential, between everyday posting and actionable knowledge. The chapter invites readers to examine the mechanisms, capabilities, and limitations of open-source intelligence, to understand how ordinary visibility produces extraordinary insight, and to grapple with the ethical and strategic ramifications of a world in which openness carries consequences far beyond the intentions of those who participate.

Virality as Signal

In 2016, a seemingly innocuous hashtag began circulating on social media in a mid-sized European city. Within hours, it had been adopted by thousands of users, shared across networks, and amplified by automated accounts. Analysts monitoring digital trends noticed an unusual pattern: rapid adoption in clustered communities, simultaneous spikes in related content, and coordinated dissemination across platforms. By interpreting these signals as early indicators of mobilisation, authorities and civic organisations could anticipate gatherings, assess potential flashpoints, and allocate resources preemptively. What began as viral chatter—playful, spontaneous, or performative—had become actionable intelligence.

This incident exemplifies the principle at the heart of social media intelligence: virality is not merely a measure of popularity, but a signal of emergent activity. Trend detection transforms collective behaviour into early-warning indicators, revealing shifts in attention, sentiment, and coordination. Hashtags, memes, or shared content act as markers of collective focus, amplifying insight into both organised campaigns and organic social phenomena. In operational terms, understanding the rhythm of virality allows observers to anticipate mobilisation, identify influence nodes, and detect emerging risks before they crystallise.

Yet the analytical power of virality is accompanied by complexity. Not every spike signals meaningful activity. Automated accounts, coordinated campaigns, and algorithmic amplification can distort the apparent significance of trends. A meme may surge in visibility due to bot activity, virality contests, or platform-specific amplification, without corresponding to genuine human mobilisation. Analysts must discriminate between signal and noise, recognising that visibility alone does not equate to influence, intent, or impact. The precision of insight depends on contextualisation, cross-validation, and careful interpretation of patterns within broader social, cultural, and platform-specific frameworks.

The rise of virality as a form of signal is inseparable from the structural design of social platforms. Algorithms reward engagement, encourage rapid sharing, and amplify content with early traction. As a result, trends can propagate faster than traditional observational systems can monitor. This structural acceleration has operational consequences: intelligence derived from virality is both immediate and volatile, reflecting the dynamic interplay of human behaviour, algorithmic curation, and networked amplification. Predictive insight relies on recognising not only what is trending, but why, where, and among whom.

Applications of virality detection extend beyond public order monitoring. Health organisations track outbreaks through surges in relevant queries or hashtags; companies detect emerging consumer preferences or reputational risks; security analysts identify coordinated campaigns targeting political, financial, or social targets. In each case, the patterns of dissemination provide intelligence that would be invisible through conventional observation. The predictive power arises from collective amplification: the faster, broader, and denser the trend propagation, the more informative the signal.

Yet these systems are vulnerable to manipulation. State actors, interest groups, and commercial entities increasingly engineer virality through coordinated dissemination, automated amplification, and strategic seeding. Inflated signals can distort perception, provoke overreaction, or mask genuine developments. Bots and coordinated networks inject noise into otherwise organic datasets, complicating interpretation and increasing the risk of false positives. Analysts must navigate this dual reality: virality can illuminate emergent activity, but it can equally obscure, mislead, or be weaponised.

The ethical dimension of interpreting viral signals is similarly complex. Identifying early-warning indicators may require observation of communities, some of which include vulnerable populations or marginalised groups. The same data that predicts mobilisation can expose individuals to surveillance, risk, or social harm. Signal detection, therefore, operates at the intersection of utility and responsibility: the capacity to anticipate must be balanced against the potential consequences of intervention, misinterpretation, or exposure. Intelligence is not merely about insight; it is about the ramifications of acting upon that insight.

Historical parallels underscore the novelty and continuity of this phenomenon. Traditional early-warning systems relied on human observation, tip-offs, and analogue networks of information. Virality replaces these mechanisms with real-time digital amplification, allowing patterns to emerge at speeds, scales, and resolutions previously impossible. Yet the underlying logic is familiar: collective behaviour contains predictive information; those who can read it first gain operational advantage. The difference is in immediacy, granularity, and the opacity of the digital environment.

Operationalising virality as a signal requires both technological and analytical sophistication. Algorithms detect anomalies, cluster activity, and identify propagation dynamics, while human analysts provide contextual interpretation. Geospatial, temporal, and network-based analyses integrate trends with known organisational structures, social relationships, and behavioural patterns. This combination of automated detection and expert evaluation allows for early identification of mobilisation, influence operations, or emergent crises. It is the fusion of human and machine intelligence that gives virality operational efficacy.

The phenomenon of virality also illuminates broader societal dynamics. Participation, amplification, and engagement are not evenly distributed: certain communities, platforms, and networks disproportionately shape visibility. Signals extracted from these spaces may overrepresent some actors while underrepresenting others, producing insight that is precise yet partial. Understanding virality thus demands awareness of social topology, platform architecture, and the mechanics of amplification. Intelligence is never neutral; it is shaped by the networks in which it emerges and the structures through which it propagates.

Virality as Signal therefore embodies both opportunity and caution. Trend detection provides early-warning capacity, operational foresight, and insight into emergent phenomena. Yet it is embedded in a landscape of manipulation, algorithmic bias, and performative behaviour. Signals may illuminate or mislead; trends may represent genuine activity or engineered amplification. Analysts, policymakers, and observers must negotiate this duality, interpreting viral patterns with both rigor and humility.

The unresolved tension is central: in a world where information flows with unprecedented speed, visibility can produce insight before events materialise, yet the same velocity magnifies error, manipulation, and misinterpretation. Virality is simultaneously a source of intelligence and a vector of uncertainty. The challenge lies in harnessing the predictive power of trends while mitigating distortion, ensuring that signal is recognised amidst the noise, and acknowledging that the very mechanisms that amplify insight can also subvert it.

The Narrative Battlespace

In the months leading up to a national election, a coordinated campaign began to unfurl across social media. Influencers with thousands of followers shared aligned talking points, memes propagated across multiple platforms, and hashtags synchronised to amplify visibility. Simultaneously, automated accounts reposted, engaged, and tagged users to simulate organic engagement. Within days, the narrative gained traction far beyond the originators' immediate reach. Platforms, recognising spikes in content, implemented takedowns and moderation measures, yet the cycle of seeding and amplification continued. What unfolded was not merely communication; it was a battlespace, a contest over perception, influence, and attention conducted entirely in digital networks.

This is the essence of the narrative battlespace: a contested environment in which information, stories, and signals are deployed strategically, often with intent to shape behaviour, perception, or decision-making. Unlike traditional intelligence, where operations focus on facts or events, the narrative battlespace operates on meaning itself. Content becomes both instrument and theatre, where influence is exerted through propagation, repetition, and amplification. Control over narratives is pursued through seeding, engagement, and coordination, while countermeasures—platform moderation, fact-checking, or counter-messaging—seek to disrupt, attenuate, or redirect influence.

The tools and methods of narrative engagement are diverse. Influencer seeding exemplifies the modern approach: selected individuals, chosen for their reach and credibility, disseminate targeted messages in ways that appear organic to their followers. Algorithms magnify visibility, facilitating viral propagation across networks. Coordinated campaigns exploit network structure, timing, and platform affordances to maximise resonance. Each interaction, each repost, each engagement functions as both a vector of influence and a signal to algorithms, creating a self-reinforcing loop of amplification.

Countermeasures are equally complex. Platform takedowns, content moderation, and algorithmic adjustments seek to interrupt propagation, limit reach, or remove harmful narratives. Yet these interventions are often reactive, partial, and constrained by the opacity of networks. Seeding campaigns can adapt, migrate across platforms, or fragment into smaller units to evade detection. The dynamic is iterative: offensive and defensive measures evolve continuously, producing a high-velocity environment in which narratives compete for attention and legitimacy.

Analytical techniques are central to understanding and navigating this battlespace. Network analysis, temporal pattern detection, and engagement metrics allow observers to identify central actors, influential nodes, and emergent clusters. Trend detection informs early-warning capabilities, highlighting which narratives are gaining traction and which may pose operational or civic risks. Yet the abundance of data introduces both opportunity and ambiguity: distinguishing genuine organic engagement from automated amplification, or authentic sentiment from orchestrated manipulation, requires nuanced interpretation.

The stakes are profound. Narratives shape perception, guide behaviour, and influence decisions at scale. They operate across political, social, and commercial domains, affecting elections, public health responses, and consumer behaviour. Unlike traditional influence, which required proximity, persuasion, or authority, digital narratives can be propagated remotely, instantaneously, and invisibly, producing effects disproportionate to the effort expended. The battlespace is global, persistent, and multi-layered, where the velocity of information rivals the consequences it produces.

Ethical tensions are unavoidable. Analysts and platform operators navigate a dual imperative: protect against malicious or manipulative narratives while respecting freedom of expression and privacy. Decisions about which content to suppress, promote, or monitor carry weighty implications. Overreach risks censorship, bias, or misinterpretation, while underreach allows manipulation, misinformation, or harm to proliferate. The narrative battlespace is thus as much a moral and social terrain as it is an analytical and operational one.

Historical precedents illuminate the stakes. Propaganda and influence campaigns have long shaped public perception, yet digital networks amplify scale, speed, and subtlety. Messages can traverse continents, adapt in real time, and be targeted with unprecedented precision. The interplay of human behaviour, algorithmic curation, and automated amplification transforms traditional influence into a systemic, distributed, and often opaque contest over attention and interpretation. The battlespace is not a metaphor; it is a structural reality of modern information ecosystems.

The interplay of offensive and defensive operations in this domain illustrates the evolving sophistication of actors. Coordinated campaigns exploit behavioural heuristics, social dynamics, and platform affordances, while countermeasures rely on detection algorithms, human moderation, and policy interventions. Success is rarely absolute: narratives can be partially disrupted, redirected, or muted, but rarely entirely eradicated. Influence is resilient, adaptive, and intertwined with the participatory behaviour of the network itself.

Understanding the narrative battlespace requires recognising both its operational mechanisms and its structural dynamics. Influence is embedded in the architecture of platforms: algorithmic prioritisation, engagement incentives, and network topology all shape visibility and impact. Analysts must consider not only the content of messages but the medium, timing, and amplification vectors. The signal emerges not merely from the words, but from the patterns of propagation, the clustering of engagement, and the interactions between human and automated agents.

The Narrative Battlespace demonstrates that contemporary influence operates at the intersection of technology, society, and psychology. Narratives are deployed strategically, observed and countered with increasingly sophisticated methods, and continuously reshaped by platform dynamics. The contest is ongoing, dynamic, and asymmetrical: a small, coordinated group can exert disproportionate influence, while countermeasures often lag or misfire. The implications for agency, perception, and governance are substantial, revealing a landscape in which attention itself is contested, operationalised, and weaponised.

The unresolved tension is both practical and ethical. How can societies, platforms, and analysts balance the necessity of countering manipulation with the preservation of autonomy, expression, and transparency? How can influence be measured without inadvertently amplifying it? The narrative battlespace presents a persistent challenge: the very systems that enable connectivity and participation also generate environments in which narratives are contested, controlled, and continuously reshaped—

raising questions that are operational, philosophical, and profoundly contemporary.

Community Clues

On an obscure corner of the internet, a forum of a few hundred users shares advice, stories, and support around a specialised interest. At first glance, the posts appear trivial—questions about daily routines, shared photos, casual exchanges. Yet for those attuned to the patterns, these micro-communities provide an extraordinary resolution of insight. Activity levels, interaction patterns, and the emergence of central figures reveal not only social dynamics within the group but also broader behavioural signals that ripple into adjacent networks. These small clusters, often overlooked, operate as high-resolution sensors, capturing nuance and detail invisible at larger scales.

The analytical value of micro-communities lies in their density and focus. Unlike sprawling social networks, where engagement is diffuse and signal-to-noise ratios are low, micro-communities produce concentrated interactions. Relationships, norms, and behaviours manifest clearly and repeatedly. Observers can detect emerging trends, influential actors, and shifts in sentiment before these phenomena appear in broader datasets. The networked intimacy of these communities functions as a kind of magnifying glass, revealing patterns that scale alone cannot produce.

Consider online hobbyist groups, activist cells, or localised interest networks. Each participant's contributions, frequency of engagement, and connections provide signals that, when aggregated, can indicate leadership, influence, and the emergence of new initiatives. Analysts can map interactions to identify clusters, central nodes, and bridging figures. Temporal patterns—such as response times, posting rhythms, and bursts of activity—offer predictive insight into upcoming events, coordination, or behavioural shifts. Micro-communities, in essence, transform ordinary engagement into observables of remarkable specificity.

Yet this capability carries profound ethical complexities. Many micro-communities include vulnerable populations: minors, politically marginalised groups, individuals with sensitive health conditions, or communities experiencing social stigma. Observation and analysis of these spaces risk unintended consequences. Even passive monitoring can produce identifiable insights, influence behaviour, or expose participants to risk. Ethical intelligence practice must navigate the tension between analytic opportunity and potential harm, recognising that micro-communities are simultaneously sources of knowledge and sites of vulnerability.

The challenge is compounded by the permeability of digital spaces. Data generated within one micro-community can propagate into adjacent networks, often without the awareness of participants. A single shared post, comment, or interaction may cross boundaries, producing insight far beyond the community itself. Analysts must therefore consider not only the immediate context but the extended digital ecology: the ways in which micro-scale behaviours cascade, interlink, and influence broader social phenomena. The observational richness of micro-communities is inseparable from these networks of propagation.

Micro-communities also illuminate the limits of anonymity and assumed privacy. Platforms may allow pseudonymity, yet behavioural and network patterns often provide sufficient resolution to identify individuals or infer affiliations. Engagement patterns, content themes, and relational structures can reveal roles, influence, and behaviour with precision. For intelligence practitioners, these spaces are valuable precisely because they concentrate signals; for participants, the concentration creates risk. The analytical clarity that makes micro-communities useful simultaneously renders them ethically fraught.

The operational and analytical logic mirrors classical intelligence practice: small, observant groups can provide disproportionate insight, and monitoring a high-fidelity, dense environment often yields more actionable understanding than a dispersed, noisy population. Modern digital tools amplify this capability. Network visualisation, temporal analysis, and sentiment mapping transform raw interactions into structured intelligence. Analysts can track the emergence of leadership, sentiment shifts, or coordination signals with unprecedented granularity. Micro-communities, therefore, act as both magnifier and sensor, converting digital micro-behaviour into operationally relevant insight.

Yet the very methods that enable this insight are morally and socially delicate. Intervention, engagement, or exploitation of micro-community data can alter dynamics, introduce bias, or harm participants. Ethical practice requires awareness of the consequences of observation: how knowledge can affect autonomy, privacy, and trust. The richness of the signal cannot be disentangled from responsibility. Studying these spaces is not simply an analytical exercise; it is a practice entangled with social, ethical, and civic dimensions.

Micro-communities also reveal the interplay between visibility and participation. The act of posting, commenting, or liking is simultaneously expression and signal. Participants, often unconsciously, generate data that informs analysis and prediction. The dual role of these communities—as spaces of social interaction and as nodes of intelligence production—illustrates the hybrid nature of contemporary observation. Micro-communities are simultaneously human, digital, and analytic constructs: they are lived experience rendered legible through digital trace.

From an operational standpoint, the signals derived from micro-communities are invaluable for early detection, trend monitoring, and behavioural inference. Emerging movements, localised coordination, or niche behavioural shifts are often first visible in these concentrated networks. Aggregation across communities, when done responsibly, allows analysts to construct higher-level understanding of social dynamics without losing the granularity that makes insight actionable. Yet every extension of observation carries attendant risk: the closer the lens, the greater the ethical stakes.

Community Clues illustrates a fundamental tension in contemporary intelligence: the very environments that produce high-resolution insight are also fragile, vulnerable, and ethically sensitive. Micro-communities provide early-warning signals, behavioural mapping, and network insight, yet their observation raises questions of consent, autonomy, and responsibility. The challenge for analysts, policymakers, and citizens is to navigate the duality of these spaces: recognising the operational value without compromising the dignity, safety, or agency of participants.

The unresolved tension remains both practical and moral. How can analysts extract meaningful insight without causing harm? How can intelligence practice balance predictive value with ethical restraint? In a world where micro-communities act as high-fidelity sensors of human behaviour, observation is both opportunity and responsibility. The chapter invites readers to confront these questions, understanding that the very closeness which provides insight also demands careful stewardship, ethical vigilance, and critical reflection.

Archiving the Present

In 2019, a controversial post on a popular social media platform was deleted within hours of publication. The user presumed the content vanished permanently, a fleeting expression lost to the digital ether. Yet third-party archival services and web caches preserved the post in perpetuity. Analysts, researchers, and investigators could retrieve the image, timestamp, and textual content long after the user's deletion. What had been intended as ephemeral became enduring, available for scrutiny, aggregation, and operational use. This moment illuminates a paradox at the heart of modern digital life: the tension between the immediacy of expression and the persistence of observation.

Archiving the present is no longer the domain of libraries, state archives, or curated repositories. Every interaction online—posts, images, videos, and comments—creates a trace that may survive deletion, obfuscation, or platform shutdown. Scraping technologies, automated web crawlers, and caching systems systematically collect these traces, rendering digital ephemera into durable datasets. For intelligence purposes, these archives provide historical continuity, enabling analysis of behavioural trends, network evolution, and emergent narratives. Yet the persistence of these traces introduces ethical, practical, and epistemological challenges: context is easily lost, intent can be misinterpreted, and the line between public and private becomes porous.

The operational logic of archiving is straightforward but profound. Deleted content, once considered irretrievable, can be reconstructed through third-party caches, platform backups, or analytic scrapes. Geotagged images, textual posts, and video content may persist in aggregate datasets, forming longitudinal records of participation, behaviour, and association. Analysts can trace influence patterns, reconstruct timelines, and identify emergent actors. The power of archiving lies not in any single piece of content, but in the capacity to situate ephemeral data within a persistent, structured framework, creating intelligence that outlasts its apparent origin.

Scraping tools magnify this potential. Automated collection systems can systematically capture publicly available content across platforms, categorising by keywords, geolocation, user networks, or temporal activity. Combined with storage, indexing, and analytic pipelines, this content forms a continuous record of digital activity. Deleted posts, altered accounts, and transient media can be reconstructed from these datasets, enabling retrospective analysis. The ordinary flow of participation thus becomes a durable record, capable of producing insight and guiding intervention long after the initial interaction.

Yet archiving is not neutral. The preservation of context is inherently imperfect. Deleted posts may lack annotations explaining deletion, edits may obscure original intent, and the surrounding discourse may be lost. Interpretation requires caution: analytical conclusions drawn from archival data may be technically accurate but conceptually misleading. Signals derived from these traces must be contextualised, cross-validated, and interpreted with awareness of the limitations imposed by digital ephemerality and selective preservation. The archive is simultaneously enabling and constraining, providing access while framing understanding within the contours of what was captured and what was lost.

The ethics of archiving are equally complex. Individuals often assume deletion equates to erasure; archival persistence undermines this assumption. Vulnerable populations, political dissidents, and private individuals may be exposed long after they intended to withdraw from public visibility. Platforms' decisions about what to retain, cache, or make accessible shape the boundaries of privacy and accountability. Researchers and analysts must navigate these tensions, recognising that access to historical digital traces is a privilege imbued with responsibility. The archive can illuminate, but it can also endanger.

Consider the consequences for network analysis. Deleted posts may reveal affiliations, interactions, or activity that were intended to vanish. Aggregated across multiple accounts and platforms, these traces can reconstruct relationships, identify coordination, and anticipate behavioural patterns. Micro-events—once imperceptible—become legible in the context of continuous archival data. The persistence of these signals transforms fleeting actions into enduring intelligence, enabling predictive insight but also raising questions about consent, permanence, and interpretive authority.

The temporal dimension of archiving introduces further analytical complexity. Signals that are immediate in their creation may accrue significance only through longitudinal observation. Trends, influence, and behavioural shifts become visible over weeks, months, or years of preserved data. Deleted content can retrospectively reveal emergent narratives or patterns of activity that were invisible at the time of posting. In this sense, the archive operates as both a mirror and a lens: reflecting the past while enhancing visibility into previously obscured dynamics.

Archiving also intersects with operational and civic responsibility. Data that persists outside its original context can be repurposed for law enforcement, research, or commercial exploitation. The same post that appears trivial today may inform decisions about risk, reputation, or influence in the future. Analysts must weigh the potential value of archival insight against the ethical implications of using traces from individuals who expected their content to disappear. The infrastructure of digital preservation thus generates power that is continuous, diffuse, and often opaque.

Platforms themselves shape the archival landscape. Policies governing retention, caching, and accessibility determine which content survives and how it can be leveraged. Automated deletions, shadowing, and content throttling interact with third-party scraping to produce layered, heterogeneous archives. Analysts working in this environment must contend with gaps, redundancies, and noise, translating fragments into coherent intelligence while acknowledging the partiality of the preserved record. The archive is as much a product of design choices as it is of human behaviour.

Archiving the Present illuminates a fundamental transformation: ephemeral expression has become persistent observation. Scraping, preservation, and the resilience of third-party caches render the digital present simultaneously immediate and enduring. Intelligence derived from these traces can map activity, identify networks, and anticipate behaviour with unprecedented granularity. Yet each advantage carries ethical, practical, and epistemological questions. The past is never fully gone, context is never entirely preserved, and the act of observation is inseparable from the architecture of preservation itself.

The unresolved tension is striking: digital ephemerality is an illusion. Posts can vanish from view but survive in systemic memory; the present is archived, analysed, and operationalised without participants' full awareness. How should societies, analysts, and platforms navigate the balance between insight, accountability, and privacy? In a world where the digital present is instantly archived, every act of expression becomes potentially enduring, raising questions about agency, interpretation, and the moral stakes of observation.

Chapter 4

Predictive Policing and Its Discontents

In a mid-sized American city, police officers received a digital map each morning, colour-coded to indicate streets, intersections, and neighbourhoods where crime was statistically most likely to occur. Patrol hours were allocated accordingly, resources concentrated where algorithms predicted the highest risk. On paper, the system promised efficiency: fewer burglaries, faster response times, and data-driven decision-making replacing guesswork. Yet the reality was more complex. Areas flagged as "high risk" were disproportionately populated by communities already heavily policed, and patterns generated from past arrests perpetuated cycles of scrutiny. The promise of predictive policing—precision and fairness—clashed with the lived experience of those who found themselves repeatedly under watch, often for minor or misclassified incidents.

This chapter explores the rise of predictive policing: the use of data, statistical models, and algorithmic systems to forecast crime and guide law enforcement deployment. From place-based hotspot mapping to individual risk scores, predictive tools are designed to optimise limited resources and anticipate criminal behaviour. Yet the translation of patterns into patrols is neither neutral nor infallible. Algorithms are trained on historical data, susceptible to biases encoded by social, economic, and systemic inequalities. Feedback loops reinforce these inequities: more policing generates more records, which feed models, which in turn justify increased scrutiny in the same locations or communities. Predictive insight, intended to improve efficiency, can therefore entrench disparities.

The allure of predictive policing lies in its promise of objectivity. By analysing arrest records, incident reports, and environmental indicators, police agencies seek to identify "hotspots" of criminal activity. Burglary forecasts, for example, may direct patrol units to streets with statistically higher risk, ostensibly preventing crime before it occurs. Place-based prediction transforms policing from reactive to proactive, replacing intuition with data-driven strategy. Yet the apparent neutrality of the algorithm masks deeper complexities: the data reflect human behaviour and human decision-making, including historic biases in enforcement, reporting, and social marginalisation.

Individual risk scores add another layer of complexity. Algorithms assign numeric risk ratings to persons, incorporating criminal history, location, social networks, and sometimes socioeconomic indicators. These scores inform watchlists, stop-and-search decisions, and prioritisation of investigative resources. The stakes are immediate and personal: a false positive can affect livelihoods, freedom, and social standing. The same tools that promise efficiency can misclassify, disproportionately targeting individuals from communities already subject to systemic oversight. Here, the promise of predictive policing meets the ethical and practical challenge of error—when the algorithm errs, the consequences are borne by real lives.

Audits, baselines, and independent evaluation are critical in addressing these tensions. Verification mechanisms can assess predictive accuracy, detect bias, and provide transparency. Benchmarks against historical outcomes, cross-validation across datasets, and rigorous scrutiny of model assumptions help ensure that predictive tools do not operate unchecked. Yet in practice, such oversight is uneven. Many agencies implement predictive systems without external review, or maintain internal evaluations that are opaque to the public. Readers will find in this chapter guidance on pragmatic tests and transparency measures that can anchor predictive policing in accountability.

Beyond algorithmic models, alternatives that reduce reliance on surveillance and prediction illustrate a different approach. Community-led interventions, environmental design, and social infrastructure can prevent crime without the compounding effects of algorithmic oversight. Improved street lighting, accessible communal spaces, and targeted social programmes have demonstrably reduced certain crimes without concentrating scrutiny on already vulnerable populations. These interventions emphasise that predictive policing is not the only path to public safety: human judgement, civic design, and local engagement remain indispensable complements to data-driven systems.

The chapter also interrogates the social and ethical implications of predictive policing. Who decides what constitutes risk? How are assumptions encoded into models? What mechanisms exist for affected communities to contest or appeal algorithmic decisions? Predictive policing operates at the intersection of statistics, policy, and lived experience, raising questions about fairness, equity, and the distribution of state power. By unpacking patterns, feedback loops, and risk scores, this chapter situates predictive policing within a broader societal context, highlighting both its technical sophistication and its potential to exacerbate inequality.

Predictive Policing and Its Discontents invites readers to examine the promises and pitfalls of algorithmic law enforcement. It situates models within their social and historical contexts, analyses operational mechanics, and provides tools for understanding the consequences of decisions guided by data. The chapter traces the pathway from pattern recognition to patrol allocation, scrutinises feedback loops that entrench inequality, and explores both person-based and place-based prediction. In doing so, it bridges technical, ethical, and civic perspectives, challenging assumptions about efficiency, objectivity, and fairness.

The tension at the heart of predictive policing is structural and enduring: systems designed to optimise resource allocation simultaneously interact with human and societal biases, producing outcomes that may reinforce the very disparities they were intended to mitigate. The chapter opens the door to critical questions: how can data-informed policing coexist with accountability, fairness, and community trust? How can society harness the predictive power of algorithms without sacrificing dignity, equity, or justice? Readers are invited to engage with these dilemmas, recognising that the contours of algorithmic oversight are not only technical, but profoundly social, ethical, and civic.

From Patterns to Patrols

On a quiet Tuesday morning, a police precinct receives its daily briefing: a digital map highlighting streets, intersections, and neighbourhoods flagged as high-risk for burglaries. Patrol schedules are adjusted accordingly, and officers are redirected to areas where predictive models indicate a heightened likelihood of criminal activity. At first glance, the process seems straightforward—data informs deployment, resources are concentrated where they are most needed, and law enforcement acts with precision rather than guesswork. Yet beneath the surface of this ostensibly neutral, algorithm-driven allocation lies a web of assumptions, historical biases, and cascading consequences that shape who is watched, where attention is focused, and how communities experience policing.

This subchapter examines the foundational mechanism of predictive policing: the translation of patterns into action. Hotspot mapping and place-based prediction convert historical incident data into forecasts that guide resource allocation, transforming policing from reactive response to proactive strategy. Burglary hotspots, traffic accident clusters, and patterns of minor offences are quantified, visualised, and codified into operational directives. The goal is efficiency—concentrate efforts where risk is highest—but the pathway from data to patrol is fraught with complexity. Models are constructed from prior enforcement records, which themselves reflect structural inequities in policing, reporting, and societal attention. The result is an interplay between statistical inference and lived reality, where operational logic meets social consequence.

Hotspot mapping exemplifies the allure of predictive systems. Using geospatial analysis, analysts identify areas with elevated incidence rates, generating maps that inform patrol schedules. The approach relies on the principle that crime is not uniformly distributed; certain streets, blocks, and intersections consistently exhibit higher levels of activity. By focusing resources on these areas, agencies aim to prevent crime, deter repeat incidents, and optimise limited personnel. However, the models assume that past patterns are reliable indicators of future behaviour, a presumption that can obscure deeper social dynamics. Areas historically over-policed may appear perpetually high-risk, while emerging patterns in less-monitored neighbourhoods remain invisible.

Place-based prediction extends beyond static maps. Temporal factors—time of day, day of the week, seasonality—intersect with spatial data to produce dynamic risk profiles. Patrols are scheduled not merely to cover locations but to anticipate when criminal activity is likely to occur. The operational logic is seductive: data-driven timing, guided by statistical patterns, seemingly replaces intuition with objectivity. Yet these patterns are only as reliable as the inputs. Arrest records, reported incidents, and community complaints feed the models, embedding prior biases into predictive outputs. The consequence is a form of algorithmic inertia: predictive systems may perpetuate the same cycles of scrutiny that produced the historical data in the first place.

The feedback loop inherent in hotspot policing illustrates this dynamic. Increased patrols generate additional observations, arrests, and citations, which are recorded and subsequently fed back into the system. The algorithm interprets these outputs as confirmation of risk, reinforcing the allocation of attention to the same areas. Communities already heavily monitored experience heightened enforcement, while areas with less scrutiny may appear safer than they truly are. In effect, the system is self-validating: data informs action, action generates more data, and the cycle repeats. Patterns from the past shape patrols in the present, producing outcomes that may reinforce inequality under the guise of statistical objectivity.

The operational mechanics are complemented by technological affordances. Geospatial information systems (GIS), predictive analytics platforms, and visualisation tools allow agencies to overlay multiple data sources—crime reports, demographic information, environmental indicators—and produce actionable insights. These systems make the invisible visible, translating numerical and temporal patterns into maps, alerts, and schedules. Yet the human element remains indispensable. Analysts interpret the data, contextualise anomalies, and calibrate models to reflect operational realities. Technology amplifies capacity, but it does not replace judgment; rather, it shapes the lens through which officers perceive risk and opportunity.

The deployment of patrols based on predictive models also has psychological and social ramifications. Communities subject to concentrated oversight may experience heightened surveillance, eroding trust between residents and law enforcement. Residents may adjust behaviour in response to perceived monitoring, while local dynamics—such as informal social networks, community engagement, and collective problem-solving—may be altered by the presence of predictive policing. The operational efficiency of patrol allocation intersects with social perception, illustrating that data-informed strategies are not value-neutral. They shape both practice and experience.

Empirical studies highlight both the promise and the limitations of hotspot-based predictive policing. Targeted deployment can reduce certain types of crime, such as property offences, in specific areas. Yet reductions are not uniformly distributed, and interventions may displace rather than eliminate criminal activity. The predictive lens captures patterns observable in historical data but may miss novel behaviours, emergent hotspots, or subtler social dynamics. The efficacy of patrol allocation is contingent on the quality, representativeness, and contextualisation of the underlying data—a reminder that operational sophistication does not guarantee equitable outcomes.

The ethical dimension is inseparable from the operational. Predictive deployment raises questions about fairness, proportionality, and accountability. Who decides what constitutes risk? How are thresholds for "high-risk" areas determined? How can oversight ensure that algorithmic guidance does not amplify systemic inequities? Even well-intentioned models carry the potential to concentrate scrutiny, enforce stereotypes, and inadvertently criminalise vulnerable populations. Hotspot mapping is not merely a technical exercise; it is a site where data, decision-making, and social consequence intersect.

From Patterns to Patrols situates the reader at the nexus of data, decision, and consequence. It examines how historical patterns are transformed into operational directives, the mechanics of place-based prediction, and the feedback loops that reinforce allocation decisions. The chapter interrogates the tension between efficiency and fairness, between predictive capacity and human judgement, and between operational objectives and community impact. By tracing the pathway from patterns observed in data to patrols deployed on the street, it reveals the architecture, assumptions, and consequences of contemporary predictive policing.

The unresolved tension is fundamental: predictive models promise foresight and efficiency, yet they operate within systems shaped by historical bias, social inequities, and uneven observation. Patterns may guide patrols, but the act of policing shapes patterns in return. The chapter invites readers to consider how operational decisions, informed by statistical inference, translate into lived experience. It asks whether predictive insight can coexist with justice, whether efficiency can be balanced with equity, and whether the promise of data-driven allocation can avoid perpetuating the disparities it seeks to address.

Feedback Loops

In a densely populated urban district, officers were dispatched repeatedly to the same few streets, responding to incidents that were ostensibly predicted by a crime-forecasting algorithm. Each patrol generated data: arrests, citations, reports of suspicious activity. This new data was fed back into the predictive model, reinforcing the notion that these streets required continued monitoring. In practice, the algorithm was not merely forecasting risk; it was shaping it. The very act of surveillance and enforcement became a generator of further "evidence," creating a cycle in which the areas most heavily monitored appeared most criminalised.

Feedback loops in predictive policing are at once elegant and insidious. The premise is straightforward: algorithms ingest historical data—arrests, incident reports, calls for service—and produce forecasts of future risk. Resources are deployed accordingly, patrols are concentrated, and interventions follow predicted hotspots. Yet the data is not neutral. Arrests and reports are influenced by social bias, reporting practices, and enforcement priorities. When these biased inputs are treated as objective measures, they produce outputs that reinforce pre-existing disparities. The algorithm, in effect, perpetuates the very patterns it purports to anticipate.

Consider the lifecycle of a single block flagged as high risk. Officers are directed there based on past crime data. Their presence results in new encounters, some resulting in arrests or citations for minor offences. These outputs are then fed back into the model, validating and amplifying the initial prediction. Over time, the block accrues a disproportionate share of enforcement activity relative to its actual risk profile. Meanwhile, nearby streets with fewer historical interactions remain under-observed, potentially harbouring unrecorded activity. The cycle is self-reinforcing: predictions shape deployment, deployment shapes data, and data shapes predictions.

This dynamic illustrates the broader phenomenon of algorithmic amplification. Biases encoded in historical enforcement—whether reflecting socio-economic disparities, racial profiling, or uneven reporting—become structural features of predictive systems. Models assume that past observations are accurate representations of underlying crime patterns, yet these observations are mediated by human judgement, community engagement, and systemic inequities. The result is a form of digital determinism: outputs appear objective, but they are inseparable from the social context that produced the input data.

The feedback loop is not merely theoretical. Empirical research demonstrates its effects. In multiple studies, predictive policing models concentrated attention on minority or lower-income neighbourhoods, even when crime rates were comparable across other areas. Areas heavily patrolled generated more reports and arrests, confirming the model's predictions and justifying further enforcement. This recursive process produces a skewed representation of risk, reinforcing inequality while giving the illusion of algorithmic objectivity. Data does not merely describe reality—it helps produce it.

Beyond spatial patterns, feedback loops operate in temporal and social dimensions. When models generate forecasts of when and where crime is likely to occur, officers are deployed at predictable intervals. Communities under continuous surveillance experience heightened attention, altering behaviour and social interaction. Residents may self-censor, avoid public spaces, or adjust routines, while unmonitored areas retain greater autonomy. Surveillance thus reshapes social landscapes, producing feedback not only in numerical data but in lived experience. The loop is simultaneously operational, perceptual, and sociological.

The human consequences of feedback loops are acute when applied to person-based models. Risk scores derived from prior encounters can influence police attention, stop-and-search decisions, and pre-emptive interventions. An individual flagged as "high risk" may be subjected to repeated scrutiny, resulting in additional records that reinforce their risk classification. Error compounds: misclassification produces new interactions, which generate more data, which further entrenches the initial prediction. The cycle illustrates how predictive systems can inadvertently criminalise and constrain individuals, with tangible effects on freedom, opportunity, and social standing.

Operationally, mitigating feedback loops requires both technical and procedural interventions. Independent audits, transparency in model design, and recalibration against unbiased baselines can reduce recursive amplification. Agencies may adjust weighting, incorporate community reporting, and apply randomness to patrol allocation to prevent overconcentration. Yet no technical adjustment fully resolves the underlying social and historical biases embedded in the data. The feedback loop is not merely a computational artefact—it is a reflection of the complex interplay between human behaviour, institutional practice, and algorithmic interpretation.

Philosophically, feedback loops challenge assumptions about objectivity, neutrality, and the role of data in decision-making. Predictive models are often framed as scientific, depersonalised, and rational. Yet the recursive amplification of biased inputs demonstrates that data-driven systems cannot be divorced from social context. Intelligence derived from these models is entangled with power, history, and inequality. Patterns observed are patterns produced, and insight is inseparable from action. The promise of objectivity masks the subtle perpetuation of pre-existing disparities.

Feedback loops also illuminate the fragility of predictive certainty. Even well-intentioned models may misallocate resources, distort perceptions of risk, or obscure emergent patterns outside historically monitored areas. The system reinforces itself in predictable ways while remaining blind to anomalies, innovation, or shifts in community behaviour. Intelligence, in this sense, is contingent, contextual, and mediated by the recursive structure of observation and intervention.

Feedback Loops therefore reveals both the operational sophistication and the social complexity of predictive policing. It demonstrates how algorithms translate biased inputs into reinforcing cycles of enforcement, shaping not only numerical outcomes but the lived experience of communities. It challenges readers to consider the consequences of relying on historical data as a foundation for action, and to interrogate the implicit assumptions embedded in systems that claim objectivity. The chapter sets the stage for subsequent discussion of individual risk scores, audits, and alternative approaches, highlighting the tension between predictive capacity and ethical responsibility.

The unresolved tension is stark: feedback loops can improve operational efficiency while simultaneously entrenching inequality. Predictive policing is at once a tool for foresight and a mechanism for reinforcement. The questions it raises are enduring: how can systems that generate recursive effects be designed or monitored to minimise harm? How should society balance the operational benefits of predictive insight against the social costs of reinforced bias? Feedback loops underscore that in data-driven policing, patterns do not merely describe reality—they help create it.

Individual Risk Scores

When Ahmed, a mid-level office worker, attempted to board a flight for a routine business trip, he was stopped by security personnel. His name had flagged an automated watchlist, the product of an algorithmic risk-scoring system designed to identify potential threats. Ahmed had no criminal record, no suspicious associations, yet the automated score assigned to him placed him in a category warranting scrutiny. For him, a false positive translated into hours of interrogation, professional disruption, and a profound sense of being surveilled and judged by an invisible system. His experience is neither unique nor isolated; it exemplifies the human consequences of person-based predictive policing.

Individual risk scores are quantitative assessments generated from personal data, past behaviour, social networks, and other digital traces. Agencies and platforms use these scores to prioritise attention, guide interventions, or restrict access. They promise efficiency: resources are focused on those deemed highest risk, and low-risk individuals are ostensibly left unmonitored. Yet the process is fraught with uncertainty. Risk scores condense complex human lives into numerical proxies, inherently imperfect and influenced by biases embedded in the underlying data. The act of scoring an individual is simultaneously analytical and moral—it evaluates probability while imposing consequences.

Person-based models range from algorithmic watchlists for terrorism screening to credit-like scores applied to criminal justice or policing contexts. These systems ingest diverse data streams: prior arrests, social media activity, travel patterns, and demographic indicators. Machine learning techniques identify correlations between these variables and adverse events, producing a predictive output: the individual's score. While statistically informed, these models cannot capture nuance, intent, or context. They are blunt instruments, translating multidimensional human behaviour into a scalar measure. The appeal is operational: officers, analysts, and decision-makers receive actionable guidance. Yet the human stakes remain immediate, tangible, and unevenly distributed.

Errors in these systems carry real-world consequences. False positives can lead to heightened surveillance, restricted mobility, increased scrutiny during routine interactions, or social stigma. False negatives, conversely, may allow actual threats to go undetected. The asymmetry of impact is significant: the costs of misclassification are borne disproportionately by individuals flagged incorrectly, often intersecting with social, economic, and racial vulnerabilities. Unlike statistical abstraction, these errors manifest in human lives, shaping experiences of freedom, privacy, and dignity.

A striking example comes from law enforcement applications. In predictive policing, individuals flagged by algorithmic risk models may face repeated stop-and-search encounters, surveillance, or inclusion on watchlists. The data that informs these scores—prior arrests, residential location, and association networks—often reflect historical biases. Communities historically subjected to over-policing may generate data that inflates risk scores for residents, perpetuating cycles of scrutiny. Here, predictive models do not merely forecast behaviour; they reinforce structural inequalities, translating systemic bias into operational outcomes.

The opacity of these models compounds the challenge. Risk scores are often calculated within proprietary systems, with little transparency into variable selection, weighting, or thresholding. Individuals affected may lack meaningful recourse, unaware of the data contributing to their classification or the mechanisms by which it influences decisions. Accountability is diffuse: algorithms operate at the intersection of data science, policy, and law enforcement practice, making it difficult to contest errors or evaluate fairness independently. The human cost of opacity is heightened by the automated authority assigned to numerical outputs.

Operationally, the use of individual risk scores necessitates both technical sophistication and ethical vigilance. Auditing, validation, and calibration are essential to identify bias, measure accuracy, and understand error rates. Benchmarks against independent datasets can illuminate disparities, while interpretability tools reveal which features most strongly influence scoring outcomes. Yet these technical measures alone are insufficient. Ethical governance requires mechanisms for review, contestation, and redress. Without these, efficiency comes at the cost of human dignity and social equity.

The philosophical stakes are equally profound. Condensing human complexity into numerical risk invites a subtle form of determinism: individuals are judged and treated based on past data and algorithmic inference, rather than personal agency or context. The score becomes a lens through which behaviour is interpreted, and the interpretation carries operational weight. In this sense, predictive scoring is both analytic and normative—it describes probability while influencing how society treats the scored individual. The act of measurement is inseparable from the act of intervention.

Emerging research and practical experience illustrate potential mitigations. Transparency protocols, independent audits, and threshold adjustments can reduce false positives. Incorporating human-in-the-loop review ensures that context, nuance, and discretion temper algorithmic outputs. Community-informed oversight and feedback mechanisms provide additional checks against disproportionate enforcement. Yet no intervention entirely eliminates error. The tension between predictive power and ethical responsibility persists, underscoring the inherent fragility of person-based intelligence.

Individual risk scores illuminate the broader challenges of algorithmic governance: the interface between data, decision, and consequence. They demonstrate how predictive systems translate historical data into operational action, creating a landscape in which probability guides attention, and misclassification produces tangible human effects. These systems amplify the scale and speed of enforcement decisions, yet their humanisation—understanding error, bias, and social impact—is essential.

Individual Risk Scores foreground the human dimension of predictive policing. Patterns, feedback loops, and data infrastructure intersect with lived experience, producing outcomes that are measurable, consequential, and ethically charged. The chapter invites readers to interrogate how personal data is transformed into authority, the consequences of misclassification, and the mechanisms that might reconcile operational insight with human dignity. The unresolved tension remains: can society harness predictive models to allocate attention and resources while ensuring that individuals are not unjustly burdened by errors embedded in the data from which those models learn?

Audits and Baselines

In 2018, a metropolitan police department unveiled a predictive policing system designed to allocate patrol resources and pre-empt criminal activity. Months later, investigative journalists revealed that the model disproportionately targeted minority neighbourhoods, amplifying historic enforcement biases. The system had passed internal performance checks, yet independent scrutiny exposed the gaps between algorithmic output and social consequence. The episode illustrates a central truth: predictive systems, however sophisticated, cannot be assumed fair or accurate without rigorous evaluation, transparency, and benchmarked accountability. Audits and baselines are the instruments that transform abstract data into trustworthy, actionable insight while safeguarding against systemic harm.

Predictive policing, person-based risk scores, and algorithmic resource allocation systems operate on the assumption that past patterns reliably inform future outcomes. Yet every dataset reflects human decisions: which incidents are recorded, how reports are categorised, and which interactions are deemed relevant. Without independent evaluation, these assumptions remain untested, hidden behind the veneer of technical objectivity. Audits—systematic, critical examinations conducted by neutral parties—serve to interrogate the integrity, validity, and social impact of predictive models. Baselines establish comparators: what would have occurred without the model, or with a neutral allocation, providing context for evaluating performance and fairness.

Independent evaluation operates on multiple levels. At the technical layer, auditors verify the statistical properties of models: their predictive accuracy, sensitivity, and robustness to noise. They examine training datasets, highlighting potential biases in representation or variable selection. For instance, an arrest-based predictive model may overrepresent certain communities due to historic policing practices rather than actual differential risk. By measuring model performance across subpopulations, evaluators can detect systemic disparities that would otherwise go unnoticed. Beyond the statistics, independent scrutiny examines operational impact: how predictions influence deployment, who is affected, and whether interventions exacerbate inequality.

Baselines function as a critical point of comparison. Without them, any evaluation risks conflating correlation with causation. Did a hotspot map reduce burglaries, or did crime decline naturally due to seasonal or social factors? Did targeted patrols improve safety, or merely displace incidents to neighbouring areas? By establishing counterfactual scenarios—comparable measures of what would have occurred absent the predictive system—baselines provide context, enabling meaningful assessment of model efficacy. These benchmarks anchor interpretation, transforming numerical outputs from raw predictions into accountable knowledge.

Transparency underpins both audits and baselines. Agencies and private vendors frequently operate predictive systems as proprietary "black boxes," limiting access to model specifications, datasets, and evaluation procedures. Such opacity impedes meaningful scrutiny, leaving affected communities and oversight bodies without the tools to question outcomes. Transparency is not merely procedural; it is ethical. It allows for the verification of claims, the identification of unintended consequences, and the incorporation of diverse perspectives into the evaluation process. Publicly accessible documentation, explanatory reports, and data-sharing agreements constitute essential mechanisms for holding predictive systems accountable.

Pragmatic tests can be demanded even within constrained institutional environments. Observers might compare model outputs to historical data, examine false-positive and false-negative rates across demographic groups, or assess the distribution of interventions relative to population density and need. Scenario testing, sensitivity analysis, and simulation exercises reveal vulnerabilities in model design and deployment. These evaluations translate technical scrutiny into operational relevance: they allow policymakers, oversight bodies, and citizens to assess whether a predictive system aligns with social objectives, respects equity, and delivers genuine improvements rather than reinforcing entrenched patterns.

The consequences of insufficient auditing are tangible. Systems that go unchecked can perpetuate biases, erode trust, and produce harms that are both measurable and experiential. In predictive policing, for example, unexamined models may continually deploy patrols to historically over-policed areas, generating arrest data that validate the model and further concentrate scrutiny. Without independent evaluation, these feedback loops remain invisible, and harm is justified by the illusion of scientific objectivity. Audits and baselines break this cycle by revealing the underlying dynamics, exposing assumptions, and enabling corrective action.

Ethically, audits operate at the intersection of technical precision and social responsibility. The same dataset that predicts burglary hotspots or assigns risk scores also encodes human decisions, prejudices, and historical inequities. Evaluators must consider not only the numerical accuracy of predictions but their distributive impact. A system may appear highly performant statistically yet exacerbate inequality, misclassify individuals, or undermine trust in institutions. Accountability in this context is multidimensional: it demands transparency, reproducibility, fairness, and ethical reflection.

Operationalising audits and baselines requires structural commitment. Independent evaluators must have access to data, algorithms, and deployment protocols. Agencies must be willing to adapt models based on findings, incorporate mitigation strategies for identified biases, and communicate openly with stakeholders. Effective oversight is iterative: evaluations occur at multiple stages of design, implementation, and maintenance, ensuring that predictive systems remain aligned with both operational goals and social norms over time.

The philosophical stakes are equally significant. Predictive systems offer the promise of rational, data-informed decision-making, yet their authority is contingent on validation. Without audits and baselines, apparent objectivity becomes an unexamined authority, and statistical inference is conflated with ethical justification. By establishing independent evaluation and benchmarking, society affirms that predictive insight must be accountable to human values, not only to mathematical optimisation. Transparency, auditability, and baseline comparison transform abstract prediction into socially legible, ethically responsible intelligence.

Audits and Baselines therefore occupy a central role in reconciling the promise of predictive systems with their potential for harm. They provide both a technical framework for verification and an ethical scaffold for oversight, enabling stakeholders to assess accuracy, fairness, and social impact. Through independent evaluation, benchmarked comparison, and transparent reporting, predictive systems can be held accountable, ensuring that operational efficiency does not come at the expense of equity, dignity, or public trust.

The unresolved tension is persistent: predictive intelligence can guide action with unprecedented efficiency, yet it is never neutral. Audits and baselines offer a mechanism for illumination, but they rely on commitment, resources, and institutional will. The questions remain: who evaluates the evaluators? How can benchmarks reflect both technical validity and social justice? And how can transparency be meaningful in an environment dominated by proprietary algorithms and opaque datasets? The chapter invites readers to grapple with these questions, recognising that the integrity of predictive systems depends as much on scrutiny as on statistical sophistication.

Alternatives That Work

On a city street once notorious for break-ins and vandalism, residents noticed a subtle change: the dim, shadowed corners had been illuminated by a network of new streetlights, strategically placed to cover alleys, stairwells, and public pathways. Over the following months, incidents of burglary and petty theft declined, not because of increased police presence or sophisticated algorithms, but due to an environment reshaped for visibility and community engagement. This simple intervention—lighting, a centuries-old tool of crime prevention—demonstrates that effective strategies for safety need not rely on intrusive surveillance or predictive models.

In contrast to the allure of algorithmic policing, community-led, non-algorithmic approaches foreground human agency, environmental design, and social cohesion. They acknowledge that crime and disorder emerge from complex, interwoven social, economic, and spatial factors. Rather than attempting to predict individual behaviour or forecast hotspots through statistical models, these strategies work with the material and social realities of the community, leveraging local knowledge, participatory design, and low-tech interventions to prevent harm. Their efficacy is measured not in predictive accuracy but in observable outcomes: safer streets, more resilient communities, and trust preserved rather than eroded.

The principle of "situational crime prevention" exemplifies the philosophy underpinning these interventions. By altering the physical environment, communities can reduce opportunity structures for crime. Improved lighting, secure entryways, clear sightlines, and maintained public spaces all serve to deter opportunistic offences. Evidence from urban studies supports the efficacy of these measures: cities that invested in street-level visibility, including the installation of pedestrian-scaled lighting and removal of concealed spaces, consistently reported reductions in burglary, assault, and vandalism, often without increasing formal enforcement. The intervention works by shifting the environmental incentives and social perception of safety, rather than by monitoring, profiling, or targeting individuals.

Neighbourhood policing initiatives complement environmental measures. Rather than deploying predictive algorithms, these programmes emphasise relationships: residents, local organisations, and law enforcement collaborate to identify risks, mediate disputes, and co-create safety strategies. Community officers act as conduits for information, not enforcers of algorithmic outputs. In practice, this approach can prevent crime before it occurs by addressing the social conditions that foster disorder—youth engagement, mental health support, conflict mediation—without amplifying surveillance or generating data-driven feedback loops. Such interventions illustrate the potential for civic intelligence: knowledge derived from local actors and social networks, rather than extracted from digital traces or transactional records.

Social cohesion itself is a preventive tool. Communities that cultivate informal social control—where residents monitor shared spaces, support vulnerable neighbours, and establish mutual expectations—experience measurable reductions in certain types of crime. Urban ethnographies reveal that in well-connected neighbourhoods, potential offenders are less likely to act, not due to fear of algorithmic detection, but because the social costs are immediate, visible, and tangible. Informal networks of oversight function as high-resolution sensors: attuned to local dynamics, adaptable, and responsive without producing the privacy intrusions characteristic of mass surveillance systems.

Importantly, these non-algorithmic approaches avoid many unintended consequences associated with predictive policing. Feedback loops, disproportionate targeting, and errors that impinge on individuals' lives are largely absent when strategies focus on environments and social infrastructure. A lit alley does not generate a false positive. A neighbourhood watch does not assign risk scores that misclassify residents. By emphasising design, participation, and community knowledge, these interventions reduce harm while achieving meaningful improvements in safety. They operationalise intelligence differently: situational, relational, and adaptive, rather than codified, centralised, and algorithmically enforced.

There are limitations and trade-offs. Community-led interventions require investment in social capital, engagement with local institutions, and sustained maintenance of physical infrastructure. They may not produce the rapid, measurable outputs prized in algorithmically managed systems. Yet the long-term benefits—enhanced trust, resilience, and autonomy—often outweigh the short-term efficiency gains of predictive models. In essence, these approaches demonstrate that operational success need not come at the cost of civic dignity or privacy. Crime prevention can be integrated into the fabric of everyday life, not imposed through intrusive monitoring.

Empirical research underscores the viability of such alternatives. In multiple cities across Europe and North America, improvements in street lighting, traffic-calming measures, and public space redesign led to significant declines in both property and violent crimes. Programmes that incorporated residents' insights—mapping unsafe areas, suggesting modifications, and monitoring implementation—achieved results comparable to algorithmic deployment but without the accompanying ethical and social concerns. Importantly, these interventions exemplify a principle increasingly relevant in public policy: effectiveness and ethical integrity are not mutually exclusive.

Alternatives That Work also highlights the philosophical dimension of crime prevention. It reframes safety not as a function of prediction and control, but as a product of visibility, trust, and engagement. It asks readers to reconsider the assumption that technological sophistication equates to efficacy, and that surveillance is a necessary tool of social order. Intelligence, in this frame, is embedded in communities, derived from human relationships, shared knowledge, and environmental cues. By cultivating these forms of insight, societies can achieve the dual objectives of safety and dignity—a balance rarely achieved by algorithmic intervention alone.

The chapter invites reflection on the limits of technology-driven enforcement and the potential of human-centred strategies. It challenges the reader to consider: how can communities leverage local knowledge, environmental design, and social networks to reduce harm without creating pervasive surveillance? What role should civic participation play in shaping safety policies, and how can operational intelligence emerge organically rather than being imposed by centralised systems? *Alternatives*

That Work offers a roadmap for understanding and implementing effective, ethical, and scalable approaches to public safety that complement, and in some cases replace, predictive technologies.

Ultimately, these strategies demonstrate that meaningful reductions in crime do not require expanding surveillance infrastructure or embedding predictive algorithms into daily life. By focusing on environment, engagement, and social cohesion, communities can achieve tangible results while preserving agency, trust, and privacy. The chapter sets the stage for examining predictive systems critically, contrasting algorithmic insight with human ingenuity, and emphasises that the pursuit of safety can, and should, be compatible with dignity, fairness, and social justice.

Chapter 5

Cyber Espionage in the Corporate Century

In 2019, a leading semiconductor company discovered that its most sensitive design schematics had been silently exfiltrated. The breach did not originate from its own employees, nor from a nation-state embassy or consulate; it came through the quiet compromise of a software library used across the industry. The theft of intellectual property dwarfed the scale of conventional espionage—the value was not measured in diplomatic leverage but in billions of dollars of market advantage, months of research accelerated or stolen, and the subtle erosion of competitive edge. In the digital age, the frontline of intelligence has shifted: corporations, rather than embassies, are now primary targets, and the battlefield is coded into the very tools, networks, and supply chains that sustain global commerce.

The corporate century has transformed espionage from episodic, human-driven operations into a continuous, low-visibility struggle over data, knowledge, and operational advantage. Industrial targets are attractive not merely because they hold secrets but because their assets are directly convertible into power, revenue, and influence. Designs, research data, strategic plans, and proprietary algorithms can be monetised or weaponised, giving attackers leverage beyond the narrow remit of political intelligence. In many instances, the theft of intellectual property exceeds the strategic value of traditional state secrets, highlighting a fundamental pivot in the locus of competitive advantage: knowledge itself has become the primary terrain of power.

This chapter examines the mechanics, strategies, and consequences of corporate cyber espionage. It begins with the recognition that companies—particularly those at the cutting edge of technology, pharmaceuticals, and infrastructure—are now front-line intelligence objectives. Attackers exploit vulnerabilities not only within firms themselves but across supply chains, through third-party vendors, service providers, and shared software ecosystems. The sophistication lies not in brute force but in subtle persistence: low-and-slow intrusions, credential reuse, and strategic compromise of ancillary systems allow actors to maintain footholds for months or years, often undetected. Unlike high-profile hacks that make headlines, these operations prioritise stealth, continuity, and maximal operational impact with minimal exposure.

Attribution remains one of the most vexing challenges in this domain. When a breach is discovered, establishing who is responsible can be fraught, even for the most sophisticated forensic teams. Code can be obfuscated, operations routed through multiple jurisdictions, and digital fingerprints deliberately manipulated. State actors may collaborate with private proxies, while criminal groups exploit the same tools to pursue profit. The uncertainty surrounding attribution has profound diplomatic, legal, and strategic consequences: a breach may provoke political tension, yet misattribution risks escalatory responses, reputational damage, or unwarranted regulatory action. Understanding the difficulty of reliably assigning blame is critical to interpreting the operational and policy implications of corporate cyber espionage.

The nature of exfiltrated data has evolved beyond mere theft. Increasingly, attackers leverage stolen information for extortion, coercion, or influence, transforming exfiltration into a tool of leverage. Ransomware campaigns illustrate this shift: encrypted or stolen corporate data can compel strategic decisions, extract financial gain, or reshape organisational behaviour. The line between espionage, crime, and coercion has blurred. Intelligence is no longer merely about acquisition; it is about manipulation, negotiation, and shaping outcomes without physical presence or overt force. In this landscape, the interplay between data, power, and human decision-making becomes both immediate and consequential.

Yet the digital corporate battlefield is not devoid of countermeasures. Understanding the architecture of supply chains, implementing robust access controls, monitoring anomalies over time, and fostering organisational awareness are central to defence. Cybersecurity is no longer a technical exercise alone; it is strategic, organisational, and geopolitical. Firms must navigate a complex environment in which innovation, collaboration, and openness—traits essential for modern business—introduce vulnerabilities that are exploitable by actors both criminal and state-sponsored. Intelligence operations are thus embedded within commercial infrastructures, blending technical sophistication with social, economic, and legal dimensions.

Cyber Espionage in the Corporate Century invites readers to explore these transformations in depth. It examines why corporations have emerged as primary intelligence targets, the vulnerabilities inherent in modern supply chains, the strategic calculus behind persistent intrusions, and the complex problem of attribution. It traces the trajectory from exfiltration to leverage, illustrating how stolen data can reshape behaviour, influence markets, and exert power without traditional forms of force. The chapter situates these developments within the broader themes of this book: the relocation of intelligence from physical espionage to networked, data-driven operations, and the implications of pervasive digital visibility for both organisations and society.

The unresolved tension is stark: corporations operate at the nexus of opportunity and vulnerability, innovation and exposure. Data is simultaneously an asset and a potential liability, and the mechanisms designed to protect it can themselves be vectors for compromise. As the boundaries between state, corporate, and criminal actors blur, the stakes of cyber espionage extend beyond profit or competitive advantage—they shape policy, governance, and global power relations. This chapter frames these dynamics, offering insight into how intelligence, strategy, and technology converge in the corporate age, and leaving readers to consider the profound consequences of a world in which the most valuable secrets reside in code, supply chains, and the quiet persistence of intruders unseen.

Industrial Targets

In the early hours of a spring morning, engineers at a European automotive company discovered that critical design files had disappeared from their internal servers. There were no signs of physical intrusion, no broken locks or forced entry. The breach had been executed silently, remotely, and with precision, exploiting vulnerabilities in network access and proprietary software. The magnitude of the theft was staggering: entire new vehicle designs, including confidential schematics for electric powertrains, had been copied in minutes. Comparisons with traditional espionage were inevitable—here, corporate secrets, not ambassadorial cables, had become the prize, and the perpetrators, invisible behind a screen, had accomplished in hours what spies once spent months infiltrating embassies to achieve.

This episode exemplifies a broader transformation in the landscape of intelligence. Industrial targets—companies at the forefront of technology, pharmaceuticals, energy, and infrastructure—are now prime objectives for both state and non-state actors. Unlike embassies, where diplomatic activity and high-level negotiations dominate intelligence collection, corporations offer information with immediate economic, strategic, and technological value. Intellectual property, product development pipelines, and research data are directly convertible into competitive advantage. The stakes are not merely about statecraft; they involve market dominance, industrial capacity, and innovation leadership, making companies high-value targets for sophisticated intrusion campaigns.

The shift toward corporate espionage reflects both opportunity and efficiency. Traditional espionage required human agents, physical presence, and careful tradecraft. Today, digital networks, cloud storage, and integrated supply chains enable actors to access critical information remotely, often without alerting internal monitoring systems. The barriers to collection have diminished: access credentials, misconfigured servers, and unpatched software present entry points that are abundant and persistent. In this context, corporations' operational knowledge—once siloed and tangible—has become both highly portable and exceptionally vulnerable. The consequences are immediate and far-reaching: stolen designs can disrupt markets, delay product launches, and even alter the trajectory of entire industries.

Certain sectors are particularly attractive. Technology companies, for instance, possess intellectual property that can redefine global economic and military capabilities. Pharmaceutical firms hold research that can accelerate or shortcut drug development, influencing both public health and commercial advantage. Energy firms, from renewables to petrochemicals, carry technical knowledge that informs national security and environmental policy alike. The value of these data assets is amplified by their replicability: unlike a stolen document from an embassy, a digital design file can be copied indefinitely, transmitted globally, and acted upon without diminishing the original holder's resources—until the theft is detected.

Corporate espionage is not monolithic. It encompasses both state-sponsored and independent actors, with motivations ranging from strategic advantage to financial gain. State actors may seek access to technologies critical for defence or infrastructure, while commercial competitors or criminal syndicates exploit intellectual property for market manipulation or resale. What unites these efforts is the recognition that corporate data is not incidental intelligence—it is the primary source of leverage in a hyperconnected, innovation-driven world. The calculus has changed: infiltrating a company often yields more actionable insight than conventional intelligence collection against a diplomatic target.

This reality has profound implications for organisational governance. Corporations must contend with dual pressures: operational efficiency and technological innovation require openness, collaboration, and connectivity, yet these very qualities create attack surfaces. Security is no longer a matter of perimeter defence alone; it demands strategic awareness of the organisation's data value, an understanding of potential adversaries, and rigorous risk management. Cybersecurity, therefore, is inseparable from corporate strategy. Protection of intellectual property, operational continuity, and market credibility has become a cornerstone of organisational resilience.

A defining feature of industrial targets is the granularity of the information sought. Design schematics, source code, experimental results, and proprietary algorithms provide insight not only into current capabilities but into future strategic intent. Unlike general economic intelligence, which may infer trends, these assets offer predictive power: understanding a company's research trajectory can reveal emerging technological paradigms, potential competitive disruption, and strategic vulnerabilities. The information is actionable, monetisable, and often more sensitive than conventional state secrets because it directly affects economic and strategic decision-making.

Corporate espionage also complicates legal and ethical frameworks. Intellectual property law, cross-border regulations, and cybersecurity statutes intersect, often with gaps that leave companies vulnerable. Unlike state-to-state espionage, which exists in a shadowed diplomatic and legal context, corporate intrusions occur across jurisdictions, exploiting both technical vulnerabilities and regulatory inconsistencies. Attribution is challenging, remediation is costly, and consequences—financial, reputational, and strategic—are immediate. Organisations must navigate not only technical defence but also legal and diplomatic exposure, often simultaneously.

Industrial Targets underscores a fundamental shift in the practice of intelligence. Companies, once peripheral in strategic calculations, are now central nodes in a global information ecosystem. Their assets—research, designs, and operational data—are not only valuable in isolation but also constitute leverage in markets, policy, and innovation. Understanding why corporations are targeted illuminates the broader mechanics of the corporate century: knowledge, rather than territory or diplomacy, has become the decisive element of power.

The chapter invites readers to examine the nature of corporate espionage, exploring why industrial targets are particularly compelling, how attackers exploit vulnerabilities, and what this means for organisational strategy and global intelligence dynamics. It raises questions that extend beyond technical defence: How should societies value and protect corporate knowledge in a hyperconnected world? What responsibility do organisations have to anticipate and mitigate attacks that blend commercial and strategic stakes? And how does the shift from embassy-focused to corporate-focused intelligence redefine notions of national and economic security?

By foregrounding the vulnerabilities and strategic value of industrial targets, this chapter situates the reader at the intersection of technology, strategy, and ethics, laying the groundwork for a detailed exploration of supply chain risks, persistent intrusions, and the complex interplay between theft, leverage, and influence in the digital corporate landscape.

Supply Chain as Attack Surface

In 2020, a global software firm unwittingly distributed an update that contained malicious code. The compromise did not originate from its own developers, nor from a direct intrusion into its primary network. Instead, the breach had entered through a trusted third-party library—an innocuous-seeming dependency that hundreds of companies relied upon. Within days, the tainted update propagated across clients, giving attackers access to systems far beyond the initial target. This incident exemplifies the profound vulnerability inherent in modern supply chains: in an ecosystem defined by interconnectedness, trust is both a necessity and a vector for exploitation.

Companies no longer operate in isolation. Their networks, codebases, and operational processes are embedded within globalised supply chains, reliant on vendors, cloud services, and external software components. Each connection—each library, service, or vendor—is a potential point of compromise, offering attackers indirect access to highly sensitive systems. The traditional perimeter of corporate security has dissolved: a breach of a supplier or an upstream software component can cascade through multiple organisations, granting visibility and influence to those who understand how to exploit interdependencies. In this sense, the supply chain itself becomes an operational theatre, as strategic and lucrative as any direct network attack.

The mechanisms of compromise are varied. Software dependencies, APIs, and routine updates can carry hidden malware, sometimes referred to as poisoned libraries. By exploiting these trusted channels, attackers achieve propagation with minimal risk of detection. Similarly, hardware components sourced from external manufacturers can be preloaded with firmware vulnerabilities. Even human-mediated processes—outsourced IT support, shared authentication services, or consulting engagements—introduce risk, as credentials and access privileges extend beyond the immediate organisation. What unites these vulnerabilities is systemic trust: the expectation that suppliers act as stewards rather than vectors for intrusion.

High-profile examples illuminate the scale of the problem. Attacks like the SolarWinds compromise revealed how a single poisoned update could infiltrate thousands of organisations, spanning government, corporate, and critical infrastructure sectors. The attackers operated with precision, injecting malicious code into routine software deployments, ensuring that normal processes became conduits for espionage. The sophistication was not in breaching defences directly, but in exploiting the implicit confidence organisations place in their suppliers. By weaponising trust, attackers gained sustained access to networks without triggering conventional alarms.

The implications extend beyond technical security. Supply chain compromises blur lines of accountability and attribution. When a third-party vendor is exploited, responsibility becomes diffused: did the firm suffer a breach, or did the vendor fail in its security obligations? Legal frameworks and regulatory oversight struggle to adapt to these complexities. In some cases, attacks may cross multiple jurisdictions, further complicating remediation and recourse. Corporations must therefore consider risk not only within their own walls but throughout the network of relationships that sustain their operations. Security becomes inseparable from governance and strategic decision-making.

The low-and-slow nature of supply chain attacks underscores their operational subtlety. Malicious actors often prioritise stealth over immediate gain, inserting code or hardware compromises that remain dormant until activated. By avoiding overt disruption, they preserve access and extend the operational lifespan of their intrusion. Credential stuffing, lateral movement through networked partners, and persistent backdoors exemplify how patience and strategic planning replace brute force. The corporate environment, interconnected and constantly updated, provides both the tools and the opacity necessary for such attacks to flourish.

From a defensive perspective, the challenge lies in visibility and verification. Traditional security tools, focused on perimeter defence, cannot easily detect malicious code embedded within trusted dependencies. Continuous monitoring, rigorous vendor vetting, and proactive code auditing become essential. Some organisations have begun to adopt "zero trust" principles across supply chains, insisting that every component, update, or access request is verified regardless of source. Yet the complexity of global operations, combined with commercial pressures and dependency networks, means perfect security is unattainable. Risk must be managed, not eliminated.

The philosophical stakes are equally profound. Supply chain attacks illustrate a fundamental shift in the locus of vulnerability: intelligence and influence no longer depend solely on breaching an organisation directly. Instead, they emerge from understanding, manipulating, and exploiting networks of trust and dependency. Security is relational, not merely structural. Knowledge of interconnections becomes as valuable as knowledge of the target itself, and control of those pathways can yield leverage without ever confronting the immediate target. In this sense, the supply chain is both a conduit and a battleground, where subtlety, foresight, and patience define operational success.

Supply Chain as Attack Surface invites readers to consider the ways that modern corporations are exposed through the very systems designed to enhance efficiency, collaboration, and innovation. It examines how vendors, updates, and dependencies can be leveraged by attackers to bypass traditional defences, the operational consequences of such compromises, and the ethical and strategic implications of diffused responsibility. By situating supply chains at the centre of cyber vulnerability, the chapter emphasises that contemporary intelligence operations are embedded in networks far broader than the walls of a single organisation, demanding vigilance, scrutiny, and strategic foresight.

The unresolved tension is stark: organisations cannot function in isolation, yet every point of connection carries risk. How can firms maintain operational efficiency while verifying the trustworthiness of a sprawling web of vendors and partners? How do regulators and oversight bodies assign accountability in an environment defined by interdependence and opacity? The chapter sets the stage for exploring these challenges, illustrating that the most sophisticated attacks exploit not firewalls, but relationships—and that understanding the architecture of dependence is critical to defending against the corporate intelligence threats of the twenty-first century.

Quiet Persistence

In a quiet office on the outskirts of a major financial district, a security analyst noticed an unusual pattern: repeated, low-volume login attempts targeting employee accounts over several weeks. Each attempt failed, but the persistence was striking. Credential stuffing—a technique in which stolen credentials are methodically tested across multiple accounts—was at play, yet it was executed with patience and subtlety. No alarms blared, no systems froze, and yet access was gradually being established. By the time the intrusion was detected, the attackers had already mapped the internal architecture, identified high-value targets, and prepared multiple footholds for future exploitation. This was not a dramatic breach; it was a deliberate, low-and-slow campaign designed to remain invisible while accumulating strategic advantage.

The phenomenon of quiet persistence marks a profound evolution in cyber operations. Unlike the high-profile, noisy hacks that capture headlines, these intrusions prioritise stealth and endurance. The goal is not immediate disruption but long-term control. Attackers seek to establish persistent access—multiple, often redundant pathways—while avoiding detection by conventional security systems. This approach reflects a strategic calculus: in complex, interconnected corporate environments, patience and subtlety yield more enduring leverage than rapid, high-risk attacks. Over time, these intrusions can generate access to intellectual property, operational knowledge, or sensitive communications without triggering alarms, creating an asymmetric advantage for the attacker.

This methodical patience also demonstrates the intersection of technical skill and strategic foresight. Credential stuffing exploits human behaviour: password reuse across accounts, insufficient authentication mechanisms, or delayed system responses. When combined with automated tools and low-volume, distributed attacks, it allows intruders to probe extensively without alerting monitoring systems. The value of such access lies not merely in the initial breach, but in the cumulative intelligence gathered over time—patterns of workflow, organisational hierarchy, and operational rhythm. Each small piece of information contributes to a broader understanding, enabling precision in future actions.

Quiet persistence extends beyond simple account compromise. Advanced adversaries embed themselves within networks through lateral movement, privilege escalation, and subtle manipulation of system configurations. By slowly expanding access and maintaining a low profile, they can harvest data, monitor communications, and influence system behaviour without triggering alerts. Unlike conventional cyberattacks that demand immediate exploitation, low-and-slow intrusions emphasise continuity: the longer an intruder remains undetected, the more strategic value accrues. Organisations often fail to recognise the cumulative effect until a critical threshold is crossed—by which point the attackers have amassed extensive knowledge and multiple points of leverage.

The philosophical significance of quiet persistence lies in its asymmetry. Defenders operate under a zero-tolerance expectation: any breach is unacceptable, and defensive measures must be continuous and comprehensive. Attackers, by contrast, can tolerate slow progress, leveraging time as an ally. The very patience of the intruder contrasts with the urgency imposed on corporate security teams, amplifying the strategic advantage of subtlety. Success is measured not by immediate gain but by the ability to endure, accumulate access, and remain concealed—a paradigm that challenges conventional notions of control and visibility.

Historical parallels reinforce the contemporary stakes. Just as espionage agents once cultivated networks of informants and assets over years, modern attackers cultivate digital footholds, patiently mapping and exploiting vulnerabilities. The tools have changed, but the strategy—gradual accumulation of intelligence under a cloak of invisibility—remains remarkably consistent. Digital persistence is the modern analogue to long-term human intelligence operations, demonstrating that subtlety and patience often outweigh overt force.

Corporate environments exacerbate vulnerability to low-and-slow intrusions. Reliance on interconnected systems, outsourced IT functions, and third-party vendors creates a dense web of potential access points. Monitoring tools frequently focus on high-impact events, leaving minor anomalies unchecked. These gaps enable attackers to exploit systemic blind spots, leveraging small, incremental actions to gain significant footholds. The combination of technical sophistication and organisational complexity means that quiet persistence can operate at a scale and efficiency unattainable in the era of human-centric espionage.

The consequences of undetected persistence are profound. Intellectual property, sensitive communications, and operational plans can be silently extracted over months or even years. Attackers can then leverage this information for financial gain, strategic disruption, or influence campaigns. The danger is compounded when the intrusion remains invisible to internal audits and standard monitoring procedures. Unlike sudden breaches, which provoke immediate response, quiet persistence allows adversaries to shape organisational decisions, behaviours, and vulnerabilities over time—subtly altering the landscape without overt confrontation.

Defensive strategies must therefore adapt. Traditional perimeter defences and reactive measures are insufficient. Organisations must adopt continuous monitoring, anomaly detection, and behavioural analytics capable of detecting slow, incremental activity. Segmentation, multi-factor authentication, and rigorous credential management reduce the effectiveness of low-volume attacks, while regular auditing of access logs and system behaviour provides opportunities to detect subtle intrusion patterns. Yet even with these measures, the complexity and interconnectedness of corporate systems make absolute prevention elusive; the challenge lies in early detection, rapid response, and mitigation.

Quiet persistence also raises broader questions about risk perception and organisational culture. If subtle, long-term intrusions can operate beneath conventional visibility, what does it mean for trust in networks, software, and human actors? The emphasis on patience and stealth highlights a shift in operational logic: power is exerted not through immediate disruption but through enduring presence and incremental influence. For defenders, recognising and internalising this shift is essential to developing a resilient posture in an environment where time and patience are as potent as technical force.

Quiet Persistence frames low-and-slow intrusions as both a technical and strategic challenge. It illustrates how attackers exploit patience, subtlety, and systemic complexity to maintain access, acquire intelligence, and influence corporate operations without triggering conventional alarms. By examining credential stuffing, lateral movement, and patient observation, the chapter situates contemporary cyber threats within a broader historical and operational context, demonstrating that stealth can be more consequential than speed. The reader is invited to consider not only how these intrusions operate but also how organisations can anticipate, detect, and respond to persistent, patient threats in a corporate environment increasingly defined by digital interdependence and complexity.

The unresolved tension is immediate: organisations must balance operational efficiency, accessibility, and connectivity with the reality that every system interaction—every login, update, or service dependency—may be a potential vector for patient exploitation. How can security frameworks adapt to threats that are invisible, incremental, and strategically patient? The chapter leaves readers with this pressing question, setting the stage for exploration of attribution, remediation, and the broader ethical and strategic dimensions of persistent digital intrusion.

Attribution Games

In the early hours of December 13th, 2020, a multinational corporation discovered that a sophisticated intrusion had compromised its internal systems. Servers were quietly exfiltrating data, internal communications had been monitored, and proprietary designs were at risk. Within days, forensic investigators traced elements of the attack to a particular malware family and identified command-and-control infrastructure with ties to a foreign state. Yet, despite the technical breadcrumbs, the question remained unresolved: who was truly responsible? In the digital realm, evidence can be forged, misdirected, or obfuscated; certainty is elusive. Attribution, it turns out, is less a matter of forensics than of strategy, inference, and risk management.

Assigning blame for cyberattacks has always been fraught with uncertainty, but corporate espionage in the twenty-first century elevates the stakes. Unlike conventional crimes, digital intrusions can cross borders effortlessly, traverse multiple jurisdictions, and exploit layers of intermediaries. Attackers deliberately obfuscate their origins—routing attacks through compromised networks, employing encryption and anonymisation, and mimicking the tactics of unrelated groups. A single intrusion may bear the hallmarks of multiple actors simultaneously, leaving defenders, regulators, and policymakers grappling with ambiguity. Misattribution can carry consequences as severe as the attack itself: diplomatic tensions, retaliatory measures, and costly legal disputes.

The challenges of attribution are both technical and conceptual. Technically, malware signatures, IP addresses, and code artefacts provide clues, but these are easily manipulated. A malicious actor can reuse open-source code, alter metadata, or exploit shared libraries to create false trails. Social engineering, spear-phishing campaigns, and compromised third parties further muddy the waters. Conceptually, determining responsibility requires weighing intent, capacity, and opportunity—a blend of evidence and inference that straddles law, intelligence, and corporate policy. Unlike physical crimes, where fingerprints or eyewitness accounts can provide near-certainty, digital forensics rarely achieves definitive closure.

Historical precedents illustrate the stakes. Consider the SolarWinds compromise, in which attackers inserted malicious code into a routine software update. Tens of thousands of organisations were affected, spanning government agencies and private corporations. While investigations pointed toward a state-sponsored actor, definitive proof that could withstand judicial or diplomatic scrutiny remained elusive. The ambiguity itself became a tool: it allowed attackers to achieve strategic objectives without triggering immediate retaliation, exploiting the limits of certainty to their advantage.

Attribution is not merely an academic exercise; it shapes operational and diplomatic responses. Governments must decide whether to sanction, retaliate, or pursue legal action, often based on probabilistic assessments rather than incontrovertible proof. Companies face analogous dilemmas: should they publicly attribute a breach, potentially exposing themselves to reputational or regulatory risk, or manage the incident quietly, accepting operational compromise as the cost of discretion? In both cases, the decision-making process is inseparable from the limits of certainty, highlighting the strategic value of ambiguity in cyber operations.

Corporate espionage further complicates matters through indirect pathways. Supply chain compromises, outsourced IT functions, and cloud dependencies mean that breaches may originate far from the primary target. An attacker may exploit a vendor's infrastructure or embed malicious updates in trusted software, creating layers of separation between perpetrator and victim. As a result, attribution must account not only for the immediate technical origin of the breach but also for the broader ecosystem in which access was gained. Failure to consider this complexity risks misidentifying actors and miscalculating responses.

The legal stakes of attribution are equally significant. In international law, state responsibility for cyber operations hinges on demonstrating both control and intent—a standard notoriously difficult to satisfy in practice. Civil and criminal liability in corporate contexts depends on establishing causation and negligence, which are complicated by the opacity of digital pathways. False or premature attribution can trigger litigation, sanctions, or reputational damage that rival the costs of the original intrusion. Consequently, organisations and states alike must navigate a landscape in which uncertainty is the norm and the consequences of misjudgment are severe.

Beyond technical and legal dimensions, attribution intersects with psychology and perception. Public statements, media reporting, and internal communications shape beliefs about responsibility and influence subsequent action. Actors who obscure their identity exploit this, understanding that ambiguity itself can serve as a strategic lever. In some cases, the mere suggestion of involvement may be sufficient to deter competitors, manipulate markets, or influence policy decisions, even without definitive proof. The game of attribution thus becomes both a factual investigation and a contest over perception, narrative, and leverage.

Philosophically, the difficulties of attribution reflect the changing nature of agency and accountability in the digital age. In traditional espionage, responsibility was tied to identifiable agents and hierarchies. Today, attacks are distributed, automated, and mediated through complex systems. A single intrusion may involve multiple actors, automated tools, and compromised intermediaries, blurring the line between direct intent and systemic consequence. Understanding responsibility requires grappling with these layers, recognising that power and influence can operate through obfuscation and intermediation as effectively as through overt action.

At the corporate level, attribution also drives internal governance and risk management. Boards and executives must consider not only technical remediation but also strategic response: who might be behind the intrusion, what their objectives are, and how disclosure affects clients, partners, and regulators. Cyber threat intelligence teams work to develop probabilistic models of attribution, combining forensic evidence with geopolitical and industry analysis. Even when certainty is unattainable, these assessments guide defensive priorities, resource allocation, and communications strategies.

Attribution Games reveals that assigning blame in corporate cyber espionage is as much an art of reasoning as it is a science of detection. It illustrates how stealth, sophistication, and strategic ambiguity challenge conventional notions of accountability, while highlighting the profound diplomatic and legal consequences of misattribution. By tracing technical pathways, examining intermediary networks, and situating breaches within broader strategic contexts, the chapter demonstrates that understanding who is behind an intrusion—and why—is central not only to remediation, but to the exercise of corporate and state power in a digitally interconnected world.

The unresolved tension is stark: how can organisations, regulators, and states act decisively in a domain where certainty is scarce, evidence is malleable, and actors exploit ambiguity as a strategic tool? This chapter leaves readers contemplating the intricate interplay between evidence, inference, and influence, setting the stage for subsequent discussions of exploitation, leverage, and the transformation of data into coercive power.

From Theft to Leverage

In July 2021, a multinational energy company awoke to a digital siege. Ransomware had infiltrated its systems, encrypting critical files and halting operations. A message appeared on screens across the organisation: pay or risk permanent loss of proprietary data. What distinguished this attack from earlier intrusions was not the breach itself—corporate networks are perpetually probed—but the shift in purpose. The aim was no longer merely extraction of information; it was a direct instrument of influence. By holding data hostage, attackers could compel strategic decisions, dictate financial transactions, and shape operational priorities. The digital theft had transformed into leverage, a coercive tool capable of steering corporate behaviour without firing a single shot.

This evolution—from exfiltration to extortion—is emblematic of the modern corporate espionage landscape. Historically, the theft of intellectual property, trade secrets, or strategic plans was the endpoint: once stolen, the material entered the vaults of a competitor or foreign intelligence service. Today, attackers increasingly exploit the stolen information as a vector for pressure, coercion, or strategic manipulation. Ransomware campaigns, industrial-scale leaks, and reputational threats illustrate that access alone is insufficient; the true value lies in the capacity to influence decisions, extract concessions, or reshape incentives. In short, data is no longer merely a commodity; it is a lever.

The mechanisms of this leverage are varied. Ransomware offers the most visible example: encryption transforms operational data into a form of negotiation. Organisations confronted with the sudden paralysis of essential systems are forced to evaluate risk, cost, and continuity. The mere presence of confidential or proprietary information in the hands of a hostile actor creates bargaining power. Similarly, the selective disclosure of sensitive data can function as a reputational weapon. Attackers can exploit exposure of regulatory non-compliance, internal communications, or strategic vulnerabilities to extract concessions without direct physical intervention. The subtlety of these tactics lies in their indirect coercion: influence is wielded through perceived risk and uncertainty rather than overt confrontation.

This shift from theft to leverage highlights a strategic sophistication previously absent in corporate intrusions. Low-and-slow operations establish persistent access, mapping internal workflows and identifying decision-making bottlenecks. Once these pathways are understood, attackers can time actions to maximise disruption or bargaining power. For instance, encrypting financial records just before quarterly reporting or releasing sensitive project timelines during critical negotiations exerts pressure beyond the immediate technical damage. The adversary's calculus is informed by organisational rhythms, operational priorities, and market sensitivities, illustrating a deep understanding of both human and systemic behaviour.

The phenomenon also underscores a critical distinction between information possession and influence. Data alone is inert; its power emerges when it can alter behaviour or generate consequences. In early corporate espionage, stolen designs or plans were valuable primarily for replication or competitive advantage. In the contemporary landscape, stolen data can simultaneously threaten, compel, and shape corporate choices. The transformation of exfiltrated information into leverage requires foresight, patience, and strategic deployment, echoing classical principles of influence even as it leverages the peculiarities of digital systems.

Ransomware is but one instrument of this broader trend. Attackers now integrate multi-stage operations, combining theft with targeted disclosure, social engineering, and threat signalling. A breach may be accompanied by messages tailored to executives, operational managers, or partners, communicating potential exposure, financial loss, or regulatory scrutiny. In this context, the digital intrusion functions not only as a technical event but as a performative act: it signals capability, intent, and reach, creating a psychological landscape in which corporate actors must respond strategically. The mere perception of ongoing surveillance or persistent access amplifies the leverage of the initial intrusion.

Economic and legal structures magnify this effect. Corporations operate in interconnected networks of supply chains, regulatory obligations, and contractual commitments. A threat to data integrity can ripple across these networks, influencing partners, insurers, and investors. The asymmetric nature of cyber leverage—where a small group of actors can impose outsized influence through targeted disruption—reflects a structural shift in power. Traditional defences, predicated on perimeter security or reactive response, are insufficient against adversaries who manipulate timing, perception, and cascading consequences.

The ethical and strategic implications are equally profound. When stolen information becomes a tool of coercion, conventional notions of risk management are inadequate. Organisations must consider not only the likelihood of breach but the potential for behavioural manipulation, financial extortion, and reputational damage. The interplay between digital access and leverage transforms the moral calculus of cybersecurity: protecting systems is no longer solely about preventing theft; it is about preserving autonomy, decision-making freedom, and organisational agency in the face of invisible pressure.

From Theft to Leverage also illuminates the blurred boundaries between criminality, corporate competition, and geopolitical strategy. State-sponsored actors may deploy ransomware or exfiltration campaigns not merely for financial gain but to shape markets, influence strategic industries, or assert soft power. Corporate entities can be caught between conventional regulatory responsibilities and the extralegal pressures imposed by external actors, navigating a landscape in which the implications of data loss extend far beyond immediate operational impact.

Ultimately, this chapter challenges readers to reconceive the role of data in the corporate sphere. Information is no longer merely an asset to be protected or a commodity to be traded. It has become a lever—a medium through which influence, coercion, and strategic advantage are exercised. Understanding this shift is crucial for executives, policymakers, and security professionals alike, as it defines the stakes of modern corporate espionage, shapes defence and response strategies, and reframes questions of accountability and resilience.

The unresolved tension is palpable: how can organisations defend not only against the theft of data but against its weaponisation? When leverage is derived from knowledge, access, and timing rather than overt destruction, conventional approaches to security and risk management are insufficient. By exploring the transformation of exfiltrated information into instruments of influence, this chapter invites readers to grapple with the evolving nature of corporate power in the digital age and to consider strategies that protect both assets and organisational agency.

Chapter 6

The Mathematics of Sorting

In the bustling departure hall of an international airport, a man stands in the queue for security. Unseen by him, a system has already assigned him a numerical risk score—one derived not from a single suspicious gesture or overheard comment, but from layers of data accumulated across years, jurisdictions, and platforms. A combination of travel history, ticket purchases, and even mobility patterns feeds into a predictive model. Though the screen at the checkpoint remains indifferent to the individual, the algorithm has quietly judged him. This is not science fiction; it is the quiet calculus of contemporary governance, insurance, finance, and policing—a world in which human lives are increasingly evaluated, categorised, and sometimes constrained by numbers.

The rise of algorithmic scoring systems—what this chapter calls *the mathematics of sorting*—marks a profound shift in how power and knowledge intersect. Once, judgements about trust, risk, or creditworthiness were made by humans exercising discretion. Today, these decisions are increasingly delegated to models trained on historical data, optimised to produce rapid, replicable outputs. Mobility data can influence insurance premiums, social media interactions can feed into predictive policing watchlists, and subtle behavioural markers can adjust credit limits or loan approvals. Each number carries authority, each model codifies assumptions about who is likely to comply, default, or pose a threat. Yet, the precision implied by these figures masks deep complexity—and, often, hidden bias.

Consider the simple act of scoring. A person's routine movements, aggregated from mobile devices or loyalty programmes, are transformed into a risk profile. To the designer, it is an abstract problem of probability and correlation. To the subject, it is an intrusion into daily life with tangible consequences. What begins as a statistical exercise quickly becomes a tool for governance, a mechanism that shapes access, opportunity, and freedom.

The chapter will trace these transformations, unpacking the social, ethical, and technical implications of treating individuals as datasets to be sorted.

The first insight lies in the architecture of these systems: *scoring the citizen.* Across sectors, the principle is the same. Credit bureaus pioneered the logic, converting payment histories into predictive grades. Insurers, tech platforms, and even municipal authorities have adapted it, applying analogous methods to mobility, social interactions, and behavioural footprints. A city's sensor network might feed into a risk model that guides policing priorities; a bank might use online activity to adjust lending limits. In each case, data is distilled into a score whose meaning is functional rather than descriptive: it exists to inform action, not to represent truth. Yet the act of scoring is never neutral. Choices about which variables to include, how to weight them, and how to interpret outputs embed subjective judgements into ostensibly objective calculations.

Training data, trained society underscores the generational impact of these choices. Historical biases are inherited by models in ways that are subtle but consequential. An algorithm trained on decades of arrest records may encode discriminatory policing practices into its predictions. Employment screening models may perpetuate systemic inequities in hiring patterns. Remedies exist—better sampling, careful documentation, fairness audits—but they require sustained attention and structural commitment. The mathematics of sorting is thus inseparable from social history: each equation carries echoes of past inequalities, and each output can either entrench or mitigate them.

The tension between accuracy, fairness, and accountability is perhaps the most pressing conceptual challenge. High accuracy on one dataset may conceal systemic errors elsewhere; a model optimised for operational efficiency may compromise transparency or ethical standards. Readers will be invited to interrogate claims of fairness, to consider pragmatic tests that go beyond technical assurances, and to recognise that the trade-offs embedded in any scoring system are social as much as mathematical. Evaluating performance thus becomes not merely a matter of statistics, but a question of societal priorities and values.

Equally important is the problem of the *black box.* Many contemporary models operate as opaque systems, their internal logic inscrutable even to those who deploy them. Techniques like feature importance or sensitivity analysis offer partial visibility, revealing, for instance, that proxy variables—ZIP codes, device usage patterns, or social connections—stand in for sensitive attributes such as race, gender, or socioeconomic status. Yet interpretability has limits; complexity, interaction effects, and adaptive learning mean that no score can ever be fully transparent. Here lies a paradox: the more powerful and predictive the model, the harder it is to understand, contest, or correct.

Finally, the mathematics of sorting acquires its real significance when error becomes policy. Even a tiny false positive rate, scaled across millions of cases, produces profound consequences. A misclassified traveller subjected to repeated screenings experiences inconvenience and indignity; a student flagged by predictive analytics may face unjust academic scrutiny; a citizen assigned a low credit score may find housing and employment opportunities constrained. The cumulative impact transforms statistical minutiae into lived reality, demonstrating that numerical abstraction is never neutral—it is enacted through human institutions and decision-making processes.

This chapter, therefore, situates the reader at the intersection of data, society, and governance. It explores how algorithmic scoring systems operate, how historical biases propagate, and how technical decisions translate into tangible outcomes. It frames the mathematics of sorting as both an analytical tool and a mechanism of power: an apparatus that organises populations, allocates resources, and shapes the possibilities available to individuals. By unpacking these systems, their assumptions, and their limitations, the chapter provides readers with a conceptual toolkit to understand, interrogate, and challenge the ways in which algorithms increasingly mediate everyday life.

The questions raised are urgent and open-ended. How can societies reconcile efficiency with justice? How can transparency coexist with technical complexity? And, crucially, how can policy and oversight prevent small errors from cascading into systemic harms? In navigating these questions, the reader enters a landscape where mathematics meets morality, prediction collides with prejudice, and numbers exert influence far beyond their symbolic value. The journey through this chapter illuminates not only the mechanisms of sorting but the stakes of living in a world where every move can be measured, scored, and acted upon.

Scoring the Citizen

On a quiet Tuesday morning in a mid-sized American city, a driver checks their insurance app and notices an unexpected increase in their premium. There was no accident, no traffic violation, no change in policy coverage—only a subtle shift in the data feeding the algorithm that assesses risk.

Unknown to the driver, their recent commuting patterns, captured via a mobile app that tracks location, have nudged them into a higher-risk bracket. What might have once been a human decision, weighed against observable facts and context, is now distilled into a numerical value. That single score, generated by an opaque computational process, determines financial cost, access, and perception, yet its origins remain largely invisible. This is the new face of risk evaluation: ubiquitous, automated, and deeply consequential.

Across sectors, the logic is the same. Credit scoring, once limited to banks evaluating loan repayment histories, now extends to insurance companies, employment platforms, municipal authorities, and even tech firms controlling user access. Every action—buying a product online, commuting through certain neighbourhoods, or interacting on social platforms—can contribute to an individual's digital dossier. The metrics are varied, the inputs numerous, but the outcome is always a distillation of human behaviour into a single, actionable figure: the citizen as a quantified entity, assessed continuously, scored perpetually.

This subchapter examines the rise of credit-like systems beyond finance, tracing how predictive algorithms ingest behavioural, social, and spatial data to produce risk scores that travel across commercial and civic domains. The stakes are tangible. Unlike a financial ledger, which documents past transactions, these systems forecast potentiality, allocating privileges or penalties based on inferred likelihoods. They introduce the familiar illusion of objectivity: numbers seem precise, rational, and impartial. Yet they embody human assumptions, operational constraints, and systemic biases.

The architecture of these scoring systems often appears deceptively simple. Mobility data, for instance, may suggest exposure to certain environments—high-crime areas, congested zones, or regions associated with frequent insurance claims. Insurers and municipal authorities alike use this information to adjust premiums, allocate resources, or flag individuals for scrutiny. An ostensibly mundane dataset—the GPS pings of a commuter—transforms into a tool for stratifying risk. Its effects ripple outward, influencing behaviour as individuals adjust routines to align with algorithmic expectations, whether by changing driving patterns or moderating online activity.

Beyond mobility, social and digital footprints intensify the granularity of scoring. Algorithms can incorporate online purchases, search histories, and engagement patterns on social media to infer stability, reliability, or propensity for certain behaviours. Each additional layer of data enhances predictive power, but simultaneously embeds assumptions: which behaviours signal responsibility or risk, which signals are proxies for social categories, and which correlations are spurious yet amplified by the model. The resulting score is not merely predictive—it is performative, shaping the citizen as much as it describes them.

Crucially, these systems are not static. Continuous data flows ensure that risk assessments update in near real-time, reflecting behavioural shifts and environmental changes. This dynamic quality contrasts sharply with traditional assessments, which relied on periodic human evaluation. Consider a small business owner whose creditworthiness is evaluated solely on repayment history: a missed payment might be remedied in weeks, and human discretion allows for nuance. In the contemporary model, a transient change in mobility or transaction pattern can trigger immediate consequences, magnifying the impact of minor deviations and amplifying systemic inequities.

The universality of scoring introduces profound ethical and societal dilemmas. Credit-like systems create a lattice of quantification that extends far beyond commerce. Employment, insurance eligibility, housing access, and even law enforcement interventions can be guided by algorithmically generated scores. While predictive power can improve efficiency and reduce overt discretion, it also consolidates authority into opaque models that resist scrutiny. Decisions that were once human—where context, mitigation, and explanation were available—now occur silently, unobserved, and often unchallengeable.

Furthermore, the portability of scores across sectors intensifies consequences. A risk assessment derived from one domain, such as mobility or insurance data, can be leveraged elsewhere: a pattern detected for premium calculation may inform municipal surveillance priorities; a digital footprint used for marketing optimisation may feed into employment background algorithms. Each system, designed with its own purpose, inadvertently contributes to a network of influence that shapes opportunity, reputation, and social standing. Individuals, largely unaware of this interconnected architecture, confront constraints produced not by visible human judgement but by automated, distributed inference.

Yet these systems are not purely deterministic. They are malleable, contingent upon design choices: which datasets are included, which features are emphasised, how thresholds are calibrated, and what corrective mechanisms exist. Transparency, documentation, and oversight emerge as critical counterweights, enabling users and policymakers to interrogate the assumptions embedded in the scoring process. The technical sophistication of the models belies the human agency behind them: engineers, analysts, and executives make normative choices about which behaviours should carry weight, and which risks are tolerable. Understanding this human layer is essential for engaging with the mathematics of sorting responsibly.

The implications extend beyond individual experience to societal patterns. Continuous scoring can reinforce stratification, privileging those whose digital traces align with institutional expectations while marginalising those whose behaviour deviates—even in harmless or contextually justified ways. As systems scale, small misclassifications propagate, amplifying disparities across populations. A modest increase in a travel-based risk metric may shift premium pricing, which in turn affects disposable income, access to services, and longer-term social mobility. The consequences of scoring ripple through daily life, producing effects that are simultaneously invisible and consequential.

As this subchapter will demonstrate, scoring the citizen is neither inherently benevolent nor malevolent; it is a mechanism of power that codifies, enforces, and perpetuates assumptions. By unpacking its architecture, tracing its applications across sectors, and examining the human and systemic biases it reproduces, readers are invited to understand not only how scores are produced, but how they matter. Each figure, each algorithm, each dataset is a node in a complex social and technical ecosystem that demands scrutiny, accountability, and thoughtful engagement.

Questions arise naturally and urgently: How should mobility, social, and transactional data be weighted in predictive models? To what extent can scoring systems be audited, corrected, or contested? What societal values should guide the design of predictive metrics, and who gets to decide? In navigating these questions, the reader begins to see the citizen not merely as an individual subject to evaluation, but as part of an intricate network in which data, technology, and governance converge.

The exercise of scoring illuminates the contemporary tension between efficiency and justice, predictability and autonomy. It exemplifies how technology mediates opportunity, risk, and privilege in ways that are subtle yet pervasive. By examining credit-like systems across sectors, this subchapter establishes the foundational understanding necessary for later discussions on bias, fairness, and interpretability in algorithmic governance. It provides the analytical lens through which the broader consequences of the mathematics of sorting can be discerned, interrogated, and, ultimately, navigated with critical insight.

Training Data, Trained Society

In 2016, a facial recognition system deployed by a major tech company was found to misidentify women and people with darker skin tones at rates far higher than white men. The system, lauded for its precision, had been trained on millions of images scraped from the internet—images reflecting the historic imbalances of representation in digital spaces. This discrepancy was not a flaw in the algorithm's mathematics but a mirror of societal bias encoded into its training data. What the system "learned" was not neutral; it was a reflection of the world as it had been documented, collected, and classified, and in doing so, it propagated inequality under the guise of objectivity.

The story exemplifies a broader phenomenon: the labels used to teach machines carry the weight of history, culture, and institutional practices. Whether in predictive policing, credit scoring, hiring algorithms, or social services, models trained on historic datasets internalise the assumptions, omissions, and prejudices embedded within those records. A dataset that underrepresents certain communities or encodes stereotypical associations transforms into a predictive tool that may reinforce disadvantage. The technology is powerful, the stakes enormous, and the mechanisms subtle, often hidden behind technical jargon or opaque interfaces.

Understanding how training data shapes societal outcomes is essential to grasping the mathematics of sorting. Data is not simply "collected" in a vacuum; it is curated, annotated, and classified by humans with imperfect knowledge, constrained resources, and prevailing social norms. When these datasets feed into machine learning models, the patterns they carry are not inert—they guide decisions, influence policy, and affect lives. The challenge is not merely technical but deeply social: how can we design systems that learn from data without inheriting the inequities embedded within it?

At its core, the problem arises from the labels used to characterise phenomena. In supervised learning, human-assigned categories—"high risk," "creditworthy," "suspicious"—provide the ground truth against which models optimise. These labels, however, are never neutral. Consider a predictive policing algorithm trained on arrest records. Arrest data is a proxy for criminal activity, but it is also shaped by discretionary policing, historical over-policing of particular communities, and socio-economic disparities. A model trained on such labels absorbs these biases, amplifying them as predictions guide patrol deployment. The mathematics is straightforward; the ethical and social implications are anything but.

Beyond overt misrepresentation, subtler issues arise from correlation and proxy variables. Features correlated with protected characteristics—ZIP codes, purchasing patterns, or educational institutions—can serve as proxies for race, ethnicity, or socio-economic status. Even without explicit labels, models can perpetuate inequity because the training data encodes historic patterns of advantage and disadvantage. Mobility data, for instance, may indicate routine commutes that intersect with areas of higher policing or commercial activity. When models interpret these traces as risk signals, individuals are evaluated not on their behaviour per se but on societal structures embedded in the datasets themselves.

Remedies are available but require deliberate attention. Improved sampling can ensure representation of underrepresented populations, reducing skewed influence in the learned models. Documentation—transparent data sheets describing provenance, collection methodology, and known limitations—enables downstream users to interpret predictions responsibly. Techniques such as reweighting, debiasing, and fairness constraints can adjust for identified disparities, though each introduces trade-offs between accuracy, utility, and equity. These solutions highlight a central truth: technical ingenuity alone cannot resolve bias; it must be paired with social awareness and ethical governance.

The interplay between data and society extends beyond model performance to perception and trust. When individuals discover that algorithms influence decisions affecting credit, employment, or civic participation, questions of legitimacy arise. Transparency, accountability, and the ability to contest decisions become not just ethical imperatives but practical necessities for sustaining the social licence of automated systems. A well-documented, representative training dataset can reduce error rates, but it cannot substitute for mechanisms that allow affected individuals to understand, challenge, and, where necessary, correct algorithmic assessments.

Historic bias in data also illustrates the principle that technology codifies society rather than creating it anew. Algorithms do not invent inequity; they inherit and propagate it. In this sense, training data is a bridge between past and present, linking historical structures to contemporary decision-making systems. Every dataset reflects choices: who was included, who was omitted, which events were recorded, and which were deemed irrelevant. Understanding these choices illuminates the societal context within which algorithms operate and provides a foundation for intervention, whether through data curation, model design, or policy oversight.

As models increasingly influence social and economic life, scrutiny of training data becomes both urgent and complex. There is no single "correct" dataset; context matters, and the same data may yield different outcomes depending on labels, features, and objective functions. Therefore, the question is not simply whether a dataset is biased, but how bias interacts with model design, deployment context, and real-world consequences. Case studies from hiring algorithms, predictive policing, and credit scoring illustrate that even minor biases in training data can scale to systemic disadvantage, particularly when models are deployed at national or global scale.

Ultimately, the task is twofold: to understand the mechanics of bias transmission and to develop practices that mitigate harm without sacrificing the utility of predictive models. Better sampling ensures that underrepresented groups are visible to algorithms; rigorous documentation allows practitioners to contextualise predictions; post hoc auditing identifies unexpected outcomes and informs adjustments. Together, these strategies form a framework for responsible machine learning, one that recognises the inseparability of data, algorithm, and society.

The broader lesson is clear: a trained model reflects its training data, and a trained society reflects the models it adopts. Bias is not merely an error to be corrected; it is a signal of deeper structural inequities. By interrogating the provenance, labelling, and representativeness of datasets, practitioners and policymakers can begin to shape models that are not only accurate but socially informed. This subchapter invites readers to understand that technical decisions—how data is sampled, labelled, and documented—carry profound social consequences, and that responsible stewardship of training data is essential to the ethics and efficacy of algorithmic governance.

As we proceed, the focus will shift to methods for assessing fairness, transparency, and accountability in the mathematical frameworks that translate training data into actionable decisions. By tracing the lineage from labelled examples to societal impact, readers will gain the tools to critically evaluate how models influence lives and to consider interventions that mitigate historic inequities while preserving predictive power. The exploration of training data is thus both a technical and moral inquiry, situating the mathematics of sorting within the lived reality of society itself.

Accuracy, Fairness, Accountability

In 2019, a major US city deployed a predictive policing system designed to forecast areas at heightened risk of violent crime. Within months, neighbourhoods with predominantly minority populations saw an increase in patrols, despite crime rates in those areas remaining statistically consistent. Officials defended the system as accurate, citing the low overall error rate in historical testing. Critics, however, argued that "accuracy" alone obscured the broader question: accuracy for whom, and at what social cost? This episode highlights a fundamental tension in automated decision-making: the interplay between numerical performance, equitable treatment, and ethical responsibility.

The technical claim of an algorithm's accuracy—the proportion of correct predictions—is straightforward. Yet in practice, measures of accuracy interact with social realities, reflecting and amplifying historic disparities. A model might correctly predict many events in aggregate but systematically underperform for specific groups, inadvertently institutionalising inequity. Similarly, efforts to correct for bias can reduce overall predictive performance, creating a trade-off that is both mathematical and moral. Understanding these trade-offs is essential for anyone seeking to evaluate, deploy, or regulate algorithmic systems that influence human lives.

Equally pressing is accountability. Who bears responsibility when a model misfires? When a risk assessment tool denies a loan, when a hiring algorithm screens out qualified candidates, or when a policing system redirects patrols based on flawed assumptions, the consequences are tangible. Accountability demands more than technical audits; it requires transparency in design, clear metrics for evaluation, and avenues for individuals to contest decisions. The convergence of accuracy, fairness, and accountability defines the ethical boundary of algorithmic governance and shapes societal trust in predictive systems.

At the core of these concerns is the question of fairness. Unlike raw accuracy, fairness is contextual and value-laden. Consider a credit scoring system that incorporates repayment history, employment data, and mobility patterns. While it may predict default risk with high accuracy overall, certain groups may be disadvantaged due to historic inequalities embedded in the training data. Detecting and correcting these disparities requires a nuanced approach, balancing statistical criteria—such as demographic parity or equal opportunity—with societal norms and regulatory requirements. Fairness is not a single metric but a suite of considerations, each with implications for policy and practice.

One practical approach is to evaluate models across multiple dimensions simultaneously. Error rates can be disaggregated by subgroup to reveal hidden inequities, and sensitivity analyses can test how changes in input variables affect outcomes for different populations. Scenario testing allows policymakers and practitioners to assess potential harms before deployment. For instance, in predictive policing, evaluating whether hotspots align disproportionately with certain demographic communities can reveal systemic bias even when the model performs well in aggregate. By incorporating these tests into standard practice, stakeholders move from abstract claims of fairness to actionable insights.

Accountability also intersects with transparency. A system that generates recommendations but cannot explain its decisions—or offers explanations that are incomprehensible to affected individuals—limits oversight and inhibits meaningful challenge. Interpretable models, post hoc explanation tools, and comprehensive documentation of training data are crucial for creating systems that are auditable and accountable. The goal is not merely to comply with regulatory standards but to cultivate understanding among decision-makers and the public, ensuring that algorithmic processes align with social expectations of justice and responsibility.

Trade-offs between accuracy and fairness are inevitable but manageable. In some cases, slight reductions in predictive performance can yield substantial gains in equity, mitigating harms that would otherwise accrue to vulnerable populations. Conversely, prioritising aggregate accuracy without regard for subgroup performance risks entrenching structural disadvantage. Effective governance requires acknowledging these trade-offs explicitly, rather than treating them as technical footnotes. It also demands continuous monitoring: societal conditions evolve, and models trained on historical data can become misaligned with current realities, producing new forms of unfairness.

The subchapter also emphasises the importance of empirical, reader-accessible tests for claims of fairness. Simple checks—such as comparing error rates, evaluating false positive and false negative distributions, and assessing alignment with legal standards—empower stakeholders to interrogate models without needing to reconstruct complex algorithms from scratch. These tests make abstract concepts tangible, allowing researchers, regulators, and even affected individuals to form informed judgements about the systems shaping their lives. They bridge the gap between statistical performance and social consequence, turning the mathematics of prediction into a tool for scrutiny rather than obscurity.

Finally, accountability extends beyond individual systems to institutional design. Organisations deploying predictive models must establish clear governance structures, delineating responsibilities for oversight, ethical review, and response to harm. External audits, independent benchmarking, and public reporting mechanisms serve as essential checks on unexamined assumptions. A system cannot be fair solely because its creators intend it to be; fairness and accountability require continuous attention, transparent evaluation, and alignment with societal values.

This subchapter frames accuracy, fairness, and accountability not as separate concerns but as interdependent elements in the responsible deployment of predictive systems. By clearly defining trade-offs, offering practical tests, and highlighting the societal stakes of model performance, it equips readers to critically assess claims of fairness and to advocate for systems that balance technical efficacy with ethical responsibility. In a world increasingly mediated by algorithmic decisions, understanding these principles is essential for ensuring that technology serves society rather than reinforcing its inequities.

Interpreting the Black Box

In 2021, a financial institution rolled out a sophisticated credit scoring system that drew from hundreds of variables, including transaction histories, social network data, and geolocation patterns. Within months, complaints emerged from customers whose loan applications were denied, despite strong traditional credit histories. When asked for an explanation, the bank could only point to a model score and a vague statement about "weighted features." The algorithm worked, but no one—neither customer nor regulator—could fully understand why it made certain predictions. This scenario exemplifies the black-box problem: modern machine learning models often deliver accurate results without providing clear reasoning, leaving humans dependent on opaque computations.

The rise of high-dimensional, non-linear models—random forests, gradient boosting, deep neural networks—has amplified this opacity. While these models frequently outperform simpler alternatives in predictive accuracy, they do so at the cost of interpretability. Decision-makers, affected individuals, and auditors face the challenge of assessing reliability, fairness, and risk without a full view of the underlying mechanisms. Interpreting a black box is not merely a technical exercise; it is a social and ethical necessity. Decisions driven by inscrutable models have real-world consequences, from credit denials and job rejections to surveillance and policing, making transparency a critical component of responsible deployment.

Efforts to illuminate the black box focus on producing human-understandable explanations. One common technique is *feature importance*, which quantifies the influence of each input on model output. For example, in a predictive hiring model, feature importance may reveal that prior job titles contribute more to predictions than education level. This insight can uncover unintended proxies: if prior job titles correlate with gender or socioeconomic status, the model may inadvertently encode systemic bias. Identifying these hidden dependencies allows institutions to audit and mitigate inequities without dismantling the entire system.

Partial interpretability extends to model-agnostic approaches. Tools like LIME (Local Interpretable Model-agnostic Explanations) and SHAP (SHapley Additive exPlanations) approximate the local behaviour of complex models around individual predictions. These methods generate intuitive visualisations or numerical contributions for specific instances, enabling practitioners to explain why a particular loan application was flagged or why a predicted crime hotspot emerged. Despite their utility, these approximations are inherently limited; they may not capture global model dynamics, interactions between variables, or context-dependent effects, leaving residual uncertainty.

Another class of interpretable models includes inherently transparent structures such as decision trees, linear regressions, or rule-based systems. While these models trade some predictive power for clarity, they offer an explicit rationale for decisions. A linear model predicting insurance premiums, for instance, directly weights factors like mileage, age, and claims history, producing coefficients that stakeholders can inspect and debate. The trade-off between accuracy and interpretability becomes a practical and ethical consideration: in high-stakes environments, a slightly less accurate model that is understandable may be preferable to a more accurate but opaque system.

Interpreting black boxes also requires attention to *proxy variables*. Even when a model excludes protected characteristics like race or gender, correlated inputs can function as surrogates. Geolocation, income brackets, or social network connections may inadvertently encode discriminatory patterns. Identifying proxies through feature analysis or correlation studies allows organisations to adjust models, implement fairness constraints, or enhance oversight. Yet, this process is neither foolproof nor straightforward: proxies may shift over time as societal patterns change, necessitating ongoing monitoring and recalibration.

Contextual understanding is equally vital. Models do not operate in a vacuum; their predictions interact with human behaviour, institutional practices, and policy frameworks. A risk score may appear unbiased in isolation but produce disparate impacts when deployed, for instance, in policing or loan allocation. Interpretable methods provide entry points for stakeholders to scrutinise these dynamics, enabling a dialogue between model mechanics and real-world consequences. By combining technical transparency with domain expertise, organisations can better anticipate harmful outcomes and design corrective interventions.

Nevertheless, interpretability has limits. Certain interactions captured by complex models—high-order feature combinations, temporal dependencies, and non-linear dynamics—cannot always be fully articulated in simple terms. Simplifications risk misleading stakeholders or overestimating the clarity of explanations. Ethical deployment requires communicating these uncertainties clearly, acknowledging that even interpretable approximations do not guarantee perfect understanding or immunity from error. Transparency is as much about communicating uncertainty as it is about revealing mechanisms.

The subchapter emphasises a practical mindset: interpretation is a tool, not a panacea. Practitioners must combine model explanations with rigorous testing, external audits, and impact assessments. For example, examining misclassification rates across demographic groups, simulating hypothetical scenarios, and cross-validating results with alternative models provide complementary layers of insight. Interpretability enables humans to ask informed questions, evaluate risk, and make accountable decisions, even when the black box cannot be fully opened.

Ultimately, interpreting the black box is a negotiation between complexity and comprehension, between predictive performance and social responsibility. Feature importance, local approximations, transparent models, and proxy analysis are all instruments in this effort, but they operate within constraints. Recognising these constraints, and embedding interpretability as a core practice rather than an afterthought, empowers organisations to deploy models responsibly while maintaining public trust.

As algorithms increasingly mediate critical aspects of life—from finance and employment to security and healthcare—the capacity to interrogate and interpret opaque systems is not optional. Understanding what drives predictions, revealing hidden dependencies, and communicating limitations are essential steps toward accountability, fairness, and ethical oversight. This subchapter provides readers with the conceptual framework, technical methods, and philosophical grounding to navigate the complexities of the black box, translating abstract computation into actionable insight.

When Error Becomes Policy

In 2004, a businessman named Maher Arar was detained at JFK Airport on his way home to Canada. Despite having no criminal record, he was placed on a US watchlist and rendered to Syria, where he endured months of detention and torture. The error was not an isolated clerical mistake; it was a systemic failure embedded within a risk-scoring and watchlist system designed to prevent terrorism. Arar's case exemplifies the central paradox of algorithmic and bureaucratic decision-making: even a seemingly small error rate, when applied across millions of individuals, can inflict catastrophic harm.

Errors in policy-driven systems rarely remain confined to theoretical miscalculations. When risk assessments, predictive models, or automated screenings guide enforcement decisions, minor inaccuracies scale into tangible consequences for real people. In airport security, the false-positive rate of watchlists determines how many innocent travellers are stopped, questioned, or detained. In healthcare, slight misclassifications in triage systems can influence who receives urgent treatment. In social services, predictive risk scores may flag families for intervention based on limited or biased data. Across these contexts, errors are no longer abstract—they become policy enacted at scale.

Understanding how small rates of misclassification propagate is crucial. A 1% false-positive rate in a database of 10 million people translates into 100,000 individuals flagged erroneously. For those caught in the system, consequences are disproportionate: delays, legal scrutiny, financial harm, reputational damage, or physical risk. Policy amplification mechanisms further exacerbate this. Systems often feed their outputs into additional decision layers—alerts trigger further monitoring, resource allocation, or enforcement measures. An error at the first stage multiplies downstream, converting statistical noise into social and political consequences.

The phenomenon of error propagation intersects with human bias in critical ways. Historical inequities embedded in training data can skew outputs, producing disproportionate impacts on marginalised populations. For example, predictive policing models may over-represent neighbourhoods with historically higher arrest rates, irrespective of current crime levels. When these predictions inform patrol deployment, the error magnifies, reinforcing the original bias in a self-perpetuating loop. Each misclassification is thus not only a statistical issue but also a vector of social injustice, shaping perceptions of risk and institutional response.

Policy environments compound the stakes of error. Decisions grounded in algorithmic outputs are often treated as objective, masking underlying uncertainty. Legislators, regulators, and administrators may accept system outputs as authoritative, assuming statistical reliability equates to infallibility. This institutional deference transforms algorithmic error into structural injustice. Airport watchlists, automated fraud detection, or health eligibility screens illustrate how small inaccuracies can institutionalise exclusion, delay, or punitive measures. The translation from error to policy requires attention not just to model performance but to governance, oversight, and accountability.

Mitigating the harms of systemic error begins with transparent error measurement and calibration. Metrics such as precision, recall, and false-positive/false-negative rates provide insight into the likelihood of misclassification. Scenario analysis and stress testing allow policymakers to anticipate the consequences of error under different deployment scales. For instance, simulating the impact of a 0.5% false-positive rate in a national watchlist system clarifies the human burden and resource requirements. Such exercises reveal that even minor model imperfections can carry outsized social and operational costs.

Error also interacts with trust and perception. When citizens experience misclassification or misidentification, confidence in institutions erodes. Public pushback may force policy revisions or system shutdowns, but not before harm has occurred. Consider the repeated failures in airline no-fly lists: despite technical corrections, erroneous entries persisted for years, illustrating the difficulty of reversing policy harm once enacted. The interplay between algorithmic error, bureaucratic inertia, and social trust underscores the need for precautionary design, continuous auditing, and remediation mechanisms.

Importantly, error is not purely technical—it is a function of design choices, operational constraints, and social priorities. Decisions about thresholds, feature selection, or risk weighting embed values and trade-offs into the system. A higher sensitivity to capture potential threats increases false positives, while prioritising precision may allow genuine risks to go undetected. Policy choices determine which type of error is tolerable, and these choices have ethical, legal, and practical ramifications. Transparency about trade-offs is essential to avoid converting statistical compromise into unintended social injustice.

The narrative of small errors cascading into systemic harm is evident beyond watchlists. In credit scoring, minor misclassifications can deny thousands of consumers loans, affecting employment and housing opportunities. In predictive healthcare, rare misdiagnoses can propagate treatment errors across populations. In welfare systems, automated eligibility assessments may misallocate benefits, disproportionately affecting vulnerable communities. Across sectors, the lesson is consistent: scale magnifies error, and policy amplifies impact.

Understanding this dynamic demands an integrative perspective. It is insufficient to evaluate a system purely on accuracy metrics; one must consider deployment context, population scale, feedback loops, and mitigation capacity. Regulatory frameworks, auditing protocols, and human oversight serve as essential checks. Ethical implementation involves continuous evaluation of how errors interact with societal structures, recognising that even a 99% accurate system may generate unacceptable harm if applied broadly.

Ultimately, the subchapter illuminates a critical insight: errors in predictive or rule-based systems are never neutral. They are socialised through policy, enacted through enforcement, and lived by individuals. Small rates of misclassification, benign in isolation, become consequential at scale, shaping lives, perceptions, and institutional credibility. By examining cases such as airport watchlist misfires, alongside cross-sector analogues, readers gain an appreciation for the stakes of algorithmic and bureaucratic error. The challenge is not merely technical but ethical: designing, deploying, and governing systems with humility, foresight, and accountability.

Chapter 7

Law, Rights, and the Loophole Factory

In 2019, the personal data of hundreds of millions of citizens found its way across borders, purchased, transferred, or requested under opaque legal mechanisms. Corporate servers, cloud storage, and government archives became the theatre for a quiet legal arms race, where the letter of the law was followed with precision, yet the spirit of privacy was repeatedly evaded. One user might consent to location tracking on a mobile app in Berlin, only to discover months later that the same data had been sold to foreign law enforcement under a cross-border memorandum, with little oversight or recourse. The paradox is stark: the safeguards embedded in centuries of legal thought coexist alongside sophisticated pathways designed to bypass them.

This chapter explores the tension between enduring principles of privacy and the inventive workarounds that have emerged in contemporary governance. At its core lies a fundamental question: can rights designed for a pre-digital era meaningfully govern a world where data flows freely across jurisdictions, commercial contracts, and technical infrastructures? The answer is neither simple nor static. Principles such as necessity, proportionality, and purpose limitation have survived generations of legislative reform, yet their translation into practice is continually tested by new tools, vendors, and legal interpretations.

The law is rarely neutral in these contexts. Its deployment, procurement choices, and enforcement strategies shape the lived experience of privacy. A government's decision to purchase surveillance software or cloud services is not merely administrative; it embeds a set of assumptions about access, accountability, and recourse into the social fabric. Likewise, cross-border data transfers, voluntary disclosures by private firms, and nuanced interpretations of warrants introduce friction points where legal authority, technological capability, and ethical obligation collide. Across these vectors, small loopholes magnify into systemic gaps, with citizens often left with recourse only in theory.

Understanding this dynamic requires shifting focus from isolated statutes or cases to patterns of practice. Principles before provisions—emphasising the enduring goals of privacy law rather than the minutiae of individual clauses—become the compass for evaluating modern implementations. They highlight why purpose limitation matters when data collected for traffic management is later used for policing, or why proportionality is essential when expansive data sharing intersects with everyday freedoms. Each of these principles offers a lens for scrutinising loopholes, whether they arise from vendor contracts, automated data purchase schemes, or international treaties.

The interplay between procurement and rights is particularly consequential. When governments acquire software or services, they effectively delegate aspects of authority, embedding technical constraints and legal interpretations into operational practice. A contract with a cloud provider determines who may access stored data, how long it persists, and under what conditions deletion is possible. These choices shape rights more tangibly than legislation alone, revealing a form of administrative law exercised not in courtrooms but in boardrooms and procurement offices. Transparency in these agreements is therefore not a bureaucratic nicety; it is a prerequisite for meaningful accountability.

Extraterritorial entanglements further complicate the landscape. Data does not respect national borders. Servers in Dublin may hold information collected in Manila, which is accessed by authorities in Washington under treaties negotiated in secret. Jurisdictional conflicts are not merely theoretical: they influence enforcement, appeal rights, and the ability of individuals to exercise control over personal information. The legal architecture struggles to accommodate a technical reality that was unimaginable when foundational privacy principles were codified. Each cross-border transfer introduces a point of friction where law, technology, and human rights intersect.

Equally important is the question of remedies. Where rights are infringed, what mechanisms provide meaningful recourse? Independent oversight, enforceable deletion rights, and compensatory damages are not abstract ideals—they are the instruments that can recalibrate the balance of power between the state, corporations, and citizens. Without these, even the most robust statutory protections risk remaining symbolic. Remedies that bite ensure that principles retain teeth, that procedural rights translate into substantive impact, and that the design of legal and technological systems can be challenged and corrected.

Throughout this chapter, attention will move seamlessly between legal theory, technical architecture, and social consequences. Case studies will demonstrate how data flows circumvent conventional oversight, while analysis will reveal the ways enduring principles can be operationalised despite systemic loopholes. From the pathways of voluntary disclosure to the intricacies of international data transfer, readers will encounter the full spectrum of forces shaping contemporary privacy. The lens is both critical and practical: understanding loopholes is not merely an intellectual exercise but a foundation for demanding transparency, accountability, and enforceable rights.

By the chapter's conclusion, it will become evident that privacy is not a static entitlement but a negotiated condition, continuously contested by technology, policy, and law. The "loophole factory" is not a metaphor for failure alone; it is an invitation to engage critically with the structures that shape everyday freedoms. The questions posed—about procurement, cross-border entanglements, and remedial effectiveness—are urgent, not optional. They challenge readers to consider how rights can be preserved in practice, not just asserted in principle, and set the stage for a nuanced exploration of the mechanisms that enable or constrain meaningful privacy in the digital age.

Principles Before Provisions

In a quiet office in Brussels, a team of policy analysts reviewed yet another draft of a national data-protection regulation. Paragraphs of detailed provisions stretched for pages—definitions of consent, retention periods, technical standards for encryption—but beneath the formalism lay a more fundamental question: did these words, however precise, actually protect the individuals they purported to serve? Across decades and continents, privacy law has repeatedly confronted this tension between meticulous legal drafting and the enduring principles that give the law moral and practical weight. The European Convention on Human Rights, the OECD Privacy Guidelines, and countless national statutes share common themes—purpose limitation, necessity, and proportionality—yet their expression varies. The challenge is not merely reading the rules but discerning the principles that must guide interpretation, implementation, and enforcement.

The paradox is immediately apparent: in a world saturated with data, we often focus on the minutiae of compliance rather than the broader goals the law is intended to achieve. Consider a company that collects location data from millions of users. One regulation may require explicit consent, another may allow opt-out, and yet a third might defer to legitimate interests. Each path leads to different procedural outcomes, but the underlying question remains constant: is the collection necessary, proportionate, and aligned with the purpose for which it was requested? When the conversation shifts from clauses to principles, the debate becomes less about loopholes and more about the moral and practical effects of data handling.

Purpose limitation is the first principle that demands attention. At its core, it asserts that personal data should be collected for a clearly defined objective, and no further processing should occur beyond that scope without renewed justification. Historical abuses—from governments repurposing census data for surveillance to marketing firms extending behavioural profiles into credit assessment—illustrate the peril of ignoring this rule. Modern challenges extend beyond the traditional boundaries of governance: machine-learning models trained on vast, heterogeneous datasets often blend signals across multiple domains, creating emergent purposes unforeseen at the time of collection. Adhering to purpose limitation requires vigilance, not just in drafting policies but in engineering systems, auditing processes, and assessing downstream consequences.

Necessity forms the second pillar of principled privacy. Every data point should serve a clear and essential function; excessive collection is inherently suspect. In practice, necessity is often tested against technical convenience. Companies may justify storing every transaction or sensor reading because it facilitates predictive analytics, security monitoring, or personalised services. Yet necessity is not determined by internal efficiency but by societal expectations and proportional benefit. A transport authority, for instance, may argue that retaining precise GPS traces indefinitely improves route optimisation, but is such retention truly necessary to the declared public function? By foregrounding necessity, regulators, engineers, and citizens alike can evaluate not only whether data is collected legally, but whether it is collected responsibly.

Proportionality, the third principle, acts as a balance beam between intrusion and benefit. It requires that the level of data collection and processing corresponds to the legitimate aim pursued. Excessive monitoring, regardless of purpose or necessity, violates proportionality if it imposes undue risk or burden on individuals. Consider the deployment of facial recognition at airports or urban intersections. Even if the objective is security, proportionality demands scrutiny of scope, retention, accuracy, and error tolerance. The law's procedural provisions may provide technical thresholds, yet it is proportionality that ensures ethical alignment, translating abstract standards into human experience.

These principles, while enduring, are not self-enforcing. Legal drafters, corporate leaders, and technologists must actively interpret them in context. This interpretation is not static: advances in computational power, the ubiquity of cloud infrastructures, and the emergence of global supply chains continually redefine what constitutes necessary, proportionate, or purpose-aligned processing. A financial services company in New York may rely on a dataset collected in Tokyo to model fraud risk. Purpose limitation, necessity, and proportionality do not evaporate across borders; they remain essential guideposts, demanding translation into technical safeguards, contract clauses, and operational protocols.

Historical case studies illustrate the stakes. In the 1980s, national ID schemes and centralised tax databases prompted debate about proportionality: should governments centralise all personal data to improve efficiency, or are limited, purpose-specific collections safer? In the digital era, the same question arises with augmented immediacy. Sensor networks, biometric authentication, and behavioural profiling create continuous, granular records of human activity. Without principled guidance, even well-intentioned data programs risk normalising surveillance, diluting consent, and amplifying inequality. Principles before provisions serve as a compass: they provide a standard by which to assess whether legal compliance aligns with human impact.

Operationalising these principles is a non-trivial task. Purpose limitation can be codified via data inventories and strict processing policies; necessity can be assessed through rigorous data minimisation strategies and pre-deployment audits; proportionality can be evaluated by weighing expected societal benefits against the potential harm of collection. Yet the abstract nature of these principles requires interpretive skill and institutional commitment. An organisation may satisfy every checkbox in a regulation while undermining the spirit of privacy if it fails to apply these guiding concepts meaningfully. For citizens and policymakers, the principles offer both a diagnostic and aspirational framework—diagnostic in identifying misalignments between practice and intent, aspirational in setting a benchmark for responsible innovation.

Ethical reflection complements legal principles. Each decision about data collection, retention, or sharing has human consequences, often unevenly distributed. Marginalised populations are particularly vulnerable to disproportionate surveillance and exploitation. By foregrounding purpose, necessity, and proportionality, stakeholders can interrogate who benefits, who bears risk, and whether safeguards suffice. For example, predictive policing systems may claim high accuracy in aggregate, but without proportionality, they can amplify bias, targeting specific communities disproportionately. Principle-driven evaluation demands that outcomes, not only intentions, be assessed.

Yet principles encounter tension in practice. Competing purposes—security, commerce, research—frequently collide, and necessity may conflict with innovation. Resolving these tensions requires prioritisation grounded not in technical convenience or short-term gain, but in societal norms and legal ethics. The principle-first approach does not resolve all ambiguity; instead, it frames the debate, ensuring that decisions are accountable, defensible, and aligned with enduring human values.

As the chapter unfolds, readers will encounter examples from corporate data collection, government surveillance, and cross-border data flows, each demonstrating the application—and the limits—of principled guidance. From cloud service contracts to AI-driven decision-making, the interplay of purpose, necessity, and proportionality shapes practical outcomes more profoundly than any procedural provision alone. The narrative will illustrate not only what these principles demand, but also how organisations, regulators, and individuals can operationalise them in contexts of rapid technological change.

Ultimately, focusing on principles before provisions invites a fundamental shift in perspective. Rather than treating regulations as static checklists, it encourages a dynamic engagement with privacy as a living, adaptive concept. Purpose limitation, necessity, and proportionality are not mere legal fictions; they are the lenses through which society can evaluate the legitimacy of data practices, anticipate potential harms, and design systems that respect human dignity even in an era of pervasive data collection. The question lingers as the chapter concludes: how can enduring principles guide practice when law, technology, and corporate ambition continuously evolve? The exploration that follows aims to illuminate this delicate but essential balancing act, providing both conceptual clarity and practical insight.

The Warrant Workarounds

In a small conference room overlooking the city skyline, an intelligence officer scrolls through a spreadsheet that tracks access to personal data across dozens of technology companies. On paper, every request has been "voluntary," every transfer of information appears compliant with law, yet the pattern is unmistakable: law enforcement, regulators, and private entities are leveraging commercial channels to obtain what would otherwise require judicial authorisation. The ostensibly simple act of purchasing or requesting data sidesteps traditional warrants, producing a complex web of accountability gaps that blur the boundaries between lawful investigation and circumvention. Across borders, the stakes rise further: one country's privacy regulations clash with another's legal reach, creating a regulatory labyrinth where consent, cooperation, and compulsion intertwine.

The paradox is stark: while privacy laws emphasise due process, necessity, and proportionality, operational practice often finds ways to achieve the same investigative objectives without invoking judicial oversight. Companies have become inadvertent intermediaries, selling or voluntarily disclosing data that effectively substitutes for a court order. Consider location data collected from smartphone apps, often sold to analytics firms, which can then be shared with law enforcement for criminal investigations. Users are neither aware nor consulted, yet the resulting intelligence shapes enforcement decisions. Here, legal compliance and ethical accountability diverge—the procedures are followed, but the protective purpose of a warrant is diluted.

Historically, warrant requirements arose to impose restraint, ensuring that the power to access private information would be mediated by an impartial authority. Courts, acting as a check on executive power, were intended to guarantee that searches and seizures were justified, proportionate, and documented. Yet the advent of commercial data brokers, cross-border digital infrastructures, and voluntary disclosure frameworks has disrupted this equilibrium. Today, the landscape of digital investigation is defined less by courtroom petitions and more by the flow of information across corporate networks, subscription services, and intergovernmental agreements. The traditional signal of judicial oversight—the warrant—is being replaced by an intricate choreography of purchase, request, and consent-like mechanisms.

Data purchase represents the most visible of these workarounds. Analytics firms and brokers aggregate mobile, transactional, and behavioural information from countless users. Law enforcement agencies can, and increasingly do, acquire these datasets without invoking judicial procedures. A single dataset may reveal movement patterns, social associations, and consumption habits—information that, if collected directly by the state, would trigger statutory safeguards. Yet when acquired via market transactions, these checks are often absent or severely weakened. The ethical and legal implications are profound: commercial intermediaries, motivated by profit rather than procedural fidelity, occupy a critical gatekeeping role. This creates a novel form of accountability gap, where the formal legal apparatus is bypassed but the consequences for individuals remain significant.

Voluntary disclosure operates under a similar logic, but with subtle distinctions. Companies may respond to informal requests from authorities, such as subpoenas, regulatory guidance, or non-binding "letters of request," providing user data without the procedural rigour of a warrant. These disclosures exploit a grey zone: organisations comply with perceived legal obligations while sidestepping formal judicial scrutiny. In practice, voluntary disclosure can encompass everything from email content and transactional records to detailed behavioural profiles, yet the mechanisms for oversight are inconsistent, often internal, and rarely transparent. Users seldom know when their information has been shared, and accountability mechanisms—audits, remedies, or sanctions—are sporadic at best.

Cross-border requests amplify these challenges, introducing jurisdictional ambiguity. Data stored on foreign servers or managed by multinational corporations often falls under multiple, sometimes conflicting legal regimes. Mutual legal assistance treaties (MLATs) exist to formalise intergovernmental cooperation, but the process is notoriously slow and opaque. In response, agencies increasingly rely on extrajudicial channels: asking companies to voluntarily provide data held abroad, purchasing information from brokers who aggregate international datasets, or exploiting legal asymmetries where a company's home country enforces minimal privacy protections. The result is a patchwork of access, where traditional principles of oversight are undermined by the complexity of global digital infrastructure.

These workarounds raise pressing questions about proportionality and necessity. While investigators may argue that purchased or voluntarily disclosed data is critical for public safety, the lack of judicial oversight erodes the principle that intrusions should be justified and measured. Errors, overreach, and incidental collection are difficult to challenge because the pathways for accountability are fragmented. A misattributed or incorrect dataset can lead to surveillance, reputational harm, or even legal consequences, yet redress is often inaccessible. By removing the procedural safeguards embedded in warrants, these mechanisms shift the burden of verification, ethics, and oversight from courts to companies and, ultimately, to citizens who remain largely unaware of the processes governing their data.

The technological dimension further complicates the picture. Automated data aggregation, sophisticated analytics, and cloud-based storage allow vast amounts of information to be accessed and correlated instantaneously. A single cross-border request or commercial purchase can yield insight equivalent to what would have previously required multiple warrants and months of investigation. The speed, scale, and opacity of these operations make traditional legal instruments seem sluggish and reactive. Moreover, the reliance on corporate intermediaries creates incentives for compliance over scrutiny: businesses are motivated by contractual obligations, reputational concerns, or market pressures, not necessarily by the ethical or constitutional imperatives that underpin warrant systems.

This subchapter also interrogates the accountability deficits created by these practices. Who is responsible when a data acquisition circumvents due process? Is it the requesting agency, the intermediary company, or the regulators who have failed to enforce transparency? The legal frameworks remain contested and unevenly enforced, and practical oversight often relies on internal audits or voluntary reporting. Without clear lines of responsibility, individuals whose information is accessed through these channels lack meaningful recourse. Courts may not review the data, public reporting is rare, and remedies—if available—are slow and limited. These gaps highlight a critical tension in modern governance: the formal legitimacy of law can coexist with practical opacity, leaving citizens exposed even when statutory procedures ostensibly exist.

Ethically, the warrant workarounds prompt reflection on consent, trust, and societal expectations. Users may have voluntarily agreed to data collection for commercial purposes, yet this consent rarely extends to law enforcement or intelligence use. When commercial flows substitute for judicial authorisation, the boundary between private and public surveillance blurs, creating a zone in which ethical and legal norms are misaligned. The societal question is profound: how should democracies ensure that investigative imperatives do not undermine foundational rights, even when the law provides technical compliance through corporate intermediaries?

As this subchapter unfolds, readers will examine case studies illustrating data purchase arrangements, voluntary disclosure practices, and cross-border requests, revealing both the mechanics and the consequences of these workarounds. Each example will illuminate the structural tensions between legality, oversight, and the lived impact on individuals, highlighting the persistent challenge of ensuring accountability in a rapidly digitising, globally interconnected world. By tracing the contours of these practices, the narrative foregrounds the urgent need for transparency, procedural integrity, and principled governance in data access—without sacrificing operational necessity entirely.

Ultimately, exploring warrant workarounds forces a reconsideration of what it means for legal protections to function in practice. Procedural compliance alone cannot guarantee privacy, proportionality, or fairness; the interplay between corporate cooperation, cross-border infrastructures, and investigative ambition determines how rights are realised—or bypassed—in the digital age. The unresolved tension lingers: can societies reconcile the operational advantages of commercial and voluntary data access with enduring expectations of oversight and accountability, or will these mechanisms continue to erode the protective architecture of the law?

Extraterritorial Entanglements

In a brightly lit server hall somewhere in Northern Europe, racks of humming machines store terabytes of personal information, financial records, and corporate communications. The physical location of these servers is trivial to most users, yet it is of profound significance to governments, regulators, and legal authorities. When data crosses borders, the question of who has the rights to access, control, or protect it becomes tangled in a web of conflicting laws, divergent privacy standards, and competing national interests. A request from one jurisdiction may collide with restrictions in another, leaving corporations caught between compliance and obstruction, and individuals exposed to surveillance regimes far from their home.

Consider the simple act of storing cloud backups for multinational clients. A European citizen's health records might reside in servers in the United States, administered by a corporation headquartered in Asia. If law enforcement in the United States issues a subpoena, it may compel the cloud provider to release the data. Yet the European Union's privacy regulations could prohibit that transfer without explicit consent, generating a direct conflict between jurisdictions. What seems straightforward on a technical level—copying files from one machine to another—becomes a contest over sovereignty, rights, and accountability. The digital realm collapses geography, but law, by design, remains rooted in it.

Historically, territoriality was assumed in legal frameworks: data generated, held, and processed within a country's borders fell under that nation's laws. Courts could adjudicate disputes; enforcement could follow clear rules. Cloud computing and globalised infrastructure have shattered that assumption. Data flows fluidly across continents, replicated in multiple jurisdictions, creating situations where compliance with one nation's law may violate another's. These extraterritorial entanglements are not theoretical—they manifest daily in disputes over user privacy, law enforcement requests, and corporate governance.

One of the most visible arenas for these conflicts is the cross-border request. Authorities in one nation often rely on foreign service providers to obtain user data. Mutual legal assistance treaties (MLATs) are the formal mechanism, but they are slow and cumbersome, ill-suited to the instantaneous nature of digital communications. In practice, agencies may bypass these procedures by requesting voluntary disclosures or leveraging commercial agreements, yet these workarounds introduce accountability gaps. A user may be subject to surveillance authorized by a foreign government without the protections ordinarily available under their domestic legal system.

The tension between extraterritorial law and corporate practice is further complicated by differences in regulatory philosophy. Some nations prioritise national security, granting expansive surveillance powers to government agencies. Others emphasise individual privacy, enforcing strict consent, purpose limitation, and proportionality. Corporations operating internationally must navigate this mosaic, often adopting policies that satisfy the strictest applicable standards, yet even these efforts cannot fully reconcile legal contradictions. A cloud provider may comply with a local warrant while inadvertently contravening foreign privacy protections, exposing themselves to litigation, sanctions, or reputational damage.

High-profile cases illustrate these conflicts vividly. Consider disputes over access to encrypted communications where providers claim they cannot decrypt data locally, yet authorities demand access through foreign offices. The legal reasoning is complicated: does jurisdiction follow the citizen, the corporate headquarters, the server location, or the pathway of the data itself?

Courts have wrestled with these questions, producing inconsistent rulings and, at times, escalating diplomatic tensions. The Apple-FBI standoff over iPhone encryption in the United States, while domestic, foreshadowed the international complexity now emerging in cross-border data governance, showing how technology and law often advance at different speeds.

The corporate dimension cannot be understated. Vendor contracts, service-level agreements, and data-processing clauses shape the extent to which companies can resist or comply with extraterritorial requests. Procurement choices—where to host data, which cloud provider to engage, and under which legal framework to operate—effectively determine users' rights in practice. When governments purchase services from global technology providers, they may gain access to data beyond the reach of domestic law. Conversely, individuals' capacity to assert privacy rights is constrained by the layers of jurisdictional authority, contractual obligations, and operational realities.

Extraterritorial entanglements also expose a deeper philosophical challenge: the law's inherent tension between universality and locality. Rights are articulated as universal—privacy, due process, and proportionality—but their enforcement is local, bound by territory. The digital environment, by contrast, is inherently borderless. A single email, transaction, or location record may touch multiple legal domains in seconds, challenging notions of accountability and control. When rights depend on geography, yet information refuses those boundaries, the promise of protection is inherently compromised.

Operational responses to these entanglements vary. Some governments attempt bilateral or multilateral agreements to harmonise standards, while others pursue assertive extraterritorial claims, demanding compliance from foreign corporations. Companies may implement geo-fencing of data, cryptographic segregation, or transparency reporting to mitigate risk. Yet none of these strategies fully resolves the underlying conflict between legal obligations, commercial realities, and individual rights. In practice, each incident tests the boundaries of authority, accountability, and the normative assumptions underpinning privacy protections.

Moreover, the implications for individuals are concrete. A user's communications stored abroad may be subject to surveillance, disclosure, or legal requests without their knowledge. Remedies are often inaccessible: challenging foreign warrants or asserting deletion rights across borders can be legally and financially prohibitive. The layering of jurisdictional authorities produces not just technical ambiguity but practical disenfranchisement, where rights exist in principle but cannot be exercised effectively.

Throughout this subchapter, we will explore specific cases, illustrating how cloud storage, multinational service providers, and cross-border legal requests interact to create entangled regimes of access and control. We will examine the competing claims of privacy and national security, the role of corporate intermediaries, and the human impact of jurisdictional friction. Each example illuminates the operational, legal, and ethical dimensions of extraterritorial entanglements, highlighting the urgent need for harmonisation, transparency, and robust oversight in an age where data's mobility exceeds traditional legal reach.

Ultimately, extraterritorial entanglements underscore a persistent dilemma: the promise of rights against intrusion is limited when enforcement depends on static, geographic-bound legal frameworks, and information flows without restraint. For regulators, corporations, and citizens alike, navigating this terrain demands attention to principles—necessity, proportionality, and purpose—while grappling with the practical reality that law, commerce, and technology rarely align neatly. The unresolved question lingers: can meaningful protections persist in a digital ecosystem where data is everywhere, yet law is anchored to place?

Procurement Is Policy

In a conference room overlooking a glassy government complex, a small team debates the specifications of the next contract. On the table lie documents detailing vendor capabilities, compliance certifications, and pricing tiers. The discussion seems routine, the language procedural, the stakes procedural. Yet in those pages, buried among clauses and service-level agreements, reside decisions that will shape the practical contours of citizens' rights. Every sensor purchased, every software licence signed, every platform integrated into governmental operations carries with it implicit authority: the capacity to access, monitor, and influence individual lives. Procurement, far from a neutral technical act, functions as policy in action. What a government chooses to buy is not merely a reflection of administrative need—it is a declaration of whose rights will be respected, whose privacy protected, and whose liberties are negotiable.

Consider the acquisition of facial recognition technology by municipal authorities. The contracts often stipulate not only the delivery of cameras and analytic software but also integration with law enforcement databases, cloud storage provisions, and retention policies. A clause dictating indefinite storage or expansive sharing privileges can enable practices that profoundly alter the balance between public safety and personal privacy. These are not hypothetical concerns: cities that deployed such systems without robust contractual safeguards faced public backlash and legal challenges when mass surveillance of ordinary citizens was exposed. The policies embedded in procurement agreements translate directly into the lived experience of rights—or their erosion.

Procurement decisions become even more consequential when the technologies involved are opaque. Software that analyses patterns, predicts behaviour, or aggregates personal data is rarely fully understood by the purchasers themselves. Vendors may offer assurances of compliance or ethical safeguards, yet these are mediated through contract language that is technical and often non-binding in practice. A seemingly minor feature—automatic data replication across borders, for instance—may have profound implications for jurisdictional authority and the enforcement of privacy protections. In effect, the act of purchase crystallises the operational scope of a government's powers, embedding them within the infrastructure of everyday governance.

The interplay between procurement and rights is especially visible in cases involving public safety systems. Consider a government's choice to implement an integrated city-wide surveillance platform. Contracts may include vendor obligations for real-time data access, retention schedules, analytic capabilities, and user access privileges. Each contractual specification determines what is possible: who can see data, under what circumstances, and for how long. Even if legislation mandates constraints on surveillance, the technical parameters and contractual allowances may circumvent these protections, illustrating how policy is enacted through procurement before it is codified in law.

Transparency emerges as a critical mechanism to safeguard rights in this domain. When contracts are confidential or heavily redacted, the public and oversight bodies cannot evaluate the scope or legality of surveillance capabilities. Independent auditors and civic watchdogs are left unable to verify compliance with principles such as necessity, proportionality, and purpose limitation. In contrast, contracts that are accessible and detailed allow for scrutiny, comparison, and accountability. Transparency transforms procurement from an opaque administrative procedure into a site of democratic oversight, where the implications for civil liberties are visible and contestable.

Procurement is further complicated by the globalisation of technology providers. Governments rarely develop complex systems in-house; they rely on multinational corporations for software, hardware, and integrated solutions. These vendors operate under their own legal regimes, with obligations to shareholders and foreign governments. Clauses dictating data access, storage, or cooperation with other jurisdictions may be included by default, with little input from local authorities. Citizens' rights are, in effect, shaped by the intersection of domestic procurement decisions and foreign corporate policies. A government's choice of vendor can enable surveillance practices that outpace domestic legal safeguards, raising questions about sovereignty and the enforceability of local rights.

Historical examples underscore the stakes. In several European jurisdictions, procurement of digital monitoring systems by municipal authorities preceded public controversies over mass data collection. Retrospective analysis revealed that contractual clauses allowing vendor discretion over analytic features and data sharing had effectively authorised practices that regulators later deemed excessive or disproportionate. These incidents illustrate a central truth: procurement is not merely administrative; it is a form of latent policymaking, with tangible consequences for individual freedoms and systemic accountability.

Contractual provisions also shape the operational culture within agencies. Systems that include automatic alerts, predictive analytics, or integrated data feeds influence decision-making. Policymakers and operators come to rely on the affordances and constraints defined in the contracts. Over time, these technical and contractual boundaries can institutionalise particular modes of surveillance, enforcement, or data retention, embedding policy through operational practice rather than legislation. Rights are affected not by explicit laws alone but by the material realities encoded in purchased systems.

To address these concerns, procurement processes must be approached with a rights-conscious lens. Technical specifications should explicitly consider privacy, proportionality, and purpose limitation. Contractual obligations must bind vendors to ethical practices, independent auditing, and transparent reporting. Moreover, procurement decisions should be reviewed with an awareness of their long-term operational and societal consequences, recognising that once infrastructure is deployed, retrofitting rights protections is costly and politically fraught. In this sense, procurement is not a one-time transaction but a continuing policy choice, shaping the framework within which rights are exercised—or compromised—for years to come.

The broader implication is clear: rights are not guaranteed by law alone. The technologies, vendors, and contractual structures through which governments act fundamentally shape the exercise of those rights in practice. Citizens' privacy, autonomy, and capacity to contest state action are mediated through procurement choices, yet these decisions are often shielded from public scrutiny. Ensuring that procurement serves as a conduit for, rather than a barrier to, rights demands transparency, accountability, and foresight.

As this subchapter will explore, specific examples of procurement decisions reveal how technical specifications, vendor agreements, and operational integrations carry legal and ethical weight. From integrated surveillance platforms to data-analytic services, each contract codifies permissions, obligations, and limitations that affect citizens' experience of rights. The discussion highlights the necessity of proactive oversight, standardised transparency measures, and ethical frameworks that bridge the gap between administrative procurement and substantive protections.

Ultimately, understanding procurement as policy reframes the debate over digital rights. It is not sufficient to legislate protections in isolation; the operationalisation of those protections is determined at the point of purchase. The act of acquiring technology, negotiating contracts, and defining operational parameters is itself an exercise of power, shaping the boundaries of rights before law is interpreted, enforced, or challenged. The challenge for policymakers, civil society, and the public is to recognise this dynamic and demand transparency and accountability, ensuring that what governments buy aligns with the principles they profess to uphold.

Remedies That Bite

In the quiet corridors of a data regulator's office, a single case file can hold the weight of thousands of lives. Consider the individual whose personal information, harvested without consent, circulates through corporate databases, predictive algorithms, and cross-border data brokers. For most, discovery of the breach triggers anxiety, confusion, and a vague sense of powerlessness. For the regulator or court tasked with enforcing remedies, the challenge is precise and concrete: how to impose consequences that are meaningful, enforceable, and deterrent in a landscape dominated by digital opacity. Mere acknowledgment of wrongdoing or token penalties are insufficient; the architecture of modern redress demands remedies that bite. It is within this tension—between the scale of digital harm and the potency of regulatory response—that the true measure of accountability emerges.

The inadequacy of passive enforcement is starkly illustrated by repeated incidents of data misuse. Consider the case of a multinational social media platform whose privacy settings were misconfigured, exposing sensitive user information to third-party advertisers. For users, the breach was immediate and personal; for regulators, the response highlighted systemic weaknesses. Initial notifications and public apologies proved largely symbolic. It was only the imposition of enforceable deletion rights, monetary penalties proportional to harm, and the requirement for independent audits that produced tangible correction and deterrence. This illustrates the core principle: remedies must be operationally forceful, not merely declaratory, to transform abstract rights into lived protections.

At the heart of meaningful redress lies independent oversight. When enforcement relies solely on self-reporting by corporations or internal compliance reviews, conflicts of interest erode both efficacy and public trust. Oversight bodies—whether statutory regulators, judicial panels, or civic auditing organisations—must have unmediated access to data, operational authority to verify compliance, and the independence to enforce consequences. Examples from the European Union's General Data Protection Regulation (GDPR) illustrate this approach. Supervisory authorities can demand data deletion, halt processing, and levy fines calibrated to both the scale of infringement and the culpability of the entity. Such interventions do more than penalise; they actively recalibrate organisational behaviour, embedding respect for privacy and rights into operational culture.

Monetary damages are another pillar of remedies that bite. A fine assessed as a fraction of a corporation's revenue or as a nominal token often fails to incentivise change. By contrast, damages that scale with both the extent of the breach and the magnitude of systemic negligence create a tangible cost for non-compliance. Beyond corporate recalibration, financial remedies signal to the broader market that rights infringements carry real consequences, shaping industry norms. They also offer a measure of justice to affected individuals, converting abstract violations into quantifiable accountability. Yet the implementation of damages raises philosophical and practical questions: how to quantify harm in the digital realm, where loss is often intangible, diffuse, or delayed? Resolving these challenges requires methodologies that combine legal rigor, technical understanding, and ethical reasoning.

Deletion rights—commonly referred to as the "right to be forgotten"—demonstrate the transformative potential of enforceable remedies. In practice, deletion extends beyond the simple removal of a record; it requires revocation of residual copies, including backups, third-party caches, and derivative datasets. The technical and procedural complexity is non-trivial. Consider a cloud-hosted repository replicated across multiple jurisdictions. Exercising deletion rights demands coordinated action among data controllers, processors, and sometimes foreign regulatory bodies. When executed effectively, deletion rights not only restore individual control but also signal that privacy and autonomy are not passive, aspirational ideals; they are enforceable, actionable rights that alter the operational landscape of data stewardship.

The intersection of independent oversight, damages, and deletion rights creates a synergy that magnifies impact. Each mechanism reinforces the others: oversight ensures that financial penalties are justified and applied accurately; damages incentivise compliance and fund corrective actions; deletion rights restore control while setting operational boundaries. This triad embodies the principle that remedies must be multidimensional—legal, financial, and operational—to fully address the scale and subtlety of modern digital harms. Partial or symbolic measures risk perpetuating vulnerability, leaving individuals exposed even in ostensibly regulated environments.

Yet even potent remedies confront limits. Enforcement is constrained by jurisdictional boundaries, technological opacity, and the asymmetry of resources between regulators and corporate actors. Companies operating transnationally may exploit legal gaps, cloud architectures, or contractual nuances to minimise accountability. Individuals may lack awareness or capacity to initiate claims. Remedies, therefore, must be designed with both rigor and pragmatism: enforceable, scalable, and adaptable to the evolving topology of digital ecosystems. Mechanisms such as cross-border regulatory cooperation, mandatory transparency reporting, and automated compliance verification are emerging responses to these structural challenges.

Philosophically, remedies that bite recalibrate the balance of power. Digital ecosystems amplify asymmetries: corporations hold data in vast quantities, while individuals typically control only fragments. Without enforceable redress, rights exist in theory but not in practice. By embedding independent oversight, consequential damages, and effective deletion mechanisms into governance frameworks, the scales shift. Accountability is no longer aspirational; it is operational. Rights are lived through enforceable consequences, and compliance becomes an intrinsic element of organisational behaviour rather than an external imposition.

Historical and contemporary cases underscore the stakes. Instances of unauthorised surveillance, mass data harvesting, or predictive algorithmic misclassification demonstrate that tokenistic remedies fail to deter or correct systemic harm. Conversely, interventions that combine oversight, tangible penalties, and restoration of individual control have prompted demonstrable behavioural changes: organisations reassess data practices, invest in compliance infrastructure, and calibrate algorithms to reduce discriminatory or intrusive outcomes. These cases illustrate that remedies are not merely corrective; they are formative, shaping the ethics, norms, and operational reality of digital governance.

As technology continues to evolve, the principle that remedies must bite becomes ever more urgent. Emerging systems—ranging from biometric authentication to AI-driven decision-making—expand the scope and granularity of potential harms. Rights cannot be effectively protected by symbolic enforcement alone. They require mechanisms that engage with technology, law, and organisational behaviour in concert. Independent oversight ensures scrutiny; damages impose tangible consequences; deletion rights restore agency. Together, these mechanisms form the backbone of accountability in the digital age.

Ultimately, remedies that bite exemplify the operationalisation of rights. They demonstrate that legal protections, ethical standards, and societal expectations converge in enforceable, impactful actions. By demanding oversight, consequences, and restitution, policymakers, regulators, and civil society assert that rights are not mere abstractions; they are actionable, enforceable, and central to the governance of contemporary digital life. The challenge, moving forward, is to sustain these mechanisms, adapt them to technological complexity, and ensure that redress remains as powerful as the systems it seeks to regulate.

Chapter 8

Corporate Governance of Surveillance

In the gleaming boardrooms of multinational corporations, discussions often revolve around quarterly earnings, market share, and competitive positioning. Yet, lurking in the periphery are the invisible threads of surveillance: the design choices, data collection practices, and analytics pipelines that quietly shape how millions of users, employees, or clients are observed and evaluated. Despite the societal weight of these practices, surveillance risks rarely command explicit attention on board agendas. They exist in shadows, acknowledged perhaps as regulatory obligations or technological necessities, but seldom framed as matters of strategic responsibility, ethical consequence, or corporate accountability. This discrepancy—between operational reliance on data capture and the board's limited engagement with its societal impact—sets the stage for a profound exploration of governance in the age of pervasive observation.

Consider a global technology firm rolling out a new product with extensive sensor networks. Engineers focus on functionality, marketing teams on adoption metrics, and legal counsel on regulatory compliance. Meanwhile, the board may see privacy only through the lens of risk mitigation or brand reputation, rather than as an intrinsic dimension of organisational accountability. The failure to elevate surveillance to the level of strategic oversight allows blind spots to proliferate. Decisions about data retention, internal access, or vendor integration may appear operationally minor yet carry outsized social consequences: profiling of vulnerable populations, normalization of constant monitoring, and erosion of trust. Understanding these dynamics requires a shift in perspective—from viewing surveillance as a technical problem to recognising it as a corporate governance challenge with ethical, legal, and societal dimensions.

Boards equipped with risk registers that incorporate societal impact, and governance metrics that track audit frequency, access logs, and data minimisation practices, are better positioned to align operational capabilities with public accountability. These instruments translate abstract principles into tangible oversight. For example, a company might routinely measure how often third-party vendors access sensitive datasets, or whether algorithmic outputs are generated using minimised, purpose-limited information. Such metrics create a bridge between executive awareness and ethical stewardship, transforming latent risks into actionable insight.

Privacy by design and data minimisation emerge as core design principles in this context. On-device processing, selective anonymisation, and compartmentalisation of sensitive information reduce both exposure and moral liability. These strategies exemplify restraint in practice: rather than merely complying with regulatory thresholds, organisations embed respect for autonomy into product architecture. By operationalising restraint, boards can shift from reactive risk management to proactive governance, fostering a culture where surveillance is deliberate, accountable, and proportionate.

The involvement of third-party vendors complicates oversight. Data pipelines rarely end at corporate firewalls; they extend through subcontractors, cloud services, and analytics providers. A failure to conduct rigorous vendor due diligence or to codify contractual controls can undermine even the most well-intentioned internal policies. Effective governance requires that boards recognise this extended footprint, establishing accountability frameworks that encompass every link in the surveillance supply chain. Transparency clauses, audit rights, and enforceable data handling obligations are no longer optional; they are essential instruments for ensuring that corporate practices reflect ethical commitments rather than purely operational convenience.

Internal channels for reporting concerns—whistleblowing mechanisms and ethical escalation procedures—represent another critical vector for governance. Employees often occupy the frontline of surveillance operations and are uniquely positioned to identify risks, design flaws, or misuse. Yet without robust pathways for raising concerns, these insights remain invisible, reinforcing systemic blind spots. Internal review councils or designated oversight officers can institutionalise the voice of conscience, translating employee observation into board-level insight. This mechanism underscores a broader principle: governance is not solely a top-down exercise; it requires the cultivation of internal feedback loops that empower individuals to influence organisational behaviour.

Throughout this chapter, we examine how corporate boards can transform surveillance from an operational by-product into a governed, accountable activity. We consider practical instruments—risk registers, governance KPIs, privacy by design frameworks, vendor contracts, and whistleblowing channels—and explore how they intersect with ethical, legal, and social imperatives. The objective is not to prescribe a singular path but to illuminate the levers through which surveillance practices can be made transparent, accountable, and socially responsible.

Ultimately, the challenge of corporate governance in the context of surveillance is both technical and moral. Boards must reconcile profit motives, innovation imperatives, and operational efficiency with the societal consequences of pervasive monitoring. They must navigate complexity without sacrificing accountability, embedding vigilance into organisational culture rather than relegating it to episodic compliance exercises. The stakes are high: the choices made—or deferred—at the executive level shape not only corporate performance but also the lived experience of those whose data forms the substrate of the digital age.

In the pages that follow, this chapter delves into the mechanisms, metrics, and philosophies that can elevate corporate oversight from reactive compliance to proactive stewardship. By tracing the intersections of strategy, ethics, and technology, we illuminate how boards can convert the latent power of surveillance into a responsibly governed force—one that respects rights, mitigates harm, and anticipates the social consequences of digital observation. The conversation begins at the intersection of ambition and accountability, where corporate decisions reverberate far beyond balance sheets and annual reports, touching the very fabric of public trust and societal expectation.

Boards and Blind Spots

On a crisp Monday morning in a glass-walled boardroom overlooking a city skyline, a multinational corporation's directors convened to review quarterly performance. Revenue trends, market share, and operational efficiencies dominated the agenda. Among the peripheral notes and operational reports sat a brief mention of "privacy compliance" and a passing reference to a new data analytics initiative. What went unspoken was far more consequential: the organisation's surveillance footprint—internal monitoring, behavioural profiling, and data aggregation—remained largely invisible to the board, a blind spot that could shape societal impact as profoundly as quarterly earnings shaped the balance sheet.

This tension between operational invisibility and societal significance is neither accidental nor trivial. Boards are structured to weigh financial risk, regulatory compliance, and competitive strategy. Surveillance practices, by contrast, often appear technical, legalistic, or subordinate to product development timelines. Yet the aggregation, analysis, and retention of personal data carries moral, legal, and reputational weight. Decisions about who sees what data, how long it is stored, and which third parties are granted access can ripple outward, affecting employees, customers, and the broader public. The quiet accumulation of these practices in the organisational periphery fosters a paradox: companies may operate at unprecedented scale and reach while their oversight mechanisms remain insufficiently attuned to the implications of surveillance itself.

Historically, boards have deferred privacy and ethical oversight to compliance teams or IT departments, viewing such responsibilities as a matter of technical execution rather than strategic governance. Yet as corporate surveillance has expanded—through internal monitoring, location tracking, algorithmic profiling, and cloud-based data orchestration—the stakes have shifted. Risks that were once narrowly operational now intersect with human rights, public trust, and societal norms. A board that ignores these dimensions risks both regulatory penalties and a profound erosion of legitimacy. Recognising this, contemporary governance literature advocates for risk registers that incorporate societal impact: frameworks that elevate surveillance from a technical footnote to a board-level consideration.

A risk register that accounts for societal impact transforms abstract ethical concerns into actionable oversight. For example, directors might track the frequency and scope of data access across internal departments, identify which personal identifiers are retained, and evaluate whether vendor relationships amplify risk. Metrics that quantify exposure, coupled with scenario planning for reputational or regulatory fallout, allow boards to anticipate consequences rather than react to crises. In this way, surveillance is rendered visible, not merely in terms of legal compliance but as a dimension of strategic foresight.

Yet the integration of societal impact into board deliberations is not without tension. Directors face competing pressures: growth imperatives, shareholder expectations, and operational efficiency often dominate conversations, while privacy, ethics, and long-term societal effects appear abstract or intangible. Even when risk registers are populated, their interpretation depends on organisational culture, incentive structures, and the willingness of executives to elevate qualitative considerations alongside quantitative KPIs. Blind spots persist not solely from ignorance but from institutional design: boards are rarely equipped with the expertise, narratives, or evaluative frameworks necessary to weigh surveillance impact in the same register as financial risk.

Concrete case studies illustrate both the peril and promise of board engagement. Consider a firm deploying advanced behavioural analytics to optimise employee productivity. Absent board-level oversight, decisions about the granularity of monitoring, thresholds for alerts, and the retention of historical logs might proceed unchecked, leading to ethical compromises or inadvertent discrimination. Conversely, a board that incorporates societal impact into its risk assessment can mandate minimisation of sensitive data, regular audits, and internal reporting mechanisms. By foregrounding oversight, boards convert latent risk into actionable governance, curbing the potential for harm while signalling accountability to stakeholders.

Blind spots are further exacerbated by the distributed nature of modern data systems. Surveillance is rarely confined to a single department; it spans human resources, marketing, IT infrastructure, and vendor networks. The complexity of these interconnections means that isolated reports, even when accurate, rarely convey the systemic implications of data collection practices. A board that relies solely on departmental briefings may see compliance in microcosm while remaining unaware of the cumulative societal impact of data flows, algorithmic decision-making, and third-party integrations. Integrating societal impact into a risk register requires both structural foresight and interpretive literacy: the capacity to read metrics against ethical and legal benchmarks, and to interrogate assumptions embedded in operational routines.

The ethical dimension of oversight cannot be overstated. Boards are entrusted with stewardship not merely over shareholder value but over the social licence to operate. Surveillance practices touch privacy, autonomy, and the balance of power between corporations and the individuals whose data fuels them. When directors fail to recognise these stakes, they tacitly sanction risk accumulation, permitting operational expedience to outpace accountability. Conversely, boards that embrace societal impact as a governance criterion signal a commitment to deliberate, principled stewardship, cultivating trust among employees, customers, and regulators alike.

Emerging best practices illustrate ways boards can operationalise this oversight. Integrating societal impact into risk registers can take multiple forms: scenario modelling of potential harms, mapping data flows to identify sensitive intersections, and auditing third-party access. Metrics can include frequency of high-risk access events, completeness of anonymisation protocols, and responsiveness to internal reports of misuse. Beyond measurement, boards can institutionalise review cycles that elevate surveillance considerations alongside financial and operational indicators, creating iterative processes for reflection, evaluation, and adjustment.

The challenge, however, remains ongoing. Surveillance technologies evolve rapidly, and ethical expectations shift with societal norms. Boards must therefore cultivate not only structural mechanisms—risk registers, KPIs, audit schedules—but also adaptive capacity: the ability to recognise emerging risks, interpret novel forms of data collection, and weigh trade-offs between operational advantage and social responsibility. In this sense, blindness is not a static deficiency but a dynamic vulnerability: a failure to continuously calibrate governance to the shifting landscape of technology and society.

Ultimately, addressing blind spots requires a cultural as well as structural shift. Directors must move from a reactive posture—responding to regulatory infractions or public controversy—to a proactive stance that anticipates the social consequences of surveillance. Risk registers that include societal impact are instruments of visibility and deliberation, but they are only effective when coupled with inquisitive leadership, cross-functional dialogue, and an institutional ethos that values ethical foresight as highly as financial performance.

The questions for boards are stark: how much oversight is enough? How can risk registers translate qualitative societal concerns into actionable strategies? And crucially, how can corporations ensure that operational expedience does not consistently outpace ethical accountability? The answers will define the contours of corporate legitimacy in an age where data is both a commodity and a conduit of influence. Surveillance is no longer an abstract operational matter—it is a governance imperative, one whose visibility or invisibility at the board level determines the ethical and societal footprint of modern enterprise.

Metrics That Matter

In a corporate headquarters bathed in fluorescent light, a compliance officer presents a series of dashboards to the board. Rows of numbers flicker across the screen: counts of database accesses, records of internal audits, metrics on anonymisation and data retention. For the untrained eye, these metrics appear technical, almost arcane. Yet embedded within them is the pulse of organisational accountability—the tangible measure of how a company governs the information it collects, stores, and processes. The question is simple yet profound: how can boards, executives, and stakeholders discern whether a surveillance operation is responsible, proportionate, and ethically managed?

Boards frequently face the paradox of visibility. Surveillance systems generate data about the public and employees at a scale that can overwhelm conventional oversight. Yet the internal monitoring of these same systems—the governance metrics that track access, minimisation, and audit processes—is often uneven, inconsistently reported, or deprioritised. Access logs, retention schedules, audit completion rates—these are not merely administrative details; they are the measurable indicators of restraint, accountability, and operational ethics. Without them, oversight is conjecture; with them, governance becomes actionable, evidence-based, and auditable.

The imperative for practical governance metrics arises from the very scale and complexity of modern surveillance. Internal and external data flows intersect, often routed through cloud platforms, third-party vendors, and automated analytics. These systems are capable of unprecedented inference and reach, yet remain opaque to traditional board oversight. Metrics that matter—carefully defined, consistently captured, and transparently presented—translate this opacity into actionable insight. They provide the instruments by which boards can monitor not only regulatory compliance but the broader societal impact of corporate surveillance practices.

Access logs are foundational. They answer the first and most essential question of oversight: who saw what, and when? The granular recording of system interactions allows boards and compliance teams to identify irregularities, track potential misuse, and demonstrate due diligence. Consider a multinational firm that analyses employee communications for operational efficiency. Without detailed access logs, it is impossible to distinguish between legitimate analytical queries and the arbitrary monitoring of sensitive interactions. A well-maintained access log system provides both retrospective accountability and forward-looking control, establishing a baseline against which deviations are immediately visible.

Data minimisation is another crucial metric, often underemphasised but profoundly consequential. Minimisation reflects the extent to which organisations collect only what is necessary, retain it no longer than needed, and reduce the risk of incidental exposure. Metrics here can include the proportion of sensitive attributes retained beyond their operational purpose, the frequency of purging redundant data, and the success rate of anonymisation protocols. Effective minimisation is not merely a technical exercise; it embodies an ethical principle: the recognition that data about individuals carries a societal weight, and that excess collection compounds both risk and moral responsibility.

Audit rates provide a complementary dimension of insight. Regular, independent reviews validate that policies and protocols are operationally effective. Audits uncover discrepancies between intended governance and actual practice, surface hidden risks, and verify that access controls, anonymisation, and retention schedules are applied consistently. Practical metrics might include the frequency of audits, coverage breadth across systems and departments, the resolution rate of audit findings, and the lag time between detection and remediation. High audit rates, coupled with meaningful follow-up, signal a culture of continuous oversight and accountability.

The interplay of these metrics—access logs, minimisation, and audit rates—forms a governance triad. Alone, each provides partial insight; together, they offer a multi-dimensional view of surveillance ethics and operational control. They allow boards to ask nuanced questions: Are access permissions aligned with operational need? Are redundant or sensitive records being retained beyond their purpose? Do audit cycles consistently identify and correct deviations? These queries, grounded in measurable data, elevate governance from aspirational principles to evidence-based practice.

Implementing effective governance metrics requires deliberate design. First, organisations must define what constitutes meaningful measurement. Not all access events are equal; not all audits capture systemic risk. Metrics must be calibrated to context, reflecting both technical reality and ethical stakes. Second, reporting must be standardised, ensuring that data is comparable over time, auditable, and comprehensible to decision-makers without technical backgrounds. Third, metrics must be interpreted within a broader framework that balances operational efficiency with societal responsibility. Numbers alone are inert; their significance emerges only when connected to policy, ethics, and consequence.

Modern case studies illustrate both promise and peril. One technology firm instituted comprehensive access logs across its analytics pipelines, coupled with automated alerts for anomalous access. This system uncovered a previously unnoticed internal misuse, allowing rapid correction and reinforcing the credibility of governance mechanisms. Conversely, another organisation relied on ad hoc reporting of audit outcomes, leaving critical gaps unexamined. When a vendor misconfiguration exposed sensitive user data, the absence of systematic metrics delayed detection, magnifying both reputational and legal consequences. These examples underscore that metrics are not ornamental—they are instruments of operational resilience and ethical stewardship.

Boards must also recognise the relational dimension of metrics. Governance does not occur in isolation; it intersects with internal culture, third-party relationships, and regulatory expectations. Metrics must therefore extend beyond internal logs to incorporate vendor compliance, contractual adherence, and oversight of outsourced systems. For instance, third-party processors may maintain separate access and audit protocols; without integrated reporting, boards cannot discern systemic risk or enforce consistent standards. In this sense, metrics act as both mirror and lens: reflecting internal practice while revealing external vulnerabilities.

Yet reliance on metrics is not without tension. Overemphasis on quantification risks narrowing the scope of oversight to what can be measured, neglecting qualitative aspects such as employee morale, public perception, or ethical culture. Boards must complement numerical indicators with narrative reporting, contextual analysis, and scenario planning. Metrics illuminate but do not dictate judgment; they provide the substrate for informed deliberation, not the sum total of governance. Recognising this balance is essential for meaningful oversight.

Finally, the adoption of metrics that matter signals a shift in governance philosophy. It moves boards from reactive compliance—responding to incidents, fines, or public scrutiny—to proactive stewardship, anticipating risks and calibrating intervention. Metrics become instruments of foresight, enabling continuous monitoring, informed escalation, and evidence-based decision-making. They create a disciplined, auditable trail that supports accountability internally and demonstrates legitimacy externally, reinforcing both operational integrity and societal trust.

The challenge persists: which metrics genuinely matter, and how should boards interpret them amid evolving surveillance landscapes? How can quantitative measures capture the nuanced balance between utility, privacy, and societal impact? These questions demand not only technical acumen but ethical literacy, a willingness to interrogate assumptions, and a commitment to iterative governance. In doing so, organisations transform abstract obligations into measurable, actionable, and transparent practice, ensuring that surveillance is not only controlled but responsibly governed.

Designing for Restraint

The glow of a smartphone screen illuminates more than a user's face; it reflects a web of unseen processes, algorithms, and data flows that continuously observe, record, and infer. In a corporate lab, engineers configure a voice assistant, and behind the interface, a server farm stands ready to ingest audio snippets, parse linguistic patterns, and store usage histories. Yet a quiet revolution is underway: instead of centralising every bit of information, designers are experimenting with restraint, embedding intelligence directly on devices, limiting data retention, and codifying ethical boundaries into the architecture itself. How does one design systems that wield immense analytic power without succumbing to overreach?

The challenge is not merely technical but conceptual. Modern surveillance infrastructures—whether consumer-facing or enterprise-scale—tend to centralise, aggregate, and correlate. The more centralised the data, the higher the risk: a single breach can expose vast troves of sensitive information, and every dataset collected increases the potential for unintended inference. Yet entirely decentralising control without guidance risks fragmentation, inefficiency, or degraded functionality. Designing for restraint reconciles these tensions, integrating privacy by design and rigorous data minimisation into every stage of development. It is an exercise in architectural prudence, balancing capability against societal responsibility.

Early adopters of these principles demonstrate that restraint need not compromise innovation. Mobile operating systems increasingly perform natural language processing, recommendation generation, and anomaly detection on-device, sending only aggregated, anonymised results to central servers. This approach curtails unnecessary data accumulation, reduces exposure to breaches, and respects user autonomy. The lesson is clear: systems can be powerful without being omniscient, sophisticated without being indiscriminate. It is the deliberate embedding of constraints that distinguishes ethical design from passive neglect.

At its core, privacy by design insists that protection is not an afterthought. Data minimisation operationalises this principle by asking whether a particular datum is truly necessary to achieve a legitimate purpose. In a retail context, a loyalty programme might gather location histories ostensibly to personalise offers. Yet effective minimisation would assess whether aggregate mobility trends suffice, or if granular tracking is essential. Designing systems to collect only what is necessary, and to discard it once its purpose is fulfilled, reduces both risk and moral exposure, establishing a baseline for ethical operation.

Concrete strategies illustrate these abstract principles. Consider biometric authentication: rather than transmitting raw fingerprints to a central server, modern implementations store encrypted templates on devices, performing verification locally. Similarly, predictive text and autocorrect algorithms leverage on-device computation, avoiding continuous streaming of keystrokes to external repositories. Even in health applications, differential privacy and federated learning permit insights to be gleaned from collective behaviour without revealing individual histories. Each case exemplifies restraint as an active, not passive, design choice.

Yet embedding restraint is not merely a defensive posture; it can enhance performance and user trust. Systems burdened by voluminous centralised data face latency, bandwidth constraints, and heightened security risks. By processing locally, developers reduce these operational pressures while signalling a commitment to ethical stewardship. The design of restraint thus intersects technical optimisation and moral accountability, creating architectures that are lean, resilient, and socially attuned.

The corporate imperative for restraint extends beyond internal systems to encompass third-party vendors. Surveillance infrastructure rarely exists in isolation: it is supported by cloud providers, analytics platforms, and service contractors. Due diligence in procurement, contractual obligations for minimisation, and verification of on-device or anonymised processing enforce restraint across the ecosystem. A single vendor misconfiguration can undermine the ethical integrity of the entire system, underscoring the necessity of governance principles that extend through all operational layers.

Despite its virtues, designing for restraint encounters resistance. Incentives often prioritise data accumulation, monetisation, and analytic breadth. Metrics of success are framed around scale, insight, and predictive power rather than proportionality and necessity. Engineers and executives must navigate this tension, advocating for architectures that privilege ethical boundaries even when the business case emphasises unbounded collection. Restraint is thus not merely a technical mandate; it is a cultural and strategic imperative.

The philosophical dimension of restraint is subtle yet profound. Every retained bit of data embodies latent power—the capacity to influence decisions, shape perceptions, or expose vulnerabilities. Designing for restraint acknowledges this moral asymmetry, embedding a presumption against excess collection and centralised aggregation. It recognises that systems, like institutions, are instruments of influence, and that ethical engineering entails limiting the capacity to surveil beyond what is essential and justifiable.

Looking ahead, the trajectory of responsible design will increasingly favour decentralised computation, adaptive minimisation, and embedded ethical constraints. Techniques such as homomorphic encryption, secure enclaves, and federated learning allow sophisticated analysis without revealing identifiable data. On-device anomaly detection, privacy-preserving analytics, and minimal retention schemas exemplify a design philosophy that treats restraint as a feature, not a limitation. The challenge lies in embedding these principles consistently, across product lines, vendor relationships, and organisational cultures.

Ultimately, designing for restraint reframes the question from what can be collected to what should be collected. It prioritises purpose, necessity, and proportionality, translating ethical principles into technical architecture. By foregrounding privacy, minimisation, and decentralisation, designers cultivate systems that are powerful yet circumscribed, capable yet accountable. In a landscape where surveillance potential outstrips oversight, the deliberate incorporation of restraint is not optional; it is the defining criterion of responsible engineering.

The tension remains: how will organisations balance innovation, functionality, and ethical obligation in an environment driven by data-hungry imperatives? The answer will shape the next generation of surveillance technologies, determining whether they reinforce trust, respect autonomy, and embody proportionality—or whether they continue the unchecked accumulation of power that has so often defined the digital century.

Third Parties, First Problems

In 2019, a multinational technology firm discovered that a routine software update from a trusted vendor had introduced a vulnerability exposing sensitive customer data. The update itself was legitimate, digitally signed, and deployed through official channels, yet the breach demonstrated a disquieting reality: corporate surveillance and data management are never purely internal matters. When third parties hold keys to systems, networks, or datasets, the locus of control—and risk—shifts beyond the organisation's immediate sight. The problem is not hypothetical; it is a structural feature of modern digital ecosystems.

Boards and executives frequently assume that vendor relationships are a transactional concern: contracts signed, service levels agreed, and compliance assurances obtained. Yet the more a system depends on external suppliers, the greater the indirect exposure to operational, ethical, and legal risk. A single third-party compromise can reverberate across national boundaries, regulatory frameworks, and customer trust, creating consequences that far exceed any single breach's technical footprint. The question becomes urgent: how can organisations navigate these dependencies without surrendering responsibility for the very data and processes they purport to safeguard?

This subchapter examines the intricate interplay between corporate surveillance infrastructure and the ecosystem of third-party providers. It asks why due diligence often fails, how contractual safeguards can both empower and constrain, and what ethical and practical principles should guide the design of vendor relationships. At stake is not only the technical integrity of information systems, but also the capacity of organisations to uphold societal expectations for accountability, transparency, and proportionality in surveillance practices.

The first challenge is visibility. Organisations rarely possess a complete map of the third-party services embedded in their operations. Cloud platforms, analytics libraries, authentication services, and outsourced IT functions introduce layers of opacity: proprietary code, undisclosed subcontractors, and complex dependency chains. Without a comprehensive inventory, boards and compliance officers cannot assess the likelihood or impact of failures, and risk registers often omit these systemic vulnerabilities entirely. The lesson is stark: first-party controls are necessary but insufficient. Accountability begins with understanding the full topology of reliance.

Vendor due diligence is the standard remedy, yet its efficacy is uneven. Traditional assessments—security questionnaires, self-attested audits, or ISO certifications—often provide only a partial picture. Real-world incidents show that even highly rated providers can propagate weaknesses, whether through insecure software libraries, poorly managed credentials, or flawed operational procedures. Due diligence must therefore evolve from a check-box exercise into a continuous, adaptive process, incorporating live monitoring, penetration testing, and verification of contractual commitments. Only then can organisations mitigate the latent hazards embedded in third-party infrastructure.

Contracts are the formal mechanism for translating due diligence into enforceable obligations. Yet here, too, the tension is evident. Standard service-level agreements focus on uptime, performance, and basic compliance; they rarely encompass nuanced ethical responsibilities, transparency around data access, or the requirement to notify clients of emerging risks promptly. Advanced clauses—mandating regular security reporting, access audits, and breach disclosure timelines—can align incentives, but they also confront negotiation realities. Vendors often resist provisions that expose operational details or impose significant liability, leaving gaps in accountability that propagate systemic risk.

A particularly acute challenge arises when third parties operate across jurisdictions. Data stored or processed in foreign territories triggers conflicting legal obligations, from government surveillance requests to privacy protections under regional statutes. A vendor's compliance with one legal regime may inadvertently violate another, placing the contracting organisation in a regulatory bind. Boards must therefore evaluate not only technical controls but also geopolitical exposure, legal congruence, and the potential for cross-border friction. The complexity of these entanglements underscores why third-party governance cannot be delegated entirely: responsibility remains organisational, even when operational control does not.

The human dimension compounds these challenges. Third-party risks are not abstract; they affect employees, customers, and citizens. Breaches or misuse can erode trust, generate financial and reputational harm, and amplify inequities if sensitive demographic or behavioural data are exposed. Ethical stewardship requires organisations to integrate societal impact into vendor selection and monitoring. Metrics for privacy, minimisation, and accountability must extend beyond internal systems to encompass all externally managed processes. The first-party mindset—

assuming responsibility ends at the corporate firewall—is both morally and strategically untenable.

Examples abound. Supply-chain attacks in the software sector illustrate how minor vendor compromises can cascade: malicious code embedded in a widely used library infiltrates thousands of systems, each downstream organisation compelled to remediate. Outsourced call centres have, in multiple cases, exposed confidential user data due to lax internal controls, despite contracts promising rigorous safeguards. Even cloud-based AI services, marketed for ease of deployment, can generate insights or store outputs in ways that conflict with organisational privacy policies. In each case, the "first problems" lie in the assumptions made about third-party reliability and the limits of contractual enforcement.

A proactive governance strategy integrates third-party oversight into corporate risk frameworks. Risk registers should enumerate vendor dependencies, potential data flows, and the societal consequences of failure. Audit rights, periodic assessments, and continuous monitoring should be codified in contracts. Moreover, scenario planning—considering cascade effects, regulatory intervention, and reputational fallout—transforms theoretical obligations into operationally actionable intelligence. Boards that internalise these considerations gain not only legal and ethical clarity but also strategic resilience.

Yet even with diligent oversight, tension remains between operational agility and ethical accountability. Vendors often provide critical functionality efficiently, but enforcing strict minimisation, transparency, or ethical clauses may increase costs or delay deployment. Boards must navigate this balance, integrating technical assessment with policy and legal analysis, and embedding ethical evaluation into procurement decision-making. Designing these mechanisms is as much an art of organisational culture as a technical or contractual exercise.

Ultimately, "third parties, first problems" is both a warning and a guide. In contemporary surveillance ecosystems, dependency is not neutral: every external service introduces vectors for compromise, moral risk, and regulatory exposure. Successful governance demands visibility, contractual clarity, continuous verification, and an ethical framework that extends beyond corporate walls. Organisations that internalise these imperatives do more than mitigate risk; they uphold trust, reinforce societal norms, and demonstrate that surveillance infrastructure can be both powerful and responsible.

The persistent question endures: how can organisations reconcile reliance on external expertise with the imperative of accountability? The answer will define the next generation of corporate governance, determining whether technological capability amplifies ethical stewardship or magnifies blind spots hidden in complex vendor networks.

Speaking Up Inside

In 2021, an employee at a multinational technology company quietly submitted a report through the firm's internal review council. The concern was not trivial: a newly deployed data-aggregation system, ostensibly designed to improve user experience, had the potential to expose sensitive behavioural data to unauthorised personnel. The report triggered a structured internal review, and ultimately led to a redesign of key processes. No public scandal ensued, no media headlines were written, yet the internal whistleblowing channel had functioned precisely as intended. This incident exemplifies a paradox that is both practical and ethical: the most effective mechanisms for accountability often leave no trace outside the organisation, yet their impact shapes corporate behaviour, regulatory compliance, and societal trust.

Employees occupy a unique vantage point in any surveillance ecosystem. They are the eyes and hands that deploy algorithms, configure access controls, and implement data retention policies. They also perceive, in ways that auditors and executives may not, where operational practices collide with ethical or legal boundaries. Yet the channels through which these observations reach decision-makers are frequently underdeveloped, obscure, or culturally discouraged. Speaking up inside is therefore not merely a matter of procedure; it is a test of organisational ethics, resilience, and structural design.

This subchapter explores the architecture of ethical escalation within corporations, analysing why whistleblowing channels are both necessary and delicate instruments. It interrogates how internal review councils, hotlines, and reporting frameworks can be structured to empower employees while safeguarding them from retaliation. It also examines the psychological, legal, and social dynamics that influence whether an employee chooses to escalate a concern—or to remain silent—and the implications this choice has for governance and public trust.

The first consideration is accessibility. Internal reporting mechanisms must be visible, navigable, and reassuring. Employees need to understand not only how to report concerns, but what will happen afterward: who will review the information, what decision-making authority they hold, and how confidentiality is preserved. Misunderstandings or opacity can undermine trust in the system. For instance, if a reporting channel is managed by the same division responsible for the activity in question, employees may perceive bias or futility, discouraging engagement and leaving potential harms unaddressed.

Second, organisational culture shapes the willingness to speak up. Hierarchical rigidity, punitive norms, and ambiguous accountability all suppress reporting. Conversely, companies that cultivate ethical reflexivity, reward responsible disclosure, and integrate ethical assessment into leadership evaluations create an environment in which internal voices are valued rather than feared. A practical example is the use of internal review councils comprising cross-functional representatives—legal, technical, compliance, and human resources—empowered to assess reports without influence from line management. Such councils can adjudicate concerns with a balance of expertise, authority, and independence, ensuring that operational decisions are informed by ethical and legal perspectives.

Third, procedural safeguards matter. Confidentiality, anti-retaliation guarantees, and formal tracking of reports contribute to effective escalation. Employees are more likely to engage when they trust that speaking up will not imperil their career, professional relationships, or personal wellbeing. Yet these protections must be actively maintained: policies alone are insufficient if organisational behaviour contradicts them. Successful programs combine codified protections with visible enforcement, clear communication, and regular audits of reporting outcomes.

Fourth, the design of escalation pathways must recognise the spectrum of concerns. Not all reports require executive intervention; some involve minor procedural errors, others implicate systemic risk or legal non-compliance. Internal channels should provide triage, ensuring that reports are appropriately escalated according to severity and urgency. For example, a misconfigured access control affecting a small dataset might be addressed by a technical lead, while a policy violation with regulatory implications triggers board-level review. The ability to calibrate responses preserves organisational resources while signalling to employees that their insights are respected and consequential.

Fifth, integration with third-party and regulatory obligations adds complexity. Certain surveillance operations may intersect with contractual, legal, or public-interest considerations, requiring coordination beyond internal stakeholders. Internal reporting systems must be capable of identifying cases where external disclosure or regulatory notification is appropriate, balancing confidentiality with the duty to prevent harm. Failure to navigate these intersections can compound risk, undermining both organisational integrity and societal trust.

Historical and contemporary examples illustrate the stakes. In financial services, internal whistleblowers have flagged algorithmic trading models that inadvertently amplified market volatility. In technology firms, employees have exposed vulnerabilities in AI-driven content moderation systems, prompting redesigns to prevent disproportionate censorship or privacy intrusion. Each case underscores that effective internal channels can pre-empt harm, mitigate legal exposure, and sustain public confidence—yet only if employees are empowered and processes are rigorous.

Ultimately, speaking up inside is an exercise in distributed vigilance. It recognises that boards, executives, and auditors cannot perceive every risk; employees provide critical signals that inform ethical and operational judgement. Effective governance of surveillance depends on these internal feedback loops, which transform isolated observations into actionable insight. For organisations, the challenge is to design systems that are both protective and responsive: protective of employees' rights and responsive to the substantive concerns they raise.

The enduring question for corporate surveillance governance is thus: how can organisations cultivate a culture and infrastructure where ethical concerns are surfaced promptly, assessed impartially, and addressed effectively? The answer requires alignment of culture, process, and accountability—a synthesis that determines whether the internal voice of conscience becomes a catalyst for responsible innovation or remains a dormant potential, unheard and unheeded.

This subchapter navigates that terrain, offering principles, case studies, and practical mechanisms for ethical escalation. It demonstrates that whistleblowing is not merely a legal formality or compliance checkbox, but a foundational pillar for corporate integrity, societal trust, and sustainable governance in the age of pervasive surveillance.

Chapter 9

Resistance, Evasion, and Care

In a dimly lit newsroom, a journalist paused over her laptop, aware that a single misstep could expose sources, colleagues, and herself. The news story was explosive, and the digital environment surrounding it was anything but secure. Rather than panicking, she reached for her authenticator app, checked encrypted messaging channels, and coordinated with her peers through a pre-established rapid-response protocol. This was not a thriller's high-octane sequence; it was the quiet, meticulous practice of operational security—everyday habits designed to protect integrity, dignity, and human life in a world where surveillance is constant.

This chapter pivots from theoretical discourse on rights and governance to the practical, grounded actions that allow individuals and communities to navigate pervasive visibility. Resistance, evasion, and care are not heroic feats—they are disciplined, often understated, practices that preserve autonomy without relying on luck or extraordinary technical expertise. The stakes are real: journalists, activists, carers, and ordinary citizens confront adversaries ranging from state actors to opportunistic hackers, each seeking access to information or leverage over human behaviour. In such contexts, small, consistent steps—like choosing secure authentication methods over vulnerable defaults—can mean the difference between control and compromise.

The underlying paradox is profound: the tools that empower users are also the ones that can lull them into false security. Encryption, ephemeral messaging, and obfuscation technologies offer protection, yet they are not panaceas. A community-led rapid response to doxxing, for instance, may mitigate harm more effectively than a single sophisticated software solution. The narrative of care and evasion is therefore not about technology as saviour, but about embedding thoughtful, actionable practices into everyday digital life, and recognising the social networks and norms that sustain them.

At its core, the chapter examines five interrelated themes. *Everyday Operational Security* emphasises pragmatic measures accessible to anyone willing to engage deliberately with their digital footprint. Users learn to prioritise measures that offer significant risk reduction without requiring heroic technical skills—a two-factor authentication app over SMS is a canonical example. *Collective Defence* extends the lens to communities, demonstrating how shared protocols, knowledge exchange, and rapid coordination form resilient ecosystems against targeted attacks. These practices are not abstract; they illustrate the tangible benefits of mutual vigilance and preparation.

Yet, tools alone are insufficient. *The Limits of Obfuscation* confronts the critical question: what can realistically be achieved against an adversary with resources, persistence, and access to systemic vulnerabilities? By modelling threat scenarios realistically, users can avoid both overconfidence and despair, understanding the boundaries of their protective strategies. Complementing this, *Designing for Dignity* considers how services themselves can embed privacy-by-default principles. Ephemeral messaging, selective on-device processing, and transparent trade-offs demonstrate that digital systems can be structured to respect human autonomy without demanding constant vigilance from users.

Finally, the chapter situates individual practices within a civic frame. *From Users to Citizens* reframes digital self-protection as a component of civic responsibility rather than a mere technical hobby. Claiming rights, exercising discretion, and supporting community norms become habits of engaged citizenship, shaping collective resilience and reinforcing the societal conditions under which surveillance does not dictate behaviour. In this view, personal care and operational discipline are inseparable from democratic participation and ethical accountability.

Throughout, the text intertwines philosophical reflection, case studies, and practical guidance. Each narrative thread—from the newsroom example to community-led digital defence networks—illustrates the interplay of technology, human judgement, and social structures. The chapter does not promise absolute security; rather, it offers a roadmap for navigating risk with foresight, moral clarity, and collaborative energy. By centring operational competence alongside dignity and civic consciousness, it challenges the reader to reconceive resistance and evasion as deliberate, principled practices embedded within daily life.

The questions that animate this chapter are immediate and enduring: How can ordinary users cultivate resilience in the face of systemic surveillance? What balance between technical safeguards and social coordination achieves both safety and autonomy? And how do these micro-level practices aggregate into the broader civic habits that sustain rights, agency, and ethical digital environments? As the discussion unfolds, readers are invited to interrogate these questions practically and conceptually, recognising that the capacity to resist and evade is inseparable from the ethic of care that underpins responsible digital citizenship.

Everyday Operational Security

A university researcher receives an unexpected email: a login attempt from a foreign country flagged on their account. The message is terse, clinical—but it triggers a cascade of precautionary steps that will soon become second nature: a switch to an authenticator app, a review of connected devices, and a tightening of account recovery options. No dramatic hacking attempts or cinematic duels are involved; the only heroics are the deliberate, methodical actions taken to safeguard data and identity. This scene, repeated countless times across the professional and personal lives of knowledge workers, exemplifies the essence of everyday operational security: practical, achievable measures that reduce risk without requiring extraordinary expertise.

The discipline of operational security, or OpSec, has long been associated with intelligence agencies and high-stakes espionage. Yet in the modern landscape, characterised by pervasive digital surveillance, data breaches, and automated attacks, the same principles apply to ordinary users navigating daily routines. The challenge is deceptively simple: how can one maintain privacy, integrity, and control in an environment that assumes visibility? The answer does not lie in rarefied technical prowess but in the consistent application of core practices that anyone can adopt. This chapter illuminates those practices, demonstrating that security is less about extraordinary interventions and more about thoughtful, habitual choices.

At the heart of everyday OpSec lies the recognition that risk is not evenly distributed. Some accounts, devices, and behaviours are inherently more exposed than others, yet even small adjustments can have outsized protective effects. Choosing an authenticator app over SMS for multi-factor authentication, for instance, mitigates a vector that has enabled countless SIM-swap attacks. Similarly, periodically auditing connected applications, updating software promptly, and employing password managers are measures that collectively raise the barrier for potential intruders while remaining accessible to non-specialists. These steps exemplify a shift from reactive anxiety to proactive control, embedding resilience into daily routines.

Beyond individual measures, the practice of OpSec demands contextual awareness. A journalist working on sensitive reporting must calibrate security differently than a healthcare professional managing patient records or a corporate analyst handling proprietary data. Understanding threat models—who might target the information, why, and with what resources—is central. This alignment of behaviour with realistic threat assessments prevents both complacency and overreach, ensuring that security practices are proportionate and effective rather than performative. By situating everyday measures within a broader strategic framework, users can maintain operational awareness without succumbing to fatigue or paranoia.

Case studies from sectors under constant scrutiny highlight the efficacy of seemingly minor interventions. For instance, human rights activists in regions of heightened surveillance often rely on encrypted messaging platforms with on-device key storage. This reduces the risk of centralised data breaches, demonstrating how design choices can augment human diligence. Similarly, corporate teams managing sensitive intellectual property implement tiered access controls and session monitoring, reinforcing accountability without requiring continuous, manual oversight. These examples underline a fundamental truth: operational security is most powerful when it combines practical tools with disciplined behaviours.

Yet the adoption of OpSec practices is not merely technical; it is cultural. Communities develop norms around information sharing, verification, and rapid response, creating a networked buffer against compromise. Peer-to-peer guidance—such as communal checklists for secure communications or shared repositories of verified software updates—extends individual precautions across social and professional networks. In this way, operational security transcends solitary effort, embodying a collective intelligence that amplifies effectiveness while distributing responsibility. The act of caring for digital integrity becomes a shared ethical commitment, reinforcing the notion that security is inseparable from trust, reliability, and social cohesion.

Crucially, the limits of these measures must be acknowledged. No routine, however disciplined, can render users invulnerable to all adversaries.

Targeted attacks by sophisticated actors, zero-day exploits, and supply chain compromises introduce uncertainties that exceed the protective reach of everyday precautions. Recognising these boundaries is not defeatist; it is a cornerstone of practical operational security. By understanding what measures can realistically achieve, users cultivate both resilience and discernment, aligning effort with impact rather than illusion. This balance between vigilance and realism ensures that operational security remains sustainable and psychologically tenable.

Embedding these practices into daily life also entails a shift in mindset. Security becomes not an emergency response but a habitual consideration integrated into routine workflows. Password hygiene, device updates, cautious link-clicking, and verified communications evolve from optional tasks into instinctive behaviour, reducing the cognitive load of crisis-driven decisions. Over time, these habits generate a baseline of protection that enhances autonomy, mitigates exposure, and reinforces confidence in digital environments. The quotidian nature of these actions belies their strategic importance; security is cumulative, and small, consistent steps compound into meaningful resilience.

Finally, everyday operational security intersects with broader societal questions. The choices users make collectively influence the norms and expectations of digital ecosystems. Adoption of strong authentication methods, secure messaging, and cautious data-sharing practices pressures service providers to prioritise privacy by default, shaping the incentives and architectures of digital platforms. In this sense, individual diligence has systemic implications: operational security is both personal and civic, an exercise in self-protection that contributes to the resilience and ethical standards of the wider digital community.

As we explore the specific measures, frameworks, and examples in this chapter, the reader is invited to consider operational security not as an extraordinary skill but as an attainable discipline. Each section builds from simple, actionable steps to more nuanced behavioural strategies, always foregrounding accessibility, efficacy, and sustainability. The central question persists: how can users maintain meaningful control over their digital lives in a landscape designed for maximum observability? The answer unfolds through deliberate, practical, and context-aware practices that transform risk into manageable, navigable terrain, demonstrating that resilience is built in the everyday choices we make, rather than in rare acts of heroism.

Every decision—from choosing a password manager to verifying software sources—carries weight. Each routine adjustment accumulates, forming a lattice of defence that, while invisible, shapes the capacity of users to act with confidence, dignity, and agency. In this light, operational security is not merely a technical imperative but a manifestation of care: care for oneself, for one's colleagues, and for the broader communities whose trust and safety are intertwined with our choices. The chapter concludes not with an endpoint, but with an invitation to engage deliberately, recognising that security is a practice cultivated in ordinary moments, yet capable of extraordinary consequence.

Collective Defence

In the early hours of a quiet Tuesday, a network of investigative journalists receives an alert: a colleague's personal information has been leaked online, a targeted doxxing attack aimed at intimidation. The response is immediate, coordinated, and rehearsed: a shared playbook guides removal requests, alerting hosting providers, and triggering secure communications channels. Within hours, the threat has been contained, the exposed information quarantined, and affected individuals counselled. There is no single hero; the resilience stems from the collective, from a community prepared with shared strategies, trusted contacts, and predefined protocols. This scene, emblematic of the modern threats facing journalists, activists, and carers, exemplifies the principle of collective defence: security and resilience are multiplied when individuals operate within a structured, supportive community.

Collective defence is not a matter of technological wizardry alone. It is a practice of coordination, anticipation, and mutual responsibility. In the face of distributed threats—whether harassment campaigns, data leaks, or coordinated surveillance—isolated actions are often insufficient. Communities, however, can develop standard operating procedures, maintain rapid-response channels, and codify lessons from prior incidents, transforming individual vigilance into networked strength. The underlying insight is simple yet profound: risks that overwhelm an individual can be absorbed and mitigated through social organisation, trust, and shared knowledge.

This subchapter examines the mechanisms and philosophies that make collective defence effective. At its core lies a recognition that operational security and privacy cannot be siloed. A journalist may secure their own communications, yet the compromise of a peer's account or a public exposure of sensitive sources can imperil the entire network. Collective defence bridges these gaps, creating structures that anticipate interdependencies, highlight vulnerabilities, and provide actionable guidance. It treats security not as a solitary endeavour but as an emergent property of well-coordinated groups.

Practical examples abound. Activist coalitions in regions of heightened censorship maintain encrypted chat groups, supplemented by rotating secure dropboxes and anonymised reporting channels. Rapid dissemination of threat intelligence—whether via shared vulnerability alerts, device compromise reports, or phishing campaign warnings—enables members to act preemptively. Similarly, non-governmental organisations supporting caregivers of vulnerable populations have developed operational templates for emergency data protection, integrating best practices for secure record-keeping, access control, and communication contingency planning. Each instance demonstrates how shared knowledge, formalised into playbooks, amplifies resilience and reduces the cognitive burden on individuals under duress.

The architecture of collective defence extends beyond reactive measures. It encompasses preparation, rehearsal, and continuous refinement. Communities construct and test incident response procedures, simulate potential breaches, and review outcomes to incorporate lessons learned. These processes codify expertise, ensuring that best practices persist even as members rotate or as external circumstances evolve. The analogy to emergency services is instructive: training and shared protocols ensure that responses are rapid, coordinated, and predictable, minimising the chaos that could otherwise exacerbate harm.

Crucially, collective defence is also a moral practice. It embodies solidarity, care, and reciprocity. Protecting a colleague's privacy, amplifying alerts about emerging threats, or mentoring new members on secure communications are acts that reinforce trust and cohesion. Ethical responsibility is thus embedded within operational efficacy: a community that disregards the welfare of its members undermines its own resilience. The social norms governing conduct, accountability, and mutual aid become as important as any technical measure, shaping the culture that sustains the network.

Yet, the model faces inherent tensions. Diverse threat profiles, varying technical expertise, and differing access to resources create asymmetries within groups. Not every member can maintain the same security posture, and protocols must be designed to accommodate these disparities without diluting effectiveness. Moreover, the visibility of collective networks can itself attract attention from adversaries, requiring careful trade-offs between openness, coordination, and stealth. The discipline of collective defence is therefore a continuous negotiation between accessibility, operational impact, and risk exposure.

Technology underpins many aspects of collective defence, but reliance alone is insufficient. Tools—encrypted messaging, anonymisation software, or secure file-sharing platforms—amplify capability but cannot substitute for the coordination, trust, and cultural norms that give these tools their potency. A playbook without adherence, channels without monitoring, and alerts without follow-up are rendered ineffective by human factors. The interplay of social and technical systems defines the boundary between resilience and fragility.

Finally, collective defence illustrates a broader principle: security at scale is as much about community as it is about individual skill. When journalists, activists, and carers operate in isolation, they confront threats proportional to their vulnerabilities. When they operate collectively, threats are mitigated through shared intelligence, rapid response, and mutual reinforcement. This principle challenges conventional thinking about operational security, reframing it as a cooperative enterprise where preparedness, practice, and ethical engagement are as consequential as any encryption algorithm or device-level safeguard.

As the subchapter unfolds, the reader will encounter detailed case studies, methodological frameworks, and strategic insights for implementing and sustaining collective defence. From rapid response protocols to shared threat intelligence networks, each example underscores the practical, philosophical, and ethical dimensions of this approach. The questions that animate the discussion are urgent and enduring: How can communities anticipate and mitigate threats without exposing themselves? What balances between openness and secrecy preserves both efficacy and safety? And ultimately, how does collective defence transform operational security from an individual burden into a shared, resilient practice that protects both people and principles?

Through these explorations, the chapter situates collective defence not as a technical abstraction but as a lived, actionable practice—one that demonstrates the power of solidarity, preparation, and care in navigating a world where threats are distributed, persistent, and evolving.

The Limits of Obfuscation

On a rainy evening in a crowded café, a freelance journalist pulls out a laptop, activating a virtual private network and a suite of privacy-enhancing tools. The screen flickers as encrypted connections establish themselves across continents. She breathes a quiet sigh of relief; she feels shielded. Yet beyond the hum of servers and the assurance of masked IP addresses lies an uncomfortable reality: the tools themselves are neither panacea nor guarantee. A sophisticated adversary can correlate seemingly anonymous data points, exploit unpatched software, or leverage social engineering to penetrate what appears to be impenetrable. This moment encapsulates a paradox central to operational security: the technology designed to obscure identity or activity provides layers of defence, but it does not render the user invincible.

Obfuscation tools—VPNs, Tor, ephemeral messaging, or encrypted email—function as shields and fogs, altering the landscape of visibility without eliminating it. They delay, complicate, and reduce the success rate of adversaries, yet they cannot fundamentally remove risk. Users who overestimate their protective capabilities often confront sudden exposure, a stark reminder that obfuscation operates within constraints defined by design, context, and human behaviour. Understanding these limits is not a pessimistic exercise; it is an ethical imperative. Misplaced confidence can produce false security, amplifying vulnerability rather than mitigating it.

The purpose of this subchapter is to delineate what obfuscation can realistically achieve and where its boundaries lie. Effective security begins with clear threat modelling: identifying plausible adversaries, understanding their incentives and capabilities, and recognising the systemic weaknesses that tools alone cannot resolve. Obfuscation is most potent when integrated into a strategy that combines technology, social awareness, procedural rigor, and adaptive vigilance. It is not a solitary act of concealment but a coordinated practice that situates the user within a realistic risk landscape.

Consider the case of Tor users during politically sensitive reporting. While Tor conceals IP addresses and encrypts traffic within the network, timing attacks, traffic correlation, and endpoint compromise have repeatedly demonstrated that adversaries can still de-anonymise users. Similarly, encrypted messaging applications offer strong assurances that content cannot be intercepted in transit, but metadata—information about who communicated with whom, when, and from where—remains a vulnerable channel. In both instances, the tools are effective but incomplete, highlighting the necessity of integrating obfuscation into broader operational security frameworks rather than treating it as an absolute safeguard.

Another dimension emerges in the context of digital caregivers or activists managing sensitive community information. On-device encryption and ephemeral storage provide tangible mitigation against mass data exposure, yet shared devices, human error, and procedural lapses can introduce vulnerabilities invisible to the protective software. The interface between human practices and technological mechanisms defines where obfuscation succeeds and where it falters. Security is thus both a technical and social problem; one cannot be fully effective without attending to the other.

The tension between usability and protective strength is central to understanding obfuscation's limits. Highly secure configurations often impose cognitive or operational burdens that users may circumvent, intentionally or inadvertently, thereby weakening protection. Multi-factor authentication with hardware tokens, for instance, enhances security but may reduce adoption among non-technical participants, creating gaps in collective resilience. Designers and users alike must grapple with these trade-offs, recognising that security exists on a continuum: absolute protection is impractical, and partial measures must be strategically deployed and maintained.

Realistic threat modelling also requires attention to adversary incentives and resources. State actors, organised criminal networks, or sophisticated corporate surveillance programmes possess capabilities far beyond casual intrusion attempts. Obfuscation tools, while robust against generic threats, are rarely sufficient to deter actors who combine technical skill, legal leverage, and social manipulation. Anticipating such adversaries demands layered strategies: obfuscation integrated with compartmentalisation, minimal exposure, secure communication protocols, and pre-established response mechanisms. Security is not a product but a dynamic process, continuously adapted to evolving threats.

Philosophically, the limits of obfuscation invite reflection on the ethics of self-protection and responsibility. Users must reconcile the desire for privacy with the recognition that no tool absolves them of strategic foresight or careful behaviour. Over-reliance on technology can produce moral hazard: the illusion of invulnerability may encourage risk-taking or complacency. Conversely, a clear-eyed understanding of limits fosters disciplined practices, informed decision-making, and a culture of shared vigilance where communities mutually reinforce security.

Finally, obfuscation's boundaries illuminate the broader societal dimension of digital security. Individual tools operate within infrastructures controlled by corporations, legal systems, and technical standards. Endpoints, cloud providers, and regulatory frameworks mediate the effectiveness of protective measures, often in ways invisible to the user. Effective operational security must therefore engage not only with software and hardware but with the systemic environment: policies, platform behaviours, and collective norms. Obfuscation is one layer in a complex lattice of responsibility, practice, and institutional design.

As this subchapter unfolds, readers will encounter detailed examples of obfuscation in practice, analyses of attack vectors that bypass protective tools, and methodological guidance for constructing realistic threat models. From journalists safeguarding sources to caregivers protecting sensitive records, the discussion emphasises the interplay between human judgment, technological capability, and environmental constraints. Each case underlines the principle that tools can empower, but only when deployed with awareness, discipline, and strategic foresight.

Ultimately, understanding the limits of obfuscation transforms operational security from a series of technical checkboxes into a nuanced practice of vigilance, judgement, and preparedness. The questions that arise are enduring: how can individuals calibrate their protective measures against realistic threats? When does the pursuit of concealment itself introduce new vulnerabilities? And how can communities collectively interpret, learn from, and compensate for the gaps that no tool can entirely eliminate? These are not merely technical queries but inquiries into the ethics, practices, and philosophies of digital resilience in a world where visibility is inevitable and risk unavoidable.

Designing for Dignity

A mother in a small town shares sensitive health updates with her child's school nurse through an encrypted messaging app. She expects the information to remain ephemeral, accessible only to those directly involved, and to vanish once its immediate purpose is served. Yet, behind the interface, design choices silently dictate the boundaries of her privacy: default retention periods, server-side storage, metadata handling, and the very pathways through which the data travels. These are not abstract technicalities—they are moral and practical decisions that affect dignity, trust, and autonomy. The paradox is stark: technology that promises discretion often carries the power to extend surveillance by default, yet deliberate design can invert this, embedding respect for privacy into the very architecture of service.

In digital environments, defaults matter as much as user choices. When services assume consent for data collection or long-term retention, individuals are nudged into exposure, often without understanding the implications. Designing for dignity flips the script: privacy becomes the baseline, and users must opt into broader sharing rather than being coaxed into surveillance. This approach challenges prevailing assumptions that convenience and data maximisation should lead; instead, it foregrounds the human subject, treating privacy not as a secondary feature but as a guiding principle.

At the heart of this philosophy is the recognition that dignity is enacted through control, transparency, and minimisation. Ephemeral messaging provides a compelling case study: messages vanish after a designated period, limiting risk of long-term exposure. Yet, the trade-offs are clear—users sacrifice archival convenience and legal recoverability in exchange for reduced vulnerability. The choice is intentional and visible, rather than buried in opaque defaults. By foregrounding trade-offs, designers enable informed consent while constraining the potential for misuse.

Designing for dignity extends beyond ephemeral messaging to encompass broader service architectures. Consider on-device processing: facial recognition or behavioural analytics executed locally rather than transmitted to central servers drastically reduces the risk of large-scale data aggregation. Such design choices operationalise minimisation, not only lowering technical risk but signalling ethical intent. They acknowledge that the act of collecting and centralising personal data is not neutral—it carries potential for coercion, exploitation, or accidental exposure. Embedding restraint into system architecture transforms privacy from a reactive measure into a proactive stance.

The challenge of operationalising dignity lies in balancing competing values: usability, functionality, security, and trust. For instance, strong local encryption may limit interoperability or the ability to provide customer support. Automatic data deletion might disrupt legitimate continuity of service. Ethical design requires grappling with these tensions openly, providing users with clear explanations and meaningful control. The goal is not perfection—no system can eliminate all risk—but transparency and deliberateness foster informed agency.

Contextual sensitivity further sharpens this perspective. Services used by activists, healthcare workers, or journalists face threats that differ in intensity and character from those of casual consumers. Designing for dignity in these contexts means anticipating potential adversaries, understanding operational stakes, and embedding safeguards that accommodate varying threat profiles. It is a practice of empathy as much as engineering: recognising the human consequences of each default setting, data pathway, and interface prompt.

Contracts, policies, and organisational culture intersect with technological design. A service may offer ephemeral messaging, but if its terms of service permit broad internal review or involuntary disclosure to third parties, dignity is compromised. Ethical architecture therefore demands coherence between system behaviour, organisational governance, and user expectations. Designing for dignity is inseparable from responsible stewardship: privacy defaults are meaningful only when backed by enforceable accountability.

Moreover, dignity-oriented design encourages granular user choice. Simple toggles—allowing for different retention periods, selective disclosure, or pseudonymous engagement—empower individuals without imposing complex decision-making burdens. The principle is consistency: defaults are protective, while flexibility accommodates legitimate need. In doing so, systems reduce inadvertent exposure and reinforce the social contract between provider and user.

Philosophically, designing for dignity reframes digital ethics. Privacy is not merely a legal compliance metric or a technical parameter—it is a form of respect, a recognition of personal agency, and a safeguard for social trust. Each design decision echoes outward, influencing user behaviour, societal norms, and collective resilience. Platforms that embed dignity in defaults cultivate environments where individuals can act with confidence, knowing that their data is handled with intentional care.

Pragmatic examples illustrate the potency of this approach. Secure messaging platforms that default to end-to-end encryption, ephemeral messages, and minimal metadata collection consistently demonstrate reduced exposure to data breaches and surveillance. Payment apps that anonymise or tokenise transaction data preserve financial privacy without impeding functionality. Even social media interfaces that default to private posting, granular audience selection, and clear deletion policies materially shift the balance of power toward users. These cases show that dignity can be operationalised: it is not an aspirational ideal but a tangible engineering and policy goal.

Yet trade-offs remain unavoidable. Design choices for dignity may reduce efficiency, complicate analytics, or limit monetisation opportunities. These constraints are not failures; they are acknowledgements that digital environments are sociotechnical systems where ethical considerations must compete with commercial or functional pressures. The careful calibration of these trade-offs is itself an act of governance, signalling that privacy, autonomy, and trust are prioritised rather than incidental.

As readers navigate this subchapter, they will encounter layered analysis of design strategies that foreground dignity, including on-device computation, ephemeral data management, privacy-respecting defaults, and user-centric transparency. The discussion situates these measures within real-world contexts—from activism and healthcare to routine social and financial interactions—highlighting both operational feasibility and ethical imperatives. Each example reinforces the principle that technology need not be neutral: it can be actively shaped to protect, rather than expose, the human subject.

Ultimately, designing for dignity transforms service architecture from a technical specification into a moral statement. Defaults, interfaces, and processing decisions become instruments through which respect for privacy is enacted, risks are mitigated, and user agency is upheld. The unresolved question is how far these principles can be extended in an ecosystem dominated by data-driven incentives: can dignity persist when commercial and regulatory pressures favour surveillance? Navigating this tension—embedding ethics into design while engaging with real-world constraints—remains a defining challenge for digital practitioners and users alike.

From Users to Citizens

In a dimly lit newsroom, a reporter receives an anonymous tip that threatens to expose the private data of thousands. The information could illuminate corruption, yet handling it improperly could imperil both sources and the public. The choice is not merely about technology—it is about civic responsibility. What begins as a technical question of secure storage or encrypted communication is inseparable from the ethical and legal frameworks that define what it means to exercise one's rights in a digital society. Here, the distinction between being a "user" and a "citizen" crystallises: a user interacts with tools, but a citizen claims and enacts rights, shaping both the flow of information and the contours of accountability.

Across sectors—journalism, activism, healthcare, even ordinary civic participation—the difference between passive consumption and active rights-claiming is profound. One might install a privacy-focused messaging app, but without an understanding of how to assert rights to access, deletion, or contestation, the protection afforded by the tool is incomplete. Civic literacy transforms everyday digital practice into a habit of accountability, embedding vigilance, judgement, and intervention into routine actions. The paradox is clear: in the digital age, the technical competence that serves as a first line of defence is insufficient without a parallel cultivation of rights consciousness.

Rights-claiming as a civic habit also reframes the stakes. It shifts focus from individual convenience or technological novelty to the social and political ramifications of data governance. When citizens understand their entitlements and the mechanisms for enforcement, they contribute to a culture of collective responsibility. This is not abstract; it affects who can speak safely, who is protected from undue surveillance, and who has leverage over corporate and governmental power. The chapter that follows treats these issues not as an optional set of skills for enthusiasts but as essential civic competencies, akin to voting, legal literacy, or community engagement.

The journey from user to citizen begins with understanding the architecture of rights in the digital ecosystem. Platforms, services, and institutional practices define default behaviours—how data is collected, stored, and shared—but these defaults are not immutable. Citizens exercise influence by interrogating these mechanisms, asserting control where possible, and demanding transparency where it is absent. Consider a healthcare worker using a patient-record system: technical literacy enables encrypted transmission, but knowledge of access rights, deletion policies, and reporting channels transforms that literacy into civic action. The worker's choices echo beyond the individual, shaping organisational accountability and societal norms.

Collective practices reinforce individual agency. Communities of journalists, activists, and carers often operate under high-stakes conditions, where rapid dissemination of rights-critical knowledge can avert harm. Civic habit is cultivated through these networks: sharing protocols for data minimisation, coordinating rapid responses to breaches, and fostering peer accountability. These practices illustrate that citizenship in the digital sphere is inherently social; it is enacted not solely by individual decisions but through participation in structures that reinforce rights-conscious behaviour.

Yet, understanding rights is insufficient without recognising their limits and constraints. Legal frameworks vary by jurisdiction, enforcement is uneven, and technical protections are fallible. A citizen must calibrate expectations, aligning tools and actions with realistic threat models while maintaining principled vigilance. For instance, ephemeral messaging can reduce exposure, but cannot guarantee immunity from state-mandated retention or sophisticated adversaries. Recognising these boundaries transforms rights-claiming from a hobbyist pursuit into disciplined civic engagement, grounded in situational awareness and ethical foresight.

Education and transparency are critical enablers of this transition. Citizens require accessible explanations of privacy policies, rights instruments, and mechanisms for redress. Documentation, plain-language guidance, and community training convert passive knowledge into actionable civic skills. In effect, the digital public square demands competencies analogous to those of the physical one: the ability to discern risk, interpret authority, and intervene responsibly. Civic habit emerges not spontaneously but through sustained exposure, reinforcement, and practical application.

The consequences of widespread civic inattention are visible in case studies across industries. Data breaches that go unchallenged, surveillance programmes accepted passively, and opaque corporate practices persist precisely because individuals interact as users, not citizens. Conversely, when communities assert their rights collectively, companies and governments adjust behaviour: transparency increases, retention policies are moderated, and mechanisms for accountability are strengthened. Rights-claiming thus operates as both shield and lever, defending individuals while influencing institutional norms.

Transitioning from user to citizen also entails ethical reflection. Civic engagement is not merely tactical; it is normative, requiring consideration of fairness, proportionality, and impact. Decisions about data disclosure, platform use, or whistleblowing carry moral weight, shaping not only personal risk but societal conditions. In this light, civic habit becomes a practice of discernment, integrating technical skill, legal knowledge, and ethical judgment.

By framing rights-claiming as a civic habit, the chapter situates digital agency within broader notions of responsibility, participation, and societal stewardship. Individuals learn to anticipate threats, assert protections, and engage constructively with institutions, moving beyond reactive or transactional use of technology. Every decision—from selecting secure communication channels to understanding deletion policies—becomes an exercise in citizenship, a rehearsal of the norms and expectations that sustain a rights-respecting digital society.

As the reader engages with the subsequent discussion, they will encounter strategies for embedding civic consciousness into daily digital practices, case studies illustrating collective empowerment, and analytical frameworks for understanding how personal actions aggregate into societal impact. The subchapter emphasises that digital citizenship is cultivated through habit: the continuous, deliberate enactment of rights, obligations, and ethical awareness. The unresolved challenge remains: how can individuals and communities sustain these habits in environments where institutional opacity and technological complexity constantly evolve? Navigating this question is essential to transforming users into citizens who do not merely interact with technology, but actively shape the conditions under which rights are respected, defended, and extended.

Chapter 10

The Geopolitics of Data Power

In 2018, a seemingly mundane decision by a standards body in Geneva rippled across the globe: a minor adjustment to encryption protocols, ostensibly technical, quickly became a policy vector. Suppliers in Europe and Asia, adhering to the new specifications, found themselves embedding defaults that facilitated government surveillance. Across continents, enterprises complied without debate, and regulators took notice only after the consequences were visible. Here, the ostensibly neutral language of standards functioned as an instrument of influence, quietly extending the reach of state power through everyday technology. This incident epitomises a core truth: in the digital age, technical norms are inseparable from geopolitical strategy. What looks like code, chip design, or cloud architecture often carries the weight of diplomacy, economic leverage, and intelligence priorities.

The modern battleground for power has shifted from borders to bandwidth, from armies to algorithms. Nations no longer rely solely on hard military might to project influence; control over data flows, protocols, and platforms has become a decisive vector of global authority. Regional governance frameworks—from Europe's rigorous data protection regime to Asia's more permissive models—operate not just as regulatory constructs, but as soft power instruments, shaping economic ecosystems, signalling alliances, and pressuring corporate behaviour. These spheres of influence determine who can store, process, and share information, effectively translating domestic policy choices into global leverage. In this context, data governance is a form of diplomacy, and standards are a subtle yet potent instrument of statecraft.

Geopolitical advantage manifests not only through regulation but also through infrastructure and access. Semiconductor design, cloud platforms, and secure communication channels are now arenas of strategic competition. Sanctions and export controls, once the domain of trade policy, intersect directly with intelligence and cyber capabilities. A nation that dominates chip fabrication or cloud hosting can influence both commercial and state actors, controlling the architecture of digital life at a planetary scale. Alliances, whether formal data-sharing agreements or informal understandings among tech providers, multiply these effects, yet they are fraught with friction. Divergent national interests, conflicting regulatory philosophies, and asymmetrical technological capabilities ensure that even cooperative pacts are contested terrains.

For smaller states, the asymmetry of power presents both vulnerability and opportunity. Countries with limited industrial heft cannot hope to dominate chip production or enforce global standards unilaterally, yet they can leverage procurement rules, contractual oversight, and selective partnerships to exert influence disproportionate to their size. Strategic adoption of privacy-centric services, insistence on auditability, and careful alignment with regional standards can shield citizens while signalling normative priorities. These tactics demonstrate that digital sovereignty is not solely a matter of raw technological capacity; it is a practice of disciplined policy design, networked alliances, and anticipatory governance.

This chapter traces the intricate interplay between technical architecture and geopolitical ambition. It examines how standards export policy, how regional governance frameworks operate as instruments of soft power, and how hardware, cloud control, and sanctions interlock with intelligence leverage. It investigates the dynamics of alliances and the frictions inherent in collaborative data arrangements, while also exploring the avenues available to smaller states seeking to protect sovereignty and assert strategic agency. Throughout, the focus remains on the mechanisms by which seemingly neutral technology choices translate into profound global consequences.

Readers will encounter real-world examples of standards shaping surveillance capacity, cloud dependencies amplifying state leverage, and alliances producing both strategic cohesion and unexpected tension. The discussion will highlight the often-overlooked levers available to nations and institutions, revealing that power in the digital era is exercised as much through protocols and procurement as through diplomacy and force. The intellectual payoff lies in understanding that every chip, algorithm, and cloud service is embedded in a web of governance, incentives, and strategic calculation, and that the geography of data is as consequential as any map of borders and resources.

As the chapter unfolds, it will illuminate how decisions about technical norms, regulatory compliance, and infrastructure investment are inherently political, shaping not only domestic markets but global power balances. The reader will gain both analytical frameworks and illustrative cases, providing insight into a world where data is the new currency of influence and digital architecture the scaffold of statecraft. By understanding these dynamics, one can see that the geopolitics of data power is not merely an abstract concern—it is the defining context for how nations, corporations, and citizens navigate the contemporary information ecosystem.

Standards as Strategy

In 2019, a subtle but consequential shift occurred within the infrastructure of global telecommunications. A consortium released a new set of protocol specifications for 5G networks, codifying defaults for encryption, authentication, and interoperability. On the surface, these were technical adjustments: bit lengths, handshake procedures, packet routing. Yet beneath the arcane terminology lay profound political implications. Certain defaults, chosen ostensibly for efficiency, also embedded options that facilitated state-level surveillance and eased cross-border law enforcement access. Telecommunications vendors worldwide, from Shenzhen to Stockholm, implemented these standards without fanfare, and suddenly, a set of technical decisions had extended the reach of regulatory norms far beyond the drafting body's borders. This incident illustrates a crucial phenomenon: technical standards are not neutral. They are vectors through which policy, influence, and control propagate, often invisibly, through supply chains and user devices.

Standards serve as the quiet architecture of global power. When protocols are defined, software libraries sanctioned, or hardware interfaces specified, nations and corporations embed assumptions about trust, compliance, and oversight into the very fabric of technology. These assumptions migrate through the industrial ecosystem, influencing product design, user behaviour, and regulatory regimes in jurisdictions that may have had no role in their creation. In some instances, surveillance-friendly defaults become the de facto global norm, shaping the operational landscape of privacy, security, and even commercial competition. The subtlety of this mechanism lies in its plausibility: technical decisions are perceived as efficiency-driven, objective, or inevitable, yet they carry normative weight, privileging certain actors, constraining choices, and altering the balance of power in quiet but durable ways.

Consider the case of encryption standards. While a higher level of cryptographic strength is lauded for securing communications, the choice of key escrow mechanisms or default protocol flags can create systematic access points for state actors. Vendors, seeking compliance with what appears to be a widely accepted technical requirement, implement these defaults globally, effectively exporting a domestic policy preference to foreign markets. End users may be unaware that the convenience of plug-and-play interoperability comes at the cost of exposing communications to surveillance. The policy has traveled not through legislation or diplomatic fiat, but through code, chips, and firmware updates—insidious yet profoundly effective vectors of influence.

The export of policy via standards is not limited to security or encryption. Supply chains, cloud interfaces, data serialization formats, and even application programming interfaces (APIs) carry implicit assumptions about what information is exposed, how identity is verified, and what logs are retained. These choices propagate downstream, affecting multinational corporations, municipal services, and individual users alike. A seemingly technical library dependency, once included in millions of applications, can define what metadata is collected, what telemetry is permissible, and, ultimately, who has access to information. The influence is recursive: as global adoption consolidates, dissenting technical choices become costly, and compliance with dominant standards becomes a practical necessity, further entrenching the original policy assumptions.

The strategic deployment of standards has long been a tool of geopolitical manoeuvre. In the mid-20th century, control over electrical standards, communication protocols, and industrial gauges offered economic leverage. Today, the same principle applies in the digital domain. Standards bodies, whether private consortia or quasi-governmental organisations, operate as conduits for influence, allowing states to shape technological ecosystems without recourse to coercion. Decisions about packet structure, default permissions, or encryption strength can advantage domestic firms, facilitate lawful intercept regimes, or subtly undermine adversaries' security postures. They also create path dependencies: once a standard is widely adopted, modification is expensive, interoperability is fragile, and the original policy choices are difficult to reverse.

The propagation of standards as policy highlights the interdependence of governance, engineering, and commerce. Corporations implement protocols to maintain interoperability, governments incentivise adherence to shape markets, and end users inherit the consequences without visibility.

This triad underscores a tension between technical neutrality and normative effect: while engineers may pursue efficiency, scalability, and compatibility, the choices embedded in specifications invariably reflect priorities, trade-offs, and assumptions about trust and control. Understanding this dynamic requires reading code, documentation, and supply chain practices as instruments of strategic policy, not merely technical artefacts.

The effects of standards extend into privacy and civil liberties. Default behaviours—whether in authentication, data retention, or telemetry—determine the ease with which personal information is collected, shared, and analysed. Even small technical defaults can cascade: a slight adjustment in logging behaviour or API access rights, when replicated across thousands of devices and millions of users, produces an exponential increase in surveillance capacity. This highlights a subtle paradox: global adoption of ostensibly neutral technical standards can institutionalise monitoring, often outpacing formal legal mechanisms or public scrutiny. Policy has moved from statute and regulation into firmware and protocol, raising profound questions about accountability, transparency, and consent.

Yet standards as strategy are not solely instruments of control. They can also advance security, interoperability, and human rights. Careful specification of privacy-preserving defaults, open-source verification, and rigorous international review can create resilient frameworks that respect user autonomy while facilitating innovation. The same mechanism that exports surveillance-friendly policies can, in principle, propagate safeguards: default encryption, minimised data collection, and decentralised processing can travel along the same supply chains, amplifying protections globally. The challenge lies in governance: how to ensure that the arbiters of standards reflect pluralistic interests, rather than narrow commercial or national imperatives.

Debates over standardisation illustrate the tensions between globalisation, sovereignty, and technical efficiency. Multinational adoption creates economies of scale, but also concentrates power in a few decision-making bodies. Smaller states or civil society actors often lack the resources to influence specifications, yet are bound by them once adopted. Similarly, corporate actors must balance competitive pressures with regulatory compliance and ethical considerations, navigating the grey zone between technical optimisation and policy enforcement. The interplay between these forces shapes the architecture of everyday technology, from cloud platforms to the devices in our pockets, and underscores the stakes of seemingly minor technical decisions.

The deployment of standards as strategic levers also demonstrates how subtlety can eclipse overt action. While traditional foreign policy relies on treaties, sanctions, and public pronouncements, standardisation operates quietly, invisibly, and often without immediate notice. By the time the implications are apparent, they are embedded in global practices, supply chains, and user expectations. This raises a profound question for policymakers and technologists alike: how can governance structures anticipate and intervene in the diffusion of normative effects through ostensibly technical mechanisms, without stifling innovation or disrupting interoperability?

Ultimately, understanding standards as a vector of policy requires an integrated perspective, combining technical literacy with political acumen and ethical reflection. It demands recognising that bits, protocols, and device defaults are not neutral—they are carriers of strategic intent, capable of shaping markets, surveillance capacity, and societal norms at scale. Engineers, regulators, and citizens are bound together in this ecosystem, negotiating the trade-offs embedded in code and specification. Every design choice, every protocol flag, every default setting is simultaneously technical and political, mundane and consequential.

The challenge moving forward is to render visible the invisible. By scrutinising how standards propagate assumptions and influence behaviour, stakeholders can reclaim agency over technological futures. Supply chains, APIs, firmware defaults, and libraries are the new battlegrounds of influence. Awareness of this reality does not demand heroic intervention from every participant, but it does require critical attention, strategic foresight, and deliberate governance. Only by treating technical standards as instruments of policy—both as potential tools of control and as levers for protection—can societies navigate the complex interplay of innovation, commerce, and power that defines our connected world.

As we trace the contours of standards as strategy, the reader will encounter the mechanisms, trade-offs, and ethical dilemmas inherent in embedding policy within technology. From encryption defaults to API specifications, from supply chain decisions to global adoption patterns, the chapter illuminates how the quiet work of standardisation can shape outcomes at national and international scales. It challenges conventional notions of neutrality, urging a recognition that every technical decision is, in effect, a political act. In the end, the story of standards is a story of influence: subtle, pervasive, and consequential, carried in the very structures that underpin our digital lives.

Spheres of Influence

In 2018, the European Union unveiled the General Data Protection Regulation (GDPR), a sweeping framework that redefined privacy and data governance not just within Europe, but globally. Multinational corporations, from Silicon Valley tech giants to East Asian manufacturing conglomerates, scrambled to comply, rewriting privacy policies, redesigning data flows, and reconsidering cross-border transfers. While the regulation's text was geographically bounded, its influence radiated far beyond the EU's borders, shaping how firms worldwide handle personal data. GDPR exemplifies a subtle yet potent form of soft power: by establishing a regulatory standard within its own jurisdiction, the EU exported its values, norms, and expectations, creating a sphere of influence that extends through compliance pressures and market incentives rather than through military or economic coercion.

The concept of a "sphere of influence" in the context of data governance challenges traditional notions of geopolitical power. Rather than relying on physical borders or coercive leverage, regional frameworks operate by establishing normative expectations and infrastructural constraints that others must respect to participate in global markets. Countries and regions with robust regulatory ecosystems project influence through the rules they enforce, the contractual obligations they demand, and the technical architectures they codify. In effect, digital sovereignty and policy choices travel along networks of commerce, technology, and law, subtly shaping the operational landscape of organisations that span multiple jurisdictions.

Consider the contrasting approaches of the European Union and the United States. GDPR imposes strict limitations on data collection, retention, and transfer, codifying principles such as purpose limitation, data minimisation, and the right to erasure. Compliance is enforced with tangible penalties, and firms that operate internationally adjust their practices to maintain access to the lucrative European market. In contrast, the United States favours a sectoral, market-driven model, with privacy obligations often mediated by contractual arrangements and voluntary codes of conduct. American firms exporting services to Europe must bridge these regimes, effectively internalising EU standards even when domestic law imposes weaker obligations. The regulatory design of one region thus becomes a de facto influence over corporate behaviour far beyond its borders, illustrating the soft power inherent in legal frameworks and governance models.

Asia presents another axis of influence, where national security, technological sovereignty, and economic strategy intersect in complex ways. China's Cybersecurity Law and related data localisation requirements create a distinct ecosystem in which domestic control and cross-border restrictions shape both the market and the flow of information. Foreign companies seeking access to Chinese consumers or cloud infrastructure must navigate not only technical compliance but also local oversight mechanisms that embed state priorities into operational practices. Here, soft power manifests through institutional design and operational expectation: firms adapt to local norms, which in turn reinforce the state's ability to govern digital space without resorting to overt force.

Regional models do not operate in isolation; they interact, compete, and sometimes clash. Multinational firms face the delicate task of reconciling multiple, often conflicting, regulatory frameworks. Data residency rules in one jurisdiction may conflict with transnational transfer obligations in another, while differing approaches to user consent or algorithmic accountability create operational friction. These interactions underscore the political dimension of seemingly technical standards: protocols, reporting requirements, and contractual clauses are not neutral, but instruments through which states extend influence, negotiate leverage, and assert normative authority over global digital flows.

The sphere of influence concept also illuminates the strategic deployment of norms in areas where hard power is constrained. Smaller states, lacking the economic or military clout of larger powers, can nevertheless assert influence by shaping procurement requirements, contractual obligations, or technical specifications within their jurisdiction. By insisting on privacy-respecting design, transparent oversight, or interoperable security standards, these states create niches in which their policy priorities govern behaviour within bounded ecosystems. In doing so, they leverage law, technology, and commerce as instruments of soft power, demonstrating that influence need not depend solely on conventional forms of geopolitical heft.

Soft power through data governance extends beyond corporate compliance to cultural and societal norms. Regional regulations shape expectations around user consent, transparency, and digital rights, which in turn influence public understanding and civic behaviour. Citizens internalise these expectations, adjusting their digital practices and demanding certain standards from service providers. In effect, governance models project normative power not only across firms and borders but into the fabric of everyday life, subtly embedding values into the choices of individuals, communities, and institutions.

Yet this exertion of influence raises profound questions. Does the export of regulatory norms privilege particular socio-political models at the expense of local autonomy? How do states ensure that influence respects pluralism, avoids unintended consequences, and mitigates friction in the global digital ecosystem? These tensions are particularly acute in areas such as cross-border data flows, AI governance, and algorithmic transparency, where divergent expectations can produce operational complexity, compliance burdens, and potential geopolitical friction. The negotiation of these spheres is thus simultaneously technical, legal, and political, demanding that stakeholders consider not only efficiency and interoperability but also equity, accountability, and legitimacy.

Moreover, spheres of influence are dynamic and contested. Standards evolve, legal frameworks are revised, and technological capabilities shift, creating continuous negotiation over norms and expectations. Alliances form and dissolve, commercial imperatives intersect with strategic interests, and the balance of influence fluctuates as new actors emerge or existing powers recalibrate. Understanding these dynamics requires an appreciation of both the structural elements of governance—laws, regulations, standards—and the practical realities of implementation, enforcement, and adoption across diverse contexts.

Ultimately, regional models of data governance demonstrate that power in the digital era is as much normative as it is material. Control over code, protocol, data flows, and legal frameworks creates leverage that can shape global behaviour without firing a shot. Citizens, corporations, and states alike are subject to the patterns of influence embedded in these models, which translate jurisdictional choices into operational and ethical consequences. Recognising this reality shifts the conversation: sovereignty, compliance, and ethics become inseparable from strategy, and the architecture of governance emerges as both a tool and a terrain of power.

As we examine the spheres of influence in data governance, the reader will encounter a spectrum of approaches, from highly prescriptive regional regimes to market-driven frameworks, and the tensions that arise at their intersections. This chapter illuminates the mechanisms through which norms, expectations, and obligations traverse borders, highlighting the interplay of soft power, compliance, and strategic behaviour. It invites reflection on how regulatory architecture shapes global digital practice, challenges assumptions about neutrality, and reveals that the design of law and policy is inseparable from the distribution of influence in a connected world.

Sanctions, Chips, and Cloud

In 2022, the United States imposed sweeping export controls on advanced semiconductor technology destined for certain foreign markets. The headlines emphasised national security and economic competition, yet beneath the surface, these measures illustrated a subtler form of leverage: control over the hardware and cloud infrastructure that underpins the digital age. From the chips that power mobile phones and servers to the cloud platforms hosting critical services, the architecture of modern computation has become a locus of strategic influence. Nations that dominate these layers of technology can shape not only the commercial landscape but also the flow of information, the deployment of intelligence capabilities, and the contours of global surveillance. The interplay between sanctions, microchips, and cloud platforms is not merely regulatory—it is a form of infrastructural power, where the physical and virtual scaffolding of digital life becomes a vector for state influence.

Consider the semiconductor industry. The fabrication of advanced chips is concentrated in a handful of countries, with Taiwan, South Korea, and the United States supplying the most sophisticated processors. Control over these chips translates into influence over computing capacity worldwide: firms and states dependent on imported hardware must navigate compliance obligations, licensing regimes, and supply chain constraints that reflect geopolitical priorities. When export restrictions limit access to cutting-edge chips, the downstream effects ripple across industries, from consumer electronics to cloud data centres, creating a practical lever through which technological dependency shapes strategic behaviour. In essence, the availability of microchips becomes a proxy for intelligence and economic power.

Cloud infrastructure adds another layer of complexity. Leading cloud providers—predominantly headquartered in North America—host vast amounts of commercial, governmental, and personal data. Control over these platforms enables subtle, yet profound, influence: compliance with local regulations, data localisation mandates, and cooperation with law enforcement requests can shape how information flows, who can access it, and under what conditions. Cloud architecture is not neutral; it embeds assumptions about governance, security, and jurisdiction. A state with leverage over cloud services can exert pressure without firing a shot, compelling firms and foreign governments to operate within constraints dictated by policy and law.

Sanctions amplify these dynamics. Beyond the direct economic impact, sanctions signal the strategic boundaries of permissible action, constraining both technology transfer and operational decision-making. For example, prohibiting sales of certain semiconductor fabrication equipment to a nation-state not only limits that state's industrial capacity but also affects intelligence operations that rely on advanced computation, including signal processing, cryptanalysis, and artificial intelligence. Similarly, restrictions on cloud services can impede data collection, analytics, and cross-border collaboration. Sanctions, chips, and cloud services thus operate as intertwined levers: by targeting infrastructure, they shape capabilities, influence behaviour, and recalibrate the strategic environment.

Yet the leverage is not purely top-down. Firms and intermediary states play pivotal roles in modulating the impact of technological restrictions. Multinational corporations navigate complex compliance regimes, often balancing profitability against legal and ethical obligations. Countries with significant technological production can act as gatekeepers, determining how sanctions translate into operational constraints. Meanwhile, smaller or technologically dependent states must innovate through procurement strategies, contractual clauses, and regional alliances to preserve autonomy and protect sensitive data flows. Intelligence leverage, therefore, is distributed through a network of actors, where infrastructure, regulation, and commercial practice converge.

The nexus of hardware, cloud control, and sanctions also underscores the asymmetry of digital power. While data can traverse borders at near-instantaneous speed, its processing, storage, and management remain anchored to physical and regulatory domains. Control over these anchor points—fabrication facilities, server farms, and cloud platforms—enables actors to enforce constraints, monitor compliance, and influence downstream operations. Even in scenarios where adversaries possess data, limitations on computing power or cloud access can inhibit effective analysis or operational deployment, illustrating that influence derives not solely from access to information but from the capacity to process, interpret, and act upon it.

Philosophically, these dynamics challenge assumptions about the neutrality of technology. Chips and cloud services are often presented as tools, commodities, or infrastructure, yet they are embedded with social, political, and strategic significance. Access, control, and interoperability carry implications for sovereignty, privacy, and security. Entities that govern these layers can impose constraints, encode norms, and shape incentives in ways that transcend conventional diplomacy or military force. The technical scaffolding of the digital realm thus becomes an arena of power projection, with intelligence leverage inseparable from supply chain architecture, platform design, and regulatory compliance.

Operationally, the interdependencies between hardware, cloud services, and sanctions create both opportunities and vulnerabilities. States and firms can leverage these relationships to deter adversaries, incentivise alignment with regulatory norms, or shape market behaviour. Conversely, over-reliance on foreign infrastructure or concentration of capabilities can introduce strategic fragility, as disruptions, embargoes, or policy shifts cascade through interconnected systems. Risk management in this context requires not only technical foresight but also an understanding of geopolitical signalling, regulatory landscapes, and the cascading effects of policy intervention.

Emerging technologies complicate the picture further. Quantum computing, AI-accelerated analytics, and edge computing shift the balance of influence across new dimensions, potentially amplifying or circumventing existing levers. Control over semiconductor production for AI chips, cloud infrastructure capable of handling massive datasets, or secure communication nodes can redefine intelligence advantage. The strategic calculus of sanctions, supply chains, and cloud deployment will evolve in tandem with technological innovation, reinforcing the inseparability of infrastructure, policy, and power.

As this subchapter unfolds, the reader will examine concrete examples, including the 2022 semiconductor export restrictions, the role of cloud platforms in global intelligence sharing, and the operational consequences of sanctions on technology-dependent states. By tracing the interplay between hardware, cloud infrastructure, and regulatory controls, we illuminate how seemingly technical elements become instruments of state influence. The narrative invites reflection on the contours of modern power, the limits of technological autonomy, and the ways in which infrastructure, policy, and strategy intersect to shape intelligence capabilities in a digitally interconnected world.

The examination of sanctions, chips, and cloud exposes a fundamental truth: in the digital era, control over the mechanisms of computation and data storage is as consequential as control over territory or financial flows. Understanding these levers is essential not only for policymakers and corporate strategists but also for citizens and scholars seeking to comprehend how technology mediates power in a global landscape defined less by borders than by the nodes, standards, and permissions embedded in the architecture of the digital state.

Alliances of Convenience

In 2016, the "Five Eyes" intelligence alliance—comprising the United States, United Kingdom, Canada, Australia, and New Zealand—released a framework that went beyond traditional espionage agreements. While often portrayed in media narratives as a tightly coordinated surveillance network, the alliance exemplifies a more subtle phenomenon: the negotiation of trust, operational alignment, and jurisdictional compromise in an environment where data flows freely but loyalties and priorities do not. Each member shares data selectively, balancing national interests, legal constraints, and public accountability. What appears as a seamless network is, in reality, a series of negotiated compromises, frictions, and workarounds, highlighting that even in cooperative ventures, divergence in objectives, capabilities, and regulatory frameworks introduces persistent tension.

The paradox of such alliances is immediate: they are simultaneously indispensable and brittle. Governments recognise the efficiency and reach of shared intelligence; cross-border data-sharing enables early warning, investigative collaboration, and policy alignment on emerging threats. Yet each participant is constrained by domestic law, political expectations, and technological dependencies, creating a persistent need for workarounds, selective disclosure, and layered agreements. These tensions reveal the limits of convenience: alliances are not natural expressions of mutuality but engineered constructs, maintained through constant negotiation and, crucially, by accepting that full alignment is rarely achievable.

The contemporary landscape illustrates this vividly. Consider the European Union's framework for cross-border data transfers, juxtaposed against bilateral agreements with non-EU countries. Privacy Shield, for instance, sought to harmonise transatlantic data flows but collapsed amid judicial scrutiny over surveillance practices and citizen rights. Companies, states, and regulatory bodies were forced to navigate a patchwork of bilateral and multilateral agreements, highlighting that alliances—even when structured with formal legality—often encounter friction between convenience and compliance. The case demonstrates that data-sharing pacts are contingent constructs: they thrive on aligned incentives but falter when normative or operational priorities diverge.

At the heart of these alliances lies the negotiation of risk and control. Sharing data involves not merely the transmission of information but the delegation of trust, accountability, and oversight. States and organisations must weigh the operational value of access against the exposure to regulatory liability, reputational harm, or unintended intelligence consequences. In some instances, rapid access to data can avert crises, yet the same channels can inadvertently facilitate overreach or misinterpretation. The practical management of these risks often involves tiered access, compartmentalisation, and legal safeguards—measures designed to reconcile convenience with control, yet never eliminating friction entirely.

Real-world examples extend beyond traditional intelligence services. International financial crime enforcement networks, for instance, rely on shared transaction data, intergovernmental reporting, and coordinated investigative protocols. While these alliances enable rapid response to money laundering, terrorist financing, and cyber-enabled fraud, they also illustrate the tension between sovereignty, procedural compliance, and operational expedience. A nation may possess unique investigative authority but lack the legal capacity to compel information from foreign entities; conversely, partners may offer access under restrictive conditions, producing a negotiation dance that reflects both the strategic value and the limits of cooperation.

Technological architecture further complicates these arrangements. Cloud-based services, encrypted communications, and data localisation requirements impose practical constraints on data-sharing. An alliance may agree, in principle, to exchange certain categories of information, yet the format, storage location, and encryption protocols can delay or obstruct operational access. These frictions are not incidental; they shape how alliances function, determining the speed, fidelity, and scope of shared intelligence. Technical compatibility thus becomes as critical as legal harmonisation, with operational design choices amplifying or constraining the effectiveness of collaborative frameworks.

Yet alliances of convenience are more than mechanical arrangements; they are instruments of strategic signalling. States leverage participation to convey alignment with norms, assert influence over emerging standards, and cultivate political capital. Inclusion in a data-sharing pact can confer legitimacy, access, and privilege, while exclusion or marginalisation can isolate a state technologically, economically, and diplomatically. Small or medium powers, recognising their limitations, often engage selectively, using participation to extract practical benefits while protecting sovereignty—a strategy that underscores the asymmetry inherent in ostensibly cooperative ventures.

Frictions within alliances are also philosophical as well as operational. Ethical frameworks, civil liberties, and public accountability can diverge sharply among partners. One state may prioritise individual privacy protections, another operational efficacy, and yet another geopolitical leverage. Harmonising these objectives requires constant dialogue, internal oversight, and, at times, tacit tolerance of compromise. Alliances of convenience thus operate in a space where legality, morality, and expedience intersect, producing outcomes that are rarely perfect but often pragmatically sufficient.

The broader lesson is clear: data-sharing pacts function not as monolithic instruments of power but as negotiated ecosystems. Their effectiveness is contingent upon alignment of incentives, technological interoperability, and legal permissibility. At the same time, their vulnerabilities—legal disputes, differing regulatory regimes, and conflicting operational priorities—reveal the fragility of convenience as a basis for enduring cooperation. Recognising this fragility is critical for policymakers, corporate strategists, and scholars seeking to understand the mechanics of global data governance.

Emerging technological and geopolitical shifts further strain these pacts. Artificial intelligence, real-time data analytics, and increasing interdependence in cloud infrastructure amplify both the value of collaboration and the potential for misalignment. As states and organisations invest in data-sharing to enhance intelligence, security, and commercial insight, they must contend with the fact that every convenience entails compromise. The art of sustaining these alliances lies in constant calibration, rigorous oversight, and an acceptance that friction is inherent, not accidental.

This subchapter examines illustrative cases, from transatlantic law enforcement networks to regional intelligence-sharing agreements, highlighting both successes and tensions. By tracing the interplay of legal, technological, and operational factors, the discussion illuminates how alliances of convenience operate as instruments of power, negotiation, and strategic adaptation. The narrative underscores that in the geopolitics of data, collaboration is never absolute, friction is inevitable, and the capacity to navigate both defines the practical limits of shared influence.

Ultimately, alliances of convenience exemplify the paradox of modern data power: they are indispensable for operational efficiency and strategic leverage, yet inherently constrained by the diversity of laws, priorities, and technical architectures among partners. Understanding this duality is essential for any actor seeking to comprehend the nuanced reality of cross-border data governance, intelligence collaboration, and the subtle dynamics of trust, compromise, and friction that shape the global information environment.

Small States, Smart Moves

For nations with modest geopolitical weight, the global data environment can appear less like a playground and more like a gauntlet. Consider Estonia, a country of just over a million people, which has consistently punched above its weight in digital governance and cyber strategy. In 2008, Estonia faced a massive cyberattack following a political dispute with Russia—an event that could have crippled a larger, less digitally sophisticated state. Instead, Estonia turned crisis into advantage, pioneering digital resilience frameworks, e-governance, and procurement strategies that embedded oversight and accountability at the very heart of its national infrastructure. This episode underscores a fundamental principle: small states cannot rely solely on conventional leverage, but through ingenuity, institutional foresight, and precise legal and technical mechanisms, they can exert outsized influence on the governance and security of digital systems.

The central paradox is striking: limitation in scale can catalyse sophistication. Large states often assume that their sheer economic or military heft guarantees influence over data flows and technology standards. Small states, in contrast, must engineer influence indirectly, leveraging agility, transparency, and strategic procurement to shape outcomes. Procurement clauses, for instance, become instruments of governance: by embedding requirements for auditing, independent oversight, and data localisation into vendor contracts, a state transforms a transactional process into a regulatory lever. These clauses serve multiple functions—they reduce exposure to foreign surveillance, create enforceable standards for privacy and security, and signal a commitment to accountability that extends across digital supply chains. In effect, every contract becomes a micro-policy instrument, multiplying the reach of limited bureaucratic resources.

Operationalising such strategies requires a nuanced understanding of both technical systems and legal frameworks. A country cannot merely mandate that suppliers comply with abstract privacy principles; it must specify what compliance entails, how it will be verified, and what recourse exists for breaches. Estonia's approach to e-residency and digital identity systems exemplifies this rigor. By codifying auditing protocols, requiring cryptographic verification, and instituting independent oversight, Estonia has created a model where digital services are both widely adopted and tightly controlled. Similar strategies are visible in Singapore, where procurement contracts for cloud services incorporate strict requirements for data sovereignty and risk mitigation. Both examples highlight that in the absence of scale, precision—legal, technical, and operational—is the key to efficacy.

Small states also benefit from strategic alliances and partnerships, but these must be approached with a clear understanding of power asymmetries. Bilateral agreements, participation in regional data-sharing networks, and collaboration on cyber norms provide access to resources, intelligence, and technical capacity that would be unattainable independently. Yet, alliances of convenience are contingent and fraught with potential compromise. Contracts and legal instruments therefore act as buffers, allowing small states to engage without ceding operational control or sacrificing oversight. By embedding rights, limitations, and audit obligations into every agreement, these states navigate the tensions between collaboration and sovereignty, ensuring that external partnerships do not translate into disproportionate exposure.

A recurring motif in small-state strategy is the institutionalisation of accountability. Internal review boards, independent oversight agencies, and transparency reporting mechanisms are not luxuries but essential tools. They provide a credible means of monitoring compliance with procurement obligations, tracking vendor behaviour, and responding to breaches without relying on external actors. The efficacy of these mechanisms is amplified by clear legislative mandates, public disclosure, and robust civic engagement. When citizens and civil society actors can monitor and challenge implementation, the state's limited capacity is effectively multiplied, creating a distributed system of vigilance that deters malfeasance and reinforces digital resilience.

Technology design choices also intersect with strategic procurement. Emphasising privacy-preserving architecture—on-device processing, minimised data collection, ephemeral data retention—reduces systemic risk while enhancing user trust. For small states, such design principles are particularly valuable: they lower the exposure associated with centralised data repositories, limit the potential for foreign exploitation, and create operational buffers that compensate for constrained oversight resources. By embedding these principles into procurement requirements, small states shape not only vendor practices but also the functional behaviour of deployed systems, leveraging technical design as a policy instrument.

Yet, the success of small-state strategies depends on continuous adaptation. Threats evolve, vendors change, and technological landscapes shift. Procurement clauses and oversight mechanisms must therefore be living instruments, capable of adjustment and reinforcement. Regular audits, scenario planning, and iterative contract revisions are critical. Small states must anticipate emerging risks, such as cloud consolidation or AI-enabled surveillance, and ensure that contractual and institutional mechanisms remain fit for purpose. This dynamic approach transforms apparent limitations into an advantage: a culture of vigilance and flexibility allows small states to respond to developments more rapidly than larger, more bureaucratic actors.

The implications extend beyond national borders. By demonstrating that precise, enforceable policies embedded in procurement and institutional practice can achieve significant influence, small states provide a model for global digital governance. Their experience illustrates that power in the data domain is not solely determined by market size or military capability, but by strategic acumen, legal foresight, and technical sophistication. Lessons from Estonia, Singapore, and other agile states suggest that well-crafted instruments—procurement clauses, oversight bodies, and enforceable standards—can multiply the impact of limited resources, yielding disproportionate resilience and leverage.

At a conceptual level, the small-state approach reframes traditional assumptions about sovereignty and capability. It underscores the idea that influence is not binary—present or absent—but operates along a spectrum, shaped by ingenuity, procedural rigour, and anticipatory strategy. Every contract clause, audit report, and design specification becomes a vector through which a state exerts normative and operational influence, turning constraint into opportunity. The practice of embedding accountability into procurement, coupled with vigilant oversight and adaptive strategy, positions small states as capable actors in a landscape often dominated by larger powers, demonstrating that strategic foresight can be as consequential as scale.

This subchapter explores these strategies in depth, examining case studies where small states have maximised their limited heft through procurement, oversight, and innovative institutional design. It evaluates the interplay of legal frameworks, technical architecture, and operational practice, offering practical insights for policymakers, legal architects, and technology strategists. By tracing the mechanisms through which small states assert influence over digital infrastructure and governance, the discussion illuminates the nuanced ways in which constraint can be converted into strategic advantage.

Ultimately, the narrative of small states making smart moves provides a broader lesson: in the global ecosystem of data power, the ability to wield influence does not depend solely on size or resources. Strategic precision, enforceable oversight, and the integration of technical, legal, and institutional instruments can achieve outcomes that rival or surpass those of larger actors. In a domain where scale often dominates headlines, the careful, deliberate, and creative exercise of leverage demonstrates that thoughtful governance can render limitation a source of strength rather than vulnerability.

Chapter 11

Measuring the Unseen

In 2015, a small civic-tech collective in Brazil began tracking municipal CCTV deployments in São Paulo. At first glance, the task seemed simple: count cameras, log locations, and note operating agencies. Yet within weeks, the team encountered a labyrinth of obfuscation. Some devices were unmarked, others embedded in streetlights or public infrastructure; permissions were inconsistently recorded, and procurement records often bore the faint trace of corporate secrecy. By the time the project concluded, the collective had not only mapped the city's visible cameras but also begun to quantify patterns of data access, retention practices, and inter-agency information flows. What had started as a local counting exercise had transformed into a sophisticated methodology for illuminating a shadowed system—a system whose operations were largely invisible to the public eye yet shaped everyday life with profound subtlety.

This paradox—how to measure what is deliberately hidden or structurally opaque—lies at the heart of the chapter. Surveillance, by design, operates in the shadows, yet its effects ripple through societies, influencing behaviour, shaping markets, and constraining political discourse. Measuring the unseen is less a matter of simple arithmetic than of strategic curiosity: defining what indicators truly matter, identifying where data traces emerge, and devising reproducible methods for translating opaque practices into observable patterns. The challenge is both technical and conceptual. One must not only ask how many cameras or algorithms exist but also interrogate access, intensity, and operational norms. A mere tally is insufficient; meaningful measurement requires insight into structure, practice, and consequence.

The significance of this work extends far beyond urban camera networks. Consider the deployment of automated licence plate readers, the use of AI-driven predictive policing tools, or the proliferation of biometric kiosks in airports. Across these domains, opaque systems affect billions of decisions without ever inviting direct scrutiny. How can citizens, researchers, or journalists hold such systems accountable when code is proprietary, procurement details are withheld, and operational logs are partial at best? Here, the logic of measurement intersects with civic empowerment. To illuminate unseen practices is to render them governable, contestable, and ultimately responsive to human norms rather than purely technical imperatives.

This chapter opens by examining the foundational question: *what to count*. Defining indicators for surveillance intensity demands careful reflection. Raw device counts are only the beginning; equally critical are patterns of access, frequency of algorithmic queries, data retention durations, and interconnections between agencies or private vendors. Drawing on case studies from public records initiatives and FOI-driven research, we demonstrate how seemingly modest metrics—like the ratio of audit logs to active devices—can reveal systemic weaknesses or points of excessive centralisation. Indicators must be chosen with an eye not only to feasibility but also to interpretive value: the ability to translate measurements into actionable insight.

Fieldwork extends these questions into operational practice. Traditional methods of social research—interviews, observation, ethnography—must be adapted to systems rather than people. How does one "interview" a process? What questions illuminate how data flows between devices, agencies, and commercial intermediaries? Through hands-on examples, including interviews with municipal IT managers, cloud service operators, and procurement officers, we explore methodologies for teasing out patterns, verifying claims, and mapping interactions that are otherwise opaque. The objective is to move from abstract description to granular understanding, producing evidence that withstands scrutiny even when direct access is restricted.

Parallel to these approaches are strategies for public accountability: transparency registers, open data portals, and Freedom of Information (FOI) mechanisms. While imperfect, these tools allow systematic extraction of operational data from official channels, providing verifiable snapshots of system scale and activity. Cases from the United Kingdom, Canada, and Australia reveal how proactive use of public ledgers can surface discrepancies between claimed and actual surveillance practices, challenging narratives promoted by both state and corporate actors. Importantly, these methods emphasise documentation, reproducibility, and the creation of records that can be analysed longitudinally—a core requirement for any robust measurement framework.

Yet measurement in this domain is rarely straightforward. Proprietary software, closed-source algorithms, and opaque procurement arrangements often obscure the most critical elements of surveillance. Replicability in the wild becomes a central concern. How can researchers validate findings when underlying systems are hidden? This chapter provides strategies ranging from synthetic data simulation to controlled observation, demonstrating how careful experimental design and triangulation across multiple evidence sources can approximate independent verification. The underlying principle is pragmatic: perfect transparency is rare, but credible inference is possible.

Finally, we turn to practical application through the lens of the "dashboard citizen." Monitoring need not be restricted to professional analysts or institutional researchers. Simple, repeatable routines—logging public camera feeds, auditing local procurement announcements, tracking algorithmic outputs—can transform individual or community practice into meaningful civic oversight. By systematically recording, visualising, and contextualising these data points, citizens gain actionable insight, creating a distributed layer of accountability that complements formal oversight mechanisms. The dashboard concept bridges the gap between technical sophistication and everyday engagement, translating abstract measurement principles into tangible practice.

Throughout the chapter, the underlying motif is one of illumination: turning obscured operations into analyzable patterns, and in doing so, empowering citizens, journalists, and researchers alike. Measuring the unseen is simultaneously a technical challenge, a methodological exercise, and a civic project. The techniques outlined—defining meaningful indicators, conducting system-informed fieldwork, exploiting public transparency mechanisms, validating claims in opaque contexts, and implementing accessible monitoring routines—combine to create a toolkit for understanding, critiquing, and influencing surveillance infrastructures.

In framing surveillance measurement as both rigorous inquiry and participatory practice, this chapter sets the stage for readers to navigate the complexity of modern oversight. It positions measurement not as an end in itself but as a lever for accountability, agency, and informed critique. By the chapter's close, readers will be equipped to approach opaque systems with both analytical rigour and practical confidence, ready to illuminate the hidden architectures that shape daily life in the digital age.

What to Count

In 2017, a civic research group in Berlin attempted a seemingly straightforward project: quantify the city's surveillance footprint. The initial goal was modest—catalogue the locations of public cameras—but the undertaking quickly revealed a deeper complexity. Cameras were hidden in façades, embedded in streetlights, or operated by private contractors with varying degrees of transparency. Some devices recorded video continuously, others only on motion detection; some streams were retained for days, others for months. The more the team investigated, the more evident it became that the simple act of counting was insufficient. To understand the intensity and impact of surveillance, they would need to define what *really* mattered—what indicators would meaningfully reflect the reach, frequency, and potential consequences of these systems.

This challenge—deciding what to count and why—lies at the heart of measuring unseen surveillance. Systems of observation rarely operate in isolation. They interconnect, layer, and sometimes conceal themselves behind opaque practices. A single camera's presence is a limited signal; its operational frequency, accessibility, the extent of recorded data, and inter-agency sharing policies are equally, if not more, informative. Indicators must capture both the *existence* and the *effectiveness* of surveillance: how much is being monitored, how often, and to what end. A simplistic tally risks producing numbers that mislead, rather than illuminate, the underlying reality.

At a conceptual level, defining meaningful indicators requires a balance between precision and interpretability. Quantitative metrics must be specific enough to allow comparison across time or jurisdictions, yet flexible enough to account for technological and procedural variation. Consider retention policies: two agencies may each operate fifty cameras, but if one deletes recordings after twenty-four hours while the other stores data indefinitely, the potential for impact diverges dramatically. Metrics must therefore encompass scope, duration, and accessibility. Similarly, algorithmic surveillance—facial recognition, predictive policing, behavioural scoring—demands measurement beyond raw counts of devices or endpoints. Queries per hour, dataset sizes, and error rates become the operational equivalent of a camera's placement and range.

Practical application of these principles can be observed in case studies ranging from municipal CCTV audits to national monitoring programmes. In the United Kingdom, investigative teams have mapped CCTV intensity using a combination of public records, direct observation, and FOI requests. Their metrics included camera density per square kilometre, frequency of audits, and public accessibility of live feeds. In Singapore, where public camera networks are integrated with license plate readers and predictive policing tools, researchers have had to combine quantitative indicators—number of active devices, average retention time—with qualitative assessments of procedural constraints and data governance. Across these contexts, it is clear that a single number—"total cameras" or "active sensors"—cannot adequately describe the surveillance landscape. Only layered, multidimensional indicators offer a faithful approximation.

Indicators also serve as a tool for revealing disparities in exposure. Surveillance rarely distributes evenly. Certain neighbourhoods, communities, or socio-economic groups may face disproportionate monitoring, while others remain relatively unobserved. Here, indicators must capture not only volume but *distribution*: spatial coverage, demographic correlation, and temporal patterns. For instance, measuring average footage collected per individual—or per unit area—can uncover systemic bias in deployment, highlighting areas where oversight and accountability are most critical. This approach transforms measurement from a passive record-keeping exercise into an active diagnostic tool, capable of revealing inequities that might otherwise remain invisible.

Beyond physical surveillance, digital monitoring requires similarly nuanced indicators. Consider the logging of online activity by government agencies or private platforms: counting the number of accounts monitored is insufficient. Metrics must incorporate frequency of access, scope of data collected, retention duration, and mechanisms for sharing or cross-referencing. For example, in assessing a social media surveillance programme, researchers might track API calls per user per day, cumulative data storage per account, and audit rates for internal compliance. Such indicators provide insight into the *intensity* of surveillance rather than merely its nominal presence.

Selecting indicators is not merely a technical exercise; it embodies philosophical and ethical considerations. What do we value enough to measure? Is the goal transparency, accountability, deterrence, or empowerment? Decisions about indicators implicitly define the scope of what constitutes acceptable or unacceptable surveillance. A system that is technically capable of intensive monitoring but rarely exercised may be treated differently than one with moderate capability but frequent utilisation. Metrics, therefore, carry normative weight: they guide both interpretation and subsequent policy or civic response. Researchers must remain vigilant against overemphasising easily measurable aspects at the expense of those with greater social significance.

Constraints and feasibility must also be considered. Data is often incomplete, inconsistent, or deliberately obfuscated. In these conditions, indicators must strike a balance between theoretical ideal and practical availability. Aggregated public records, observational surveys, and open-data portals may offer partial glimpses, while interviews with operators or FOI requests can fill gaps. Triangulation across sources increases confidence, but limitations should always be acknowledged. In this sense, the process of defining indicators is inseparable from the challenge of evaluating evidence reliability.

An additional dimension is temporal: surveillance intensity fluctuates over time. Seasonal events, political cycles, or emergent threats can drastically alter monitoring practices. Indicators must, therefore, allow for longitudinal assessment. Continuous logging of key metrics—camera activity, algorithmic queries, access logs—provides a dynamic view, revealing how systems adapt and how exposure evolves. Static snapshots risk obscuring trends, whereas repeated measurement allows patterns of escalation, reduction, or displacement to emerge.

Finally, meaningful indicators empower civic engagement. When collected and communicated effectively, they enable journalists, activists, and citizens to hold institutions accountable. A dashboard displaying camera density, retention durations, and audit frequency can transform abstract data into actionable insight. Indicators become not only a tool for measurement but a medium for transparency, participation, and informed debate. They bridge the gap between technical surveillance systems and societal oversight, translating complexity into comprehension.

Yet the task remains daunting. Surveillance is designed to be invisible, its reach diffuse, its operation opaque. Defining what to count is as much a strategic act as a technical one: selecting indicators that illuminate power, expose inequities, and enable intervention. Researchers must continually ask which metrics will reveal both the scale and the consequences of monitoring. Which aspects of operation most directly affect human behaviour, civil liberties, and trust in institutions? These are not questions with easy answers, but grappling with them is essential for meaningful measurement.

The logic of "what to count" sets the foundation for all subsequent methods in measuring the unseen. Without carefully defined, socially and operationally meaningful indicators, fieldwork, transparency investigations, and replicability exercises risk producing fragmented or misleading pictures. Thoughtful selection transforms raw data into intelligence: a lens through which to discern patterns, assess intensity, and guide civic and policy responses. In short, the act of defining what to count is itself a form of civic intervention, shaping both understanding and governance of the invisible forces that increasingly shape public life.

By foregrounding the principles of indicator selection—scope, intensity, distribution, temporal dynamics, and interpretive relevance—this subchapter equips readers with the conceptual and practical tools to navigate complex surveillance ecosystems. It frames measurement as a deliberate, disciplined process that bridges empirical observation with ethical reflection, technical insight with social significance. Readers are encouraged to see metrics not merely as numbers, but as instruments for visibility, accountability, and civic empowerment in a world increasingly governed by unseen observation.

Fieldwork with Systems

In a bustling municipal office in Madrid, a researcher sat across from a data analyst who had never considered himself a "gatekeeper" of surveillance knowledge. Yet, as he traced the flow of information—from the cameras on city streets to the central monitoring hub and finally into local law enforcement databases—he unwittingly revealed patterns, priorities, and blind spots that no public report could convey. The researcher was not merely collecting anecdotes from a human source; he was observing the *system itself*, its operational rhythms, the tacit rules governing access, retention, and analysis. Each pause, each reference to automated alerts or exception-handling procedures, became data. The process illuminated a fundamental truth: in contemporary surveillance research, understanding people alone is insufficient. One must interview the system.

This approach—interrogating processes as actively as individuals—defines the emerging practice of system-centred fieldwork. Traditional social research emphasises interviews, focus groups, or ethnography: human behaviour as the primary lens. Yet, in surveillance ecosystems, the machinery, software protocols, and bureaucratic routines often hold as much sway over outcomes as any individual decision-maker. A security dashboard might prioritise certain alerts over others; automated scoring algorithms determine which cases receive human scrutiny; internal logs dictate the operational memory of a system. Observing these flows, asking structured questions of both human actors and artefacts, reveals the unseen rules shaping privacy, power, and risk.

The challenge begins with conceptual framing. What does it mean to "interview" a system? It requires shifting from a linear conception of interaction to a networked one. A single process—say, the automated flagging of license plates—cannot be understood in isolation. One must trace inputs, processing rules, decision thresholds, and outputs. This often entails a combination of document review, software analysis, process mapping, and structured conversation with staff. The objective is to reconstruct the operational logic: how information moves, how thresholds are set, and how exceptions are handled. Each of these components becomes a locus for observation, questioning, and verification.

Practical applications abound. Consider the study of airport security watchlists. Researchers have found that interviewing the system—not just the personnel—uncovers discrepancies between official policy and practice. Access logs reveal who can override alerts, how often flags are escalated, and under what conditions items are removed or retained. Observing the interface between software, staff, and standard operating procedures exposes patterns invisible to external audits. Similarly, in municipal video surveillance projects, combining human interviews with analysis of automated alerts and data retention logs allows researchers to discern which areas receive sustained attention, which remain overlooked, and how resources are allocated.

A key tension arises between visibility and obfuscation. Systems are designed to operate efficiently, often optimising against human comprehension. Data flows may be opaque, algorithms unlabelled, and logs incomplete. Fieldwork must therefore balance rigor with creativity. Researchers develop methods to make the implicit explicit: diagramming information flows, coding exceptions, and simulating operational conditions. Triangulation—comparing human recollection, process documentation, and empirical traces from the system—is essential to avoid over-reliance on any single source. The resulting narrative captures both the intent of the system designers and the emergent behaviour shaped by real-world deployment.

Ethical and philosophical dimensions also emerge. When systems are observed as actors, researchers confront questions about accountability, transparency, and agency. Processes can amplify bias, perpetuate inequities, or operate in ways that humans may not fully understand or control. Fieldwork with systems thus becomes an exercise not only in technical documentation but also in normative assessment: what are the consequences of automated prioritisation? Which invisible rules govern access and retention? Who bears responsibility when errors propagate? The act of observation itself is an ethical engagement, highlighting the intersection between operational mechanics and societal impact.

Moreover, system-centred fieldwork demands careful attention to temporal dynamics. Processes evolve: software updates change decision thresholds, operational procedures shift in response to incidents, and personnel rotations alter interpretation of rules. A snapshot at a single point may misrepresent both intensity and reach. Longitudinal observation—tracking changes, monitoring adaptations, and noting deviations—provides a richer understanding. Systems, like societies, are dynamic; only by embedding observation in time can researchers capture trajectories rather than static configurations.

Technically, tools for system interrogation vary. Access logs, audit trails, configuration files, and dashboard outputs provide empirical traces. Shadowing staff during routine operations reveals tacit knowledge, workarounds, and informal hierarchies. Even structured interviews can be reframed: asking personnel to describe processes as if the system were a collaborator, to walk through decision trees, or to demonstrate exception handling, effectively "interviews" the system through human proxies. The skill lies in translating operational detail into structured, comparable indicators that capture both volume and consequence.

The implications extend beyond surveillance research. In corporate governance, understanding how automated compliance or risk systems operate can prevent policy gaps from translating into operational failures. In civic technology, examining how digital services handle sensitive data illuminates vulnerabilities before they manifest as breaches. Across contexts, fieldwork with systems reframes observation: it is no longer sufficient to understand only the actors who wield authority; one must map the architecture of influence embedded in processes themselves.

Ultimately, the practice of interviewing systems challenges assumptions about evidence, authority, and interpretive hierarchy. It situates the researcher at the intersection of human judgement and algorithmic operation, requiring both technical literacy and critical insight. Each interaction—tracing a process, questioning a decision pathway, logging an automated response—reveals the latent governance embedded in design choices. In doing so, it transforms fieldwork from passive documentation into a form of operational inquiry, where the system itself becomes a participant in the narrative of accountability.

In grappling with these methods, readers are invited to expand the scope of inquiry. Surveillance is not merely about the people it touches but the processes that mediate experience. Observing, interviewing, and mapping these processes allows for a fuller, more accurate depiction of intensity, bias, and impact. By treating systems as interlocutors, researchers gain access to a deeper layer of insight—one where operational logic, institutional priorities, and civic implications converge. This approach, rigorous yet reflective, forms the foundation for meaningful measurement in an age increasingly defined by automated oversight.

Public Ledgers of Power

In 2019, a civic researcher in Toronto spent weeks poring over municipal transparency registers, meticulously tracing the allocation of surveillance contracts for public cameras, licence plate readers, and data analytics tools. What emerged was more than a ledger; it was a map of influence, showing which private vendors had disproportionate access to civic data and how procurement patterns correlated with policy priorities. Each entry—a line item in a public register—became a node in a network revealing power that was nominally accountable yet functionally opaque. The researcher did not merely document transactions; they decoded the invisible architectures of control embedded within civic systems.

Public ledgers—ranging from statutory transparency registers to voluntarily disclosed corporate reports—offer a unique vantage point. Unlike interviews or leaked datasets, these sources are legally mandated or formally published, yet they require interpretive skill to transform raw entries into actionable insight. They are simultaneously authoritative and incomplete, providing both a window into institutional operations and a challenge to the researcher: how to read between the lines, understand systemic patterns, and anticipate where information gaps may conceal operational risk or inequity.

The exercise highlights a central paradox of accountability: transparency mechanisms exist to empower oversight, yet the sheer volume and form of the data can obscure rather than clarify. A register may catalogue thousands of contracts, but without context—such as the criteria for awarding a contract or the monitoring procedures applied—its utility is limited. This tension underscores the importance of methodical approaches that combine scrutiny of formal records with strategic queries under freedom of information (FOI) frameworks. These legal instruments transform static public ledgers into dynamic tools of investigation, allowing researchers to ask pointed questions and compel clarifications that illuminate otherwise hidden processes.

In practice, fieldwork using public ledgers requires careful navigation. Registers vary dramatically in structure and completeness: some are machine-readable datasets updated in real time, while others are PDFs or scanned forms requiring manual extraction. Analysts must develop heuristics for identifying meaningful indicators, such as recurring vendor names, contract values relative to service impact, or temporal clustering of acquisitions. FOI requests complement this by filling gaps: asking for communications around contract decisions, internal audit reports, or risk assessments can reveal discrepancies between documented intentions and operational realities. Through iterative cross-referencing, researchers reconstruct an operational topology of power that extends beyond what is formally visible.

Case studies illustrate the method's potency. Consider a study of national-level surveillance acquisitions: by correlating FOI responses with public procurement registers, analysts uncovered that several contracts included clauses allowing remote software updates without explicit oversight. Individually, these clauses appeared minor, but in aggregate they signalled an expansion of operational control beyond statutory safeguards. Similarly, comparative analysis across municipalities can reveal patterns of vendor concentration or shared technical standards, pointing to broader trends in how surveillance capacity is deployed, monetised, and regulated. Public ledgers thus act as both a mirror and a lens—reflecting documented reality while amplifying systemic trends that might otherwise remain invisible.

Yet there are conceptual tensions inherent in ledger-based analysis. The formality of public records may mask practical improvisations, discretionary judgements, and informal governance. Data can mislead if treated as a direct proxy for operational behaviour. Observing that a vendor holds multiple contracts does not necessarily indicate misuse; conversely, absence from a register does not guarantee absence from influence. Researchers must therefore calibrate their interpretive models, combining ledger analysis with complementary methods such as interviews, system audits, or process observation. This integration ensures that the ledger informs a nuanced understanding rather than a simplistic assumption of transparency.

FOI strategies, in particular, introduce a performative element to research. Requests are selective, time-bound, and legally framed, which shapes both the responses received and the operational behaviour of the target institution. Analysts often iterate: initial requests identify gaps or ambiguities, which in turn inform follow-up queries that probe deeper into decision-making logic. Over time, this method allows the researcher to construct a provisional model of institutional priorities, data flows, and procedural bottlenecks. Importantly, it treats the public ledger not as an endpoint, but as the entry into an investigative process where accountability is co-constructed through dialogue with formal mechanisms.

The philosophical dimension is equally critical. Public ledgers embody a principle of civic empowerment: that citizens and researchers can observe, assess, and influence the deployment of state or corporate power. Yet the very act of transforming these registers into meaningful insight demands a civic skill set—literacy in data formats, understanding of institutional logics, and interpretive acumen. Transparency, in this sense, is not automatic; it is enacted. The researcher's craft lies in making latent patterns legible, linking procedural documentation to social impact, and tracing the pathways through which policy intentions translate into operational reality.

Technically, there are strategies for maximising the analytic yield of ledgers. Structuring datasets to highlight recurring actors, integrating contract metadata with spatial or temporal indicators, and applying network analysis can reveal both concentration of influence and structural vulnerabilities. FOI responses can be coded for decision rationales, exception handling, and compliance narratives. Even partial datasets provide a scaffold for triangulation with other sources, such as media reports, regulatory filings, or whistleblower accounts. In all cases, the goal is to render the ledger intelligible in relation to the lived effects of surveillance: who is empowered, who is monitored, and how institutional choices reverberate through society.

In applying these methods, the researcher must also navigate ethical and legal boundaries. FOI requests, while public instruments, intersect with privacy, security, and proprietary considerations. Interpretation of ledgers must respect confidentiality where appropriate, avoiding inadvertent exposure of sensitive operational detail. The ethical craft lies in balancing the imperative to illuminate systemic patterns with the responsibility to protect individual actors, thereby preserving the integrity of the investigative process.

Ultimately, public ledgers and FOI strategies constitute a methodology for measuring the unseen. They transform static records into living instruments of oversight, revealing how surveillance capacity is configured, exercised, and legitimised. By engaging both the formality of registers and the strategic leverage of FOI, researchers can map institutional power, identify systemic risks, and produce evidence that informs civic discourse and policy reform. The ledger, once decoded, becomes a mirror of governance: structured, interpretable, and revealing, yet always demanding thoughtful interrogation.

In tracing these formalised pathways of authority, analysts learn to read the signatures of power in the language of administration. Each contract entry, each procedural annotation, each FOI response carries embedded assumptions about control, prioritisation, and oversight. Through rigorous engagement with these sources, the researcher reconstructs not just a record of activity, but the architecture of influence itself—offering clarity, accountability, and a framework for citizens to understand and contest the distribution of surveillance capacity.

Replicability in the Wild

In 2022, an investigative team sought to verify the effectiveness of a popular content moderation algorithm deployed across multiple social media platforms. The company declined to release the source code, citing proprietary concerns and security risks. Yet, claims about bias mitigation, user impact, and false-positive rates were abundant in marketing materials and policy statements. The researchers faced a common paradox: how to hold an opaque system accountable when direct inspection is impossible. Their answer lay not in seeing the inner workings, but in observing behaviour—the system in the wild.

Closed-source code presents a fundamental challenge to replicability, the cornerstone of rigorous analysis. In science, replication allows independent verification of claims; in technology, it ensures that assertions about performance, fairness, and risk are not merely marketing or assumption. When the mechanisms themselves are hidden, the burden shifts to external observation, reverse engineering, and inventive experiment. Analysts must treat the system as both black box and interactive environment, designing tests that elicit measurable outcomes, systematically record responses, and allow comparison across contexts. Every interaction becomes a data point; every anomaly, a clue to underlying structure.

This approach transforms the act of replication from a purely technical exercise into an epistemic strategy. Researchers do not merely test functionality; they interrogate assumptions, expose inconsistencies, and map the space between stated objectives and operational reality. Closed code is not a barrier but a constraint that encourages methodological creativity: controlled experiments, shadow testing, synthetic inputs, and comparative analyses all provide avenues to approximate the truth within bounds of feasibility. In practice, these strategies reveal not only the behaviour of algorithms but also the cultural and organisational choices embedded within their deployment.

Observing systems in the wild demands careful design. Analysts must identify relevant variables—inputs, triggers, outputs—and determine how to manipulate or measure them without violating ethical, legal, or operational boundaries. Consider a facial recognition system used at border checkpoints. Direct inspection of the software may be impossible, but by deploying controlled datasets, monitoring error rates, and cross-referencing results with demographic variables, researchers can approximate performance and assess discriminatory outcomes. Each test is a probe into a closed architecture, revealing operational characteristics without needing access to proprietary logic.

Case studies illustrate the method's potency. In one instance, a team examining automated content moderation at scale created hundreds of synthetic profiles to test algorithmic prioritisation. They recorded variations in content removal, flagging behaviour, and account suspension across different simulated identities. Patterns emerged that contradicted official claims of fairness and consistency, prompting a public discussion on accountability. Similarly, research into predictive policing tools used historical crime data to construct surrogate scenarios, revealing systemic bias even when the codebase remained inaccessible. These examples demonstrate that replicability does not require source code—it demands disciplined observation, rigorous control, and analytical transparency.

Yet external replication is not without conceptual tension. Closed systems are designed to resist inspection, often incorporating randomisation, adaptive learning, or obfuscation. Observed behaviour may vary over time, confounding simple measurement. The researcher must therefore distinguish between intrinsic properties of the system and ephemeral states influenced by deployment context, user interaction, or environmental conditions. Statistical methods, repeated trials, and triangulation with other data sources become essential. Replicability becomes a probabilistic exercise: conclusions are statements of confidence rather than absolute certainties.

Ethical considerations are equally central. Experimentation in real-world systems risks unintended consequences: users may be affected, operations disrupted, or proprietary boundaries breached. Replicability in the wild requires balancing investigative rigor with responsibility. Researchers must design minimally invasive probes, anonymise sensitive data, and document methodology for accountability. The legitimacy of findings rests on both analytic soundness and ethical integrity, reinforcing the civic purpose of examining opaque systems: to hold power accountable without inflicting harm.

Practical techniques for replicability in closed systems are increasingly sophisticated. Shadow deployments, where parallel systems mimic production environments, allow controlled testing without interfering with live operations. Synthetic inputs and adversarial datasets probe system responses systematically. Comparative benchmarking against open-source analogues provides context, highlighting divergences between claimed and observed behaviour. Even partial transparency—logs, aggregate metrics, or limited API outputs—can be leveraged to infer deeper operational characteristics. Collectively, these methods form a toolkit for rigorous evaluation in environments where direct inspection is impossible.

Philosophically, the exercise confronts a central tension between opacity and trust. In democratic and civic contexts, reliance on unverifiable claims is incompatible with accountability. Closed systems wield influence over individuals, communities, and public discourse, yet the mechanisms of that influence are hidden. Replicability in the wild asserts that oversight does not depend on proprietary exposure alone; it depends on methodological sophistication, observational skill, and civic commitment. The act of testing, measuring, and documenting becomes itself a form of accountability, translating opacity into informed critique.

Ultimately, replicability in closed systems is about translating unseen processes into verifiable patterns of behaviour. It is about creating knowledge where transparency is partial, leveraging observation, controlled experimentation, and cross-referenced data to approximate truth. Each replication attempt contributes to a body of evidence that constrains institutional claims, informs policy debate, and empowers users. Closed code may limit direct scrutiny, but it does not preclude accountability. Through disciplined methods, researchers illuminate the pathways by which algorithms shape lives, enabling citizens and scholars alike to understand, question, and act upon the power exercised by technological systems.

In this light, replicability in the wild is not merely a technical challenge; it is a civic practice. It demands patience, rigor, and creativity, transforming opacity from an obstacle into a stimulus for methodical inquiry. By interrogating closed systems through their external manifestations, analysts reclaim the capacity to measure, critique, and influence, ensuring that technology remains accountable to the societies it serves.

The Dashboard Citizen

In a quiet office in 2019, a group of civic technologists huddled over a series of spreadsheets and scripts. They were not engineers building the next viral app, nor were they regulators auditing corporate compliance. Instead, they were ordinary citizens assembling a dashboard: a simple, transparent system to monitor how local authorities collected, stored, and shared data about residents. Over time, the dashboard revealed patterns of access, instances of policy drift, and discrepancies between stated and observed practice. The organisers had discovered something powerful: when equipped with modest tools, citizens could track the often-invisible machinery that governs digital life.

The paradox is clear. Surveillance, data flows, and algorithmic governance often seem abstract, complex, and unapproachable. Yet the principles underlying their operation—frequency of access, duration of retention, procedural adherence—can be tracked using straightforward metrics and consistent monitoring. The dashboard citizen transforms opacity into actionable insight. No proprietary code or privileged access is necessary; systematic observation and disciplined recording are sufficient to produce knowledge that can inform debate, influence policy, and guide personal or community action.

This subchapter positions monitoring not as an act of technical heroics, but as a civic habit. It asks readers to shift perspective: from passive recipients of policy and data collection to active participants capable of measurement, comparison, and accountability. The focus is on sustainable routines, repeatable methods, and the creation of local intelligence that is meaningful without requiring vast infrastructure. The dashboard becomes both a tool and a metaphor: a means to observe, synthesise, and understand the impact of systems on everyday life.

Effective monitoring begins with clarity about purpose. What exactly does one want to know? Access frequency, unusual logins, data-sharing events, policy compliance—all represent meaningful indicators. A small local government might release public-facing datasets or provide transparency reports; these can be logged, visualised, and compared over time. Even in contexts where formal transparency is limited, indirect observation can provide proxies: tracking changes in service behaviour, documenting anomalies, or triangulating with public records. The goal is to make invisible actions visible, without overextending resources.

Central to the dashboard approach is consistency. Metrics must be recorded in a structured manner and evaluated over time. One-off observations are insufficient to detect trends or irregularities. A simple spreadsheet, a basic script, or a low-cost visualisation tool can enable a citizen to track patterns, compare them against declared norms, and highlight deviations. For example, monitoring a municipal API's rate of response to FOI requests can reveal delays, selective disclosures, or systemic inefficiencies. The insight gained from repetition and methodical recording often exceeds that derived from sporadic or anecdotal attention.

The dashboard citizen also navigates the tension between granularity and manageability. Too broad a focus leads to scattered attention, while excessive detail becomes unmanageable. The key is to identify a limited set of indicators that collectively capture essential dynamics. Consider a city's camera network: metrics might include the number of cameras deployed, areas covered, access authorisations, and retention policies. Even without internal documentation, these parameters can be estimated through field observation, user feedback, and requests for information. Each data point contributes to a holistic picture of governance, supporting informed advocacy or scrutiny.

Another dimension is visualisation and interpretation. A dashboard is not merely a collection of figures; it organises data into comprehensible patterns. Colour-coded alerts, trend lines, and simple charts can highlight anomalies, systemic shifts, or emerging risks. In practice, these representations allow citizens, journalists, and advocacy groups to act quickly: spotting a sudden spike in surveillance activity, flagging a new contract clause in a vendor agreement, or correlating data retention trends with legislative changes. Visualisation transforms raw observation into strategic intelligence.

Importantly, dashboard monitoring is iterative. Systems evolve, policies change, and new technologies are deployed. The citizen's dashboard must be flexible: updating indicators, adapting methods, and incorporating feedback from real-world observation. In some cases, repeated monitoring uncovers latent assumptions or systemic vulnerabilities previously unnoticed. By iterating, the citizen not only records data but also learns the contours of the system itself, becoming attuned to subtleties that static reports fail to capture.

Ethical and practical constraints are ever-present. Monitoring must respect privacy, avoid interference, and operate within legal boundaries. The citizen's role is not to hack, disrupt, or expose personal data, but to observe publicly visible behaviours, track systemic patterns, and leverage official transparency mechanisms. Civic diligence, rather than technical intrusion, forms the backbone of accountability. The power of the dashboard resides in its replicability: routines that can be shared, scaled, and adopted across communities, creating a networked form of civic oversight.

Case studies illustrate the impact of modest dashboards. In several cities, journalists used simple tools to track police body-camera usage, FOI response times, and municipal data-sharing events. Patterns emerged—discrepancies between published policies and operational reality, repeated delays in data requests, or uneven access logs—prompting public scrutiny and policy review. Similarly, community groups monitoring social service deployments discovered inequalities in service provision, enabling targeted advocacy. In each instance, the dashboard provided an accessible, evidence-based platform for action, bridging the gap between complex systems and civic agency.

Finally, the dashboard citizen embodies a philosophical shift: accountability is not outsourced solely to regulators or auditors; it is a participatory, iterative practice. By engaging in routine monitoring, citizens cultivate habits of attentiveness, critical thinking, and civic responsibility. Observation becomes an act of care: a commitment to ensuring that technology and governance serve the public interest rather than operating unchecked. The dashboard is not a panacea, but it is a tool that empowers sustained oversight, fostering transparency and responsiveness in systems otherwise shrouded in complexity.

Through structured monitoring routines, even modestly resourced individuals or groups can transform invisible dynamics into visible patterns. The dashboard citizen translates attention into action, creating knowledge where opacity prevails. By building simple, repeatable routines, documenting observations, and visualising trends, civic actors generate leverage, influence policy, and embed a culture of continuous scrutiny. In doing so, the dashboard moves beyond metaphor: it becomes an instrument of civic intelligence, illuminating the unseen mechanisms that shape collective life, and equipping ordinary people to participate actively in the governance of technology and data.

Chapter 12

Towards Accountable Intelligence

In the autumn of 2023, a mid-sized European city faced an unexpected dilemma. Its police department had invested in a sophisticated predictive policing system, designed to allocate resources efficiently and anticipate criminal activity. Within weeks, the system's outputs began to shape patrol patterns in ways that disproportionately targeted certain neighbourhoods. Despite repeated assurances from vendors about algorithmic neutrality, human officers reported feeling compelled to follow the system's "recommendations," fearing professional backlash if they ignored them. What was intended as a tool for efficiency had quietly reshaped discretion, accountability, and civic trust. The episode illuminated a central paradox of our era: intelligence systems promise clarity, yet their deployment often diffuses responsibility.

This chapter confronts that paradox head-on, framing a vision for intelligence that is not merely powerful, but accountable. It invites readers to examine the principles, architectures, and institutional practices that determine whether a system serves society or undermines it. Here, accountability is neither abstract nor optional—it is a design parameter, embedded in procurement choices, operational workflows, and oversight structures. The focus is on creating intelligence that can be interrogated, corrected, and restrained, even as it scales.

The stakes are immediate and enduring. From predictive policing to healthcare triage algorithms, decisions made by machines ripple outward, affecting human lives, civic liberties, and public trust. Yet the conversation often stalls at the level of regulation or ethics statements, leaving the technical and operational levers unexamined. This chapter shifts the lens: it examines the levers, showing where discretion must remain human, how institutions can audit and intervene, and how minimalism—collecting only what is necessary—can itself be a potent safeguard. The aim is to equip readers with both understanding and practical insight, bridging theory, policy, and everyday organisational reality.

The first principle, *Minimalism as Default*, argues that restraint must be designed in from the outset. Excessive collection is not a problem that arises later; it is baked into architecture, contracts, and deployment choices. Consider procurement clauses that specify data retention limits, or system designs that process information on-device rather than centralising it in a cloud. Each design decision becomes a moral and civic statement, influencing the scale and scope of potential harm. Minimalism is not merely a technical guideline—it is a philosophy of accountability.

Equally vital is the retention of human judgement. The notion of *Human-in-the-Loop, For Real* insists that certain decisions, especially those with tangible consequences for individuals or communities, cannot be delegated entirely to opaque systems. Human discretion must be structured, observable, and reviewable. The city's predictive policing example demonstrates the cost of neglecting this principle: officers followed machine outputs not out of choice, but out of fear, producing patterns of bias and disempowerment. Integrating humans meaningfully requires both procedural design and cultural reinforcement: roles, responsibilities, and escalation pathways must be explicit and enforced.

Yet humans alone cannot suffice. Intelligence systems often span technical, organisational, and societal domains. *Independent Eyes* advocates for cross-disciplinary oversight that extends beyond internal audit teams or legal compliance officers. Philosophers, sociologists, engineers, and civic advocates can each illuminate blind spots inaccessible to a single perspective. Crucially, oversight must have authority: the capacity to interrogate, intervene, and mandate correction. Without teeth, accountability risks becoming performative. Independent review is not ceremonial; it is a mechanism through which power is checked and systems are constrained.

The chapter also explores the power of imagination. *Democratic Imagination* asks readers to conceive institutions that can tame complex systems. How might city councils, public health agencies, or corporate boards structure themselves to anticipate the unintended consequences of automation? What cultural, procedural, or architectural safeguards can ensure that intelligence amplifies public interest rather than erodes it? By envisioning accountable structures before crises arise, societies can shift from reactive mitigation to proactive governance.

Finally, *A Playbook for Now* translates principles into action. Policymakers, technology firms, and citizens alike can adopt measures immediately: procurement requirements that enforce minimal collection, mandatory human review for high-stakes decisions, cross-disciplinary audit protocols, and routines for monitoring outcomes. The playbook emphasises feasibility and pragmatism, recognising that accountability is both urgent and incremental. Small, well-structured steps can create leverage far beyond their immediate scope, cultivating a culture in which intelligence systems are responsive, legible, and constrained by public values.

This chapter positions accountable intelligence not as an aspiration but as a practical imperative. It challenges assumptions about automation, data, and decision-making, insisting that power—digital or institutional—must be harnessed responsibly. Through principles, examples, and actionable guidance, readers are invited to move from observation to intervention, from passive acceptance to active stewardship. In doing so, intelligence ceases to be an uncontested force; it becomes a tool shaped by civic judgement, ethical design, and sustained oversight—a system whose outputs are not only effective, but just, legible, and accountable.

Minimalism as Default

In the winter of 2019, a major metropolitan transit authority deployed a suite of facial recognition cameras across its subway system, promising enhanced safety and operational efficiency. Within months, the volume of captured biometric data was staggering: every commuter, every visitor, every incidental passerby was catalogued in a growing database. Technical staff insisted that the system was designed with security in mind, yet the scale of collection soon outpaced both oversight mechanisms and practical use. What was intended as a targeted security measure became a sprawling repository of personal information, much of it irrelevant to its stated purpose. This episode encapsulates a fundamental challenge: systems designed without limits tend to collect everything, and in doing so, erode trust, constrain accountability, and increase the risk of abuse.

The principle of *minimalism as default* responds to precisely this challenge. It insists that restraint must be embedded at the earliest stages of system design, procurement, and deployment. Rather than retrofitting limits after a system is operational, organisations should define the essential data needed to meet their objectives—and nothing more. Minimalism is not merely a technical preference; it is an ethical and civic stance, signalling respect for the individuals whose information is being processed and for the society whose norms frame its legitimacy.

Consider procurement. Contracts often specify functional requirements—accuracy, speed, and coverage—without articulating boundaries on data collection. Minimalist procurement inverts this logic: contracts delineate explicit limits on what can be gathered, stored, and shared. For instance, a law enforcement agency purchasing predictive analytics software may stipulate that only anonymised, aggregated data is permitted beyond immediate operational use. Clauses can enforce automatic purging schedules, prohibit bulk retention, and restrict access to identifiable records. By translating minimalism into binding contractual language, organisations embed accountability upstream, long before deployment.

Architecture reinforces procurement. Data pipelines, storage schemas, and processing workflows can either amplify or constrain collection. Centralised architectures often encourage hoarding: every sensor, every log, every user interaction funnels into a single repository. Minimalist architecture, by contrast, prioritises localisation and purpose limitation. On-device processing, ephemeral caches, and selective sampling reduce the creation of comprehensive central stores, limiting both potential exposure and surveillance creep. A healthcare application that analyses user activity locally to deliver recommendations, transmitting only aggregate statistics to a central server, exemplifies this approach. The technical design becomes a form of policy enforcement: the architecture itself upholds restraint.

The tension between functionality and minimalism is not purely technical; it is conceptual. Critics argue that collecting more data provides flexibility, adaptability, and unforeseen analytic possibilities. Yet empirical evidence suggests diminishing returns: sprawling datasets increase noise, complicate analysis, and introduce new vectors for error. Minimalist systems, by contrast, encourage focus, transparency, and interpretability. When less is collected, every datum carries weight, and governance structures can meaningfully oversee its use. Moreover, minimalism reduces moral hazard: when organisations accumulate vast troves of personal data, incentives shift towards extraction and exploitation rather than stewardship.

Real-world applications illustrate the principle's potency. Consider a municipal smart lighting system: cameras and sensors track pedestrian flow to optimise illumination. A non-minimalist deployment would store continuous video, GPS traces, and biometric indicators. A minimalist design, however, collects only anonymised footfall counts, processed at the edge, with automatic deletion of raw sensor logs after brief intervals. Operational goals are met, yet individual privacy is preserved, and auditability is enhanced. Minimalism, in effect, operationalises the ethical dictum that surveillance should only reach as far as necessity demands.

Procurement and architecture intersect in the design of audit mechanisms. Minimalist systems inherently simplify oversight: fewer data points, more comprehensible flows, and restricted access make it feasible for internal and external reviewers to trace operations, detect anomalies, and enforce compliance. Conversely, maximalist systems often become black boxes: oversight is overwhelmed, accountability diffused, and errors magnified. In this sense, minimalism is not only a privacy strategy but an enabler of robust governance.

The principle extends to retention policies. Data persists only as long as operationally required, after which it is irreversibly destroyed or anonymised. Automatic purging schedules, combined with robust logging of access and deletion events, create a verifiable record of compliance. Organisations that adopt minimalism as default can demonstrate restraint not only in theory but in observable practice—a critical distinction in sectors where public trust is fragile.

Minimalism also shapes culture. Engineers, managers, and policymakers must internalise the idea that *more is not better* by default. Incentives and evaluation metrics should reward judicious collection, precision, and ethical restraint alongside performance outcomes. Procurement officers, system architects, and operators should share a conceptual framework where each design choice is weighed against necessity, proportionality, and potential harm. This cultural embedding transforms minimalism from a guideline into an organisational norm.

Yet challenges persist. Determining the "minimal" dataset is inherently context-dependent: operational needs, threat models, and societal expectations all influence what counts as essential. Minimalism does not imply arbitrary limitation or the abdication of analytic ambition. Rather, it requires deliberate deliberation, iterative review, and responsive adaptation. A balance must be struck between efficiency and ethics, functionality and restraint—a balance that is as dynamic as the environments these systems inhabit.

Technological innovation complicates matters further. AI systems, in particular, thrive on large volumes of data. Minimalism, in this domain, demands creative architectural and procedural solutions: federated learning, synthetic data, and privacy-preserving computation techniques can allow algorithmic advancement without wholesale accumulation of sensitive records. The pursuit of minimalism need not stall innovation; it can guide it toward methods that respect human dignity while delivering analytic utility.

Ultimately, *minimalism as default* reframes the conversation around intelligence systems. It positions collection decisions not as technical footnotes but as moral and civic choices, shaping both the scale of risk and the contours of accountability. By embedding restraint into procurement, architecture, retention, and organisational culture, minimalism transforms surveillance from an uncontrolled expansion into a system governed by design, principle, and foresight.

As systems proliferate and data volumes continue to grow exponentially, the question becomes urgent: how can organisations design for sufficiency, rather than surplus? How can the ethics of restraint be codified into technical practice before patterns of overcollection ossify into default behaviour? Minimalism is not a compromise; it is a framework for power that respects limits, amplifies oversight, and preserves the social licence upon which legitimate intelligence depends. It challenges practitioners to imagine not just *what can be collected*, but *what should be collected*, and in doing so, sets a new standard for accountable design in a data-saturated world.

Human-in-the-Loop, For Real

In the early hours of a quiet Tuesday, an automated decision system flagged a financial transaction as potentially fraudulent. Within milliseconds, the algorithm had scanned thousands of parameters—transaction history, device fingerprints, behavioural heuristics—and assigned a risk score. The alert reached a compliance officer, who, guided by the system, froze the account. A week later, it became apparent that the flagged transaction was legitimate: a parent sending tuition fees across borders. The consequence? Temporary account suspension, bureaucratic friction, and a loss of trust that technology alone could not repair. This incident underscores a critical lesson: while algorithms excel at speed and pattern recognition, discretion—the nuanced understanding of context, intent, and human consequence—cannot be fully automated.

The concept of *human-in-the-loop* is often invoked in abstract terms: a safeguard against error, a bridge between computational efficiency and moral judgement. In practice, however, it is rarely implemented with the depth or rigor that its name suggests. Too often, "human oversight" is a token checkbox: a late-stage reviewer with limited authority, constrained by opaque outputs and rigid system parameters. Real human-in-the-loop design requires more than cursory review; it demands that human discretion is central, informed, and accountable. It is not a symbolic gesture but an operational imperative.

Consider automated policing systems, where predictive algorithms recommend individuals for heightened scrutiny or intervention. The ethical stakes are immediate and high: errors can amplify bias, compromise civil liberties, and inflict lasting social harm. Here, human oversight cannot be perfunctory; officers must understand the logic underpinning the recommendations, interrogate anomalies, and retain the authority to override machine outputs. Crucially, the decisions themselves must be reviewable, traceable, and documented. Without these features, the human becomes a rubber stamp, and accountability evaporates.

The tension between automation and discretion reveals a broader paradox: technology promises objectivity, yet the complexity of social reality demands empathy, judgement, and moral reasoning. Human-in-the-loop is not simply a control measure; it is the recognition that intelligence—both artificial and organisational—must operate within a framework that preserves human responsibility. Discretion, in this sense, is not a flaw but a feature: it ensures that decisions remain legible, contestable, and aligned with societal norms.

Embedding effective human-in-the-loop mechanisms begins with architecture. Systems should present interpretable outputs, highlight uncertainty, and offer decision pathways that guide but do not dictate human choices. For example, in content moderation, algorithms can flag potentially harmful material, but moderators should receive contextual cues, explanatory signals, and flexible interfaces that support nuanced judgement. Interface design, transparency of algorithmic reasoning, and actionable feedback loops collectively shape the quality and integrity of human oversight.

Training and organisational culture are equally essential. A human reviewer is only as capable as the understanding, authority, and incentives provided by the organisation. Ethical escalation protocols, scenario-based training, and cross-disciplinary review councils can reinforce human judgement while mitigating the risk of mechanical compliance. The "human" in human-in-the-loop must be empowered, informed, and accountable—a custodian, not a passive observer.

Procurement and policy further define the scope of human discretion. Contracts for AI or automated decision tools should stipulate not only functional requirements but also accountability mandates: clear thresholds for human review, logging of override decisions, and mechanisms for independent auditing. Policies that enshrine reviewable human discretion convert abstract oversight into enforceable practice, ensuring that automated systems cannot circumvent human authority.

Real-world cases illustrate the stakes. In healthcare, AI-driven triage tools recommend resource allocation during crises. Without structured human-in-the-loop processes, errors can disproportionately affect vulnerable populations, eroding public trust. Conversely, systems that integrate human judgement—paired with transparency, traceability, and clear escalation protocols—demonstrate both efficacy and ethical robustness. The balance between speed and deliberation, between computational efficiency and human judgement, is delicate but non-negotiable.

A critical dimension of human-in-the-loop is auditability. Every automated recommendation that carries social consequence should be traceable to both machine logic and human intervention. Review logs, decision rationales, and override records transform oversight from an abstract concept into an actionable safeguard. When combined with independent review bodies, cross-functional ethics councils, and policy frameworks that demand accountability, human-in-the-loop moves from performative to substantive.

Yet challenges remain. Cognitive overload, overreliance on algorithmic outputs, and opaque models can compromise human judgement. Humans may defer excessively to perceived computational authority, allowing errors and biases to propagate. Mitigating these risks requires deliberate design: interpretability, alerts for anomalies, and clear thresholds for when human review is mandatory versus advisory. The architecture of oversight itself must reflect the limits of both human and machine cognition.

Ultimately, *human-in-the-loop, for real* reframes the relationship between technology and responsibility. It asserts that discretion must be preserved where stakes are high, outcomes are consequential, and moral judgement is required. Human oversight is not a convenience—it is the safeguard that upholds trust, accountability, and legitimacy. It challenges organisations to embed human agency not at the margins but at the core of automated systems, ensuring that intelligence serves humanity rather than displacing it.

The imperative is clear: as algorithms increasingly permeate decision-making, the question is not whether humans should be involved, but how their involvement can be structured, empowered, and verified. How can organisations prevent the human element from becoming performative, reducing oversight to a ritual rather than a substantive check? What mechanisms ensure that human discretion remains informed, actionable, and enforceable? Addressing these questions is central to designing systems that respect both operational goals and societal values—a challenge that defines accountable intelligence in the twenty-first century.

Independent Eyes

In 2019, a whistleblower revealed that a widely deployed facial recognition system misidentified people of colour at disproportionately high rates. The disclosure prompted widespread concern, but it also revealed a more profound issue: the system had undergone internal testing, overseen by teams steeped in engineering metrics and technical benchmarks, yet no independent review had scrutinised its social or ethical implications. Errors, bias, and potential harms persisted precisely because the oversight was neither broad in perspective nor authoritative in enforcement. This moment highlights a critical truth: without independent, cross-disciplinary scrutiny, even the most sophisticated systems can operate unchecked, with consequences that ripple far beyond their immediate context.

The notion of *independent eyes* is often invoked rhetorically, but operationalising it demands more than nominal committees or advisory boards. It requires oversight bodies endowed with both the expertise and the mandate to interrogate not just technical outputs but the organisational, ethical, and societal dimensions of intelligence systems. Independence is not a procedural nicety; it is a structural necessity. It ensures that scrutiny is rigorous, critical, and insulated from conflicts of interest, corporate inertia, or bureaucratic complacency.

Consider predictive policing tools, which have been deployed in numerous municipalities to identify potential crime hotspots. Internal audits frequently emphasise algorithmic accuracy and system uptime, yet fail to account for the broader social impact: disproportionate targeting of marginalised communities, reinforcement of historical inequities, and erosion of public trust. Independent oversight—ideally combining legal scholars, ethicists, social scientists, and technologists—can identify these patterns and demand corrective action. Such cross-disciplinary perspectives are essential precisely because no single lens, technical or otherwise, can apprehend the full scope of harm.

The architecture of independent review must be carefully designed. Expertise alone is insufficient; the body must possess authority, resources, and access to data. It must be able to compel transparency, request explanations, and mandate changes where systems fall short. Otherwise, independence is nominal—a badge without teeth. Historical precedents in financial auditing and environmental regulation demonstrate that oversight without enforcement tends to be performative rather than transformative. Lessons from these domains can inform the creation of truly potent review mechanisms in the intelligence and surveillance context.

Independence also entails cross-functional composition. Technical reviewers provide insight into algorithmic logic, data pipelines, and model robustness; ethicists interrogate normative implications; legal experts interpret compliance with domestic and international law; and social scientists assess societal impact. Each lens illuminates blind spots that others might overlook. The synergy of these perspectives transforms oversight from a procedural checkpoint into a substantive safeguard, capable of identifying emergent risks before they crystallise into harm.

Case studies illustrate the stakes. In healthcare AI, tools for triaging patients or predicting treatment outcomes can dramatically affect human wellbeing. Internal audits focusing solely on performance metrics risk ignoring systemic inequities, data biases, and ethical dilemmas. Independent panels that integrate medical practitioners, patient advocates, statisticians, and ethicists can challenge assumptions, highlight latent risks, and recommend mitigations that preserve both efficacy and justice. Similar principles apply to intelligence systems where human rights, privacy, and civil liberties intersect with technological power.

An independent eye is not merely reactive; it is proactive. By scrutinising system design choices, procurement contracts, and data governance policies, oversight bodies can influence architecture upstream. They can advocate for minimal data collection, privacy-preserving defaults, and mechanisms for human-in-the-loop intervention. In effect, independence shapes the development process itself, ensuring that accountability is built into systems rather than appended as an afterthought.

Yet independence carries its own challenges. Oversight bodies can be co-opted, under-resourced, or siloed. Experts may disagree on interpretations or priorities. Decision-making authority can be contested between organisational leadership and the oversight entity. Mitigating these risks requires transparent governance structures, statutory backing where possible, and clear channels for public accountability. Authority must be matched by credibility, expertise, and procedural integrity.

Beyond organisational or national contexts, the principle of independent eyes has international relevance. Cross-border data flows, multinational deployments, and transnational AI tools complicate the landscape of accountability. Independent review that incorporates diverse jurisdictional, cultural, and legal perspectives can identify frictions, anticipate regulatory conflicts, and propose harmonised standards. Without such oversight, the global diffusion of technology risks replicating inequities, concentrating power, and sidestepping local norms.

Ultimately, the call for independent eyes is a call to recognise that technological power is inseparable from human and institutional responsibility. Expertise, mandate, and authority converge to ensure that systems are not only technically sound but socially accountable. Oversight without independence is a hollow promise; with independence, it becomes a bulwark against error, abuse, and the erosion of trust. The challenge, then, is to institutionalise scrutiny that is not only knowledgeable but empowered, rigorous, and enduring—a safeguard for both technology and the societies it serves.

How can institutions guarantee that these eyes remain truly independent, able to challenge organisational orthodoxy without fear or favour? What mechanisms can ensure that oversight translates into action rather than symbolic review? The answers lie at the intersection of design, governance, and civic imagination, and they will define the shape of accountable intelligence for the decades to come.

Democratic Imagination

In 2022, a small European country enacted a law mandating that all algorithmic decision-making systems used in public administration be subject to citizen review panels. Ordinary residents were invited to evaluate outcomes, question assumptions, and scrutinise the logic underlying automated determinations affecting welfare, policing, and urban planning. The initiative was met with scepticism: how could non-experts meaningfully assess complex systems? Yet, as the first panel deliberated, it became clear that the act of engagement—asking what is being measured, why, and to whose benefit—shifted power dynamics. This was democracy in its most experimental form: not merely voting on candidates or policies, but actively interrogating the machinery that shapes everyday life. The episode demonstrates a broader imperative: societies must cultivate a *democratic imagination* capable of envisioning institutions that both harness and constrain technology.

The challenge is immediate and profound. Intelligence systems, predictive algorithms, and pervasive data infrastructures operate with opacity, scale, and speed that far exceed traditional governance mechanisms. Citizens rarely see the full chain from data collection to automated decisions, let alone the embedded assumptions or trade-offs. Left unchecked, these systems can subtly, yet systematically, erode rights, entrench biases, or concentrate power in ways that evade scrutiny. Democratic imagination does not call for blind optimism or technocratic naivety; it demands thoughtful speculation on how institutions, civic practices, and oversight frameworks can be designed to *tame* these forces.

Consider urban surveillance networks. Sensors, cameras, and algorithmic analytics gather vast quantities of personal and environmental data. Engineering teams focus on optimisation: coverage, accuracy, and throughput. Lawmakers may legislate broadly on privacy or retention periods, but rarely intervene in the architectural choices shaping everyday life. A democratic approach asks a different set of questions: could neighbourhood councils access anonymised data to verify public safety claims? Might independent review bodies simulate the system's social consequences before deployment? Could whistleblowing channels or public dashboards be built into operational design? Each of these considerations arises from imagining civic institutions not as passive observers, but as active participants shaping technological realities.

At its core, democratic imagination intersects the practical and the philosophical. It recognises that governance is not merely regulatory compliance; it is an exercise in collective judgment. Ethics, law, social science, and technology converge to form a lens through which societies can anticipate, critique, and guide emergent systems. Historical precedents illuminate this potential. In the post-war period, industrial safety laws and environmental regulations were drafted in response to accidents and ecological crises. Citizens, scientists, and inspectors collaborated to embed oversight into industrial processes. The principle remains consistent: meaningful constraint arises from institutionalised engagement, grounded in knowledge yet accountable to public values.

Translating imagination into operational institutions requires structural creativity. Citizen juries, cross-disciplinary advisory boards, independent audit units, and participatory policy labs are more than aspirational concepts—they are prototypes for embedding deliberation within systems. Their legitimacy stems from transparency, procedural fairness, and the capacity to influence outcomes. Systems are tamed not by abstract rules alone but by the very people who experience their effects. Engagement must be iterative: panels review algorithms, feedback loops inform redesign, and policy frameworks adapt to emergent insights. Democratic imagination thus functions both as a conceptual tool and a method for sustained institutional experimentation.

Yet tension remains. The scale and complexity of modern intelligence systems can overwhelm participatory structures. How can ordinary citizens meaningfully engage with millions of decisions per second? The answer lies in abstraction and delegation: institutions can curate representative samples, highlight high-stakes cases, and translate technical complexity into digestible scenarios. Civic literacy is essential, but so too is institutional architecture that scaffolds understanding without diluting scrutiny. The goal is not universal technical mastery but *informed agency*: a society capable of asserting values, identifying harms, and demanding accountability.

International contexts add further layers. Global data flows, transnational AI platforms, and multinational cloud infrastructures often escape the purview of any single democratic polity. Imagining institutions capable of taming these systems requires transnational networks of oversight, harmonised transparency standards, and mechanisms for cross-border civic engagement. Alliances of democracies, multi-stakeholder consortia, and international review panels become instruments of collective imagination, translating national ideals into operational checks on global technologies.

Finally, democratic imagination is iterative and reflective. It does not assume perfection in foresight or implementation. Rather, it acknowledges uncertainty and embeds mechanisms for correction, adaptation, and learning. Systems evolve; so too must institutions, informed by empirical evaluation, ethical reflection, and civic debate. By fostering structures where citizens, experts, and policymakers interact continuously, societies can cultivate resilience against misuse, bias, and unanticipated consequences.

Ultimately, democratic imagination challenges the very notion of passive technological governance. It invites us to envision institutions that are not reactive, but anticipatory; not purely regulatory, but constitutive of civic life. These are bodies capable of *taming systems*, translating human values into operational constraints, and ensuring that intelligence infrastructures serve the public rather than dominate it. The central question remains: how can societies institutionalise this imaginative capacity, so that oversight is not episodic but enduring, participatory yet effective, aspirational yet actionable? The answers will shape the contours of accountable intelligence for generations to come.

A Playbook for Now

In the summer of 2023, a coalition of civic technologists, privacy lawyers, and municipal policymakers convened in a Berlin workshop to map immediate actions for governing emerging intelligence systems. The agenda was deceptively simple: what can be done today, without waiting for international treaties or grand institutional reform, to ensure that technology serves the public rather than dominates it? The discussion ranged from hardware procurement clauses to citizen-facing transparency dashboards, from algorithmic audit trails to whistleblowing protocols. What emerged was not a theoretical manifesto but a concrete, operational playbook: a sequence of steps that policymakers, firms, and citizens can implement now, each reinforcing the others. This subchapter distils that ethos into actionable guidance, bridging lofty principles with immediate possibilities.

The urgency is palpable. Intelligence infrastructures—automated decision systems, pervasive surveillance networks, predictive policing platforms—are expanding in both reach and sophistication. Governments, firms, and civil society face a stark choice: react to harms after they occur or proactively embed accountability and restraint into the systems themselves. The former risks perpetuating cycles of damage and public mistrust; the latter requires deliberate orchestration across regulatory frameworks, technical design, and civic engagement. This playbook treats accountability as multidimensional, recognising that no single actor can fully supervise complex socio-technical systems. Instead, it emphasises coordinated action, where each stakeholder's role is clear, measurable, and enforceable.

For policymakers, the imperative is structural and anticipatory. Decisions about procurement, architecture, and contracting must be evaluated not solely on cost and efficiency but on long-term societal impact. Mandates for minimal data collection, privacy-preserving defaults, and human-in-the-loop review are not abstract ideals—they can be embedded in tender specifications, procurement contracts, and standards compliance. Jurisdictions that have experimented with such frameworks, from Scandinavian data protection authorities to municipal digital oversight offices in the Netherlands, illustrate how proactive regulation can shape systems at their inception, rather than attempting to correct them ex post facto.

Firms occupy a parallel terrain of responsibility, balancing innovation, market pressures, and societal expectations. The playbook emphasises design choices that anticipate oversight and embed transparency: audit logs that are easily interpreted, access controls that limit internal overreach, and system architectures that permit meaningful review without compromising functionality. Case studies in financial services illustrate the stakes: automated credit scoring systems, when deployed without human review or robust traceability, can replicate and amplify biases, sometimes affecting thousands of applicants before errors are detected. Firms that adopt continuous auditing, cross-disciplinary ethics reviews, and accountable design principles not only mitigate reputational risk but contribute to a normative baseline where responsible innovation becomes the industry standard.

Citizens, too, are active participants in this ecosystem. The playbook frames engagement as both practical and habitual: monitoring dashboards that track local surveillance intensity, FOI requests that uncover deployment patterns, and participation in public consultations or advisory panels. Individuals gain leverage not by mastering code but by cultivating informed agency—observing, questioning, and escalating anomalies within institutional frameworks. Collective literacy initiatives, exemplified by journalism consortia tracking algorithmic content moderation or civic tech organisations mapping municipal sensor networks, show that sustained citizen engagement can complement formal oversight and create feedback loops that reinforce accountability.

Interconnections between these spheres matter profoundly. Policies without operational follow-through yield little; corporate systems without civic scrutiny risk becoming opaque; citizen activism without structural leverage may generate awareness but not change. The playbook insists on alignment: procurement clauses inform system design; design choices facilitate audit and review; reviews and audits empower both regulators and citizens. Each component amplifies the others, producing a resilient lattice of accountability rather than isolated interventions.

Yet challenges persist. Resource disparities, technical complexity, and uneven legal frameworks can undermine even the most carefully constructed interventions. Implementing human-in-the-loop review may be straightforward in theory but cumbersome at scale. Transparency dashboards require sustained maintenance and interpretation to avoid superficial metrics. Citizen monitoring hinges on accessible, comprehensible data. The playbook acknowledges these frictions, advocating iterative refinement: actions must be continually evaluated, recalibrated, and integrated with emerging technologies and shifting social expectations.

Crucially, the playbook resists the notion that immediate action is synonymous with minor adjustments or symbolic compliance. Each step—whether a contractual clause, an audit routine, or a civic reporting mechanism—carries material consequences for system behaviour, power distribution, and societal trust. Acting now does not substitute for long-term reform but establishes the foundations upon which robust, accountable intelligence systems can be built. By embedding constraints, transparency, and civic engagement into operational practice today, societies can shape trajectories of technological development rather than remain passive observers.

Ultimately, this agenda is a call to coordinated pragmatism. It recognises that intelligence systems are neither inherently benevolent nor malevolent; their social impact depends on the structures, decisions, and actors that govern them. Policymakers, firms, and citizens each hold levers of influence, and by acting in concert—through procurement policies, accountable design, and informed oversight—they can collectively orient these systems toward public benefit. The challenge, and the opportunity, lies in translating principle into practice: moving from abstract aspirations for accountable intelligence to concrete, verifiable actions that can be implemented today, monitored tomorrow, and refined indefinitely.

The playbook does not claim completeness. Emerging technologies, novel architectures, and shifting socio-political contexts will continually test these strategies. But it establishes a shared baseline: a tangible, actionable framework for navigating the complexities of modern intelligence systems with foresight, responsibility, and civic awareness. It invites all stakeholders to engage actively, iteratively, and thoughtfully, transforming accountability from a distant ideal into an operational reality. The pressing question lingers: as technology accelerates and systems evolve, can societies maintain the discipline, imagination, and coordination necessary to ensure that intelligence serves citizens, rather than the other way around?

About the Author

Ronan Khoury is a Lebanese-French historian of cyber intelligence whose work traces how power migrated from listening posts to lines of code. After years as a digital analyst contributing to international investigations, he now writes about the politics of platforms, policing, and privacy with a focus on how ordinary people are sorted by unseen systems. Raised between Beirut and Marseille, he draws on a Levantine tradition of border-crossing scholarship and the Mediterranean habit of reading empires by their ports and cables. His mission is simple: to make complex infrastructures legible so that citizens, not only technicians, can argue for limits and accountability. Khoury's essays and lectures examine how incentives, not intentions, drive surveillance, and how practical guardrails can protect both safety and dignity without surrendering to fatalism.

www.ingramcontent.com/pod-product-compliance
Lightning Source LLC
Chambersburg PA
CBHW031323230926
51848CB00001B/71
* 9 7 8 9 3 4 7 4 3 6 6 0 4 *